DATE DUE			

The Minutemen and Their World

The Minutemen and Their World

ROBERT A. GROSS

American Century Series

HILL AND WANG · NEW YORK
A DIVISION OF FARRAR, STRAUS AND GIROUX

First edition, 1976
Published simultaneously in Canada
by McGraw-Hill Ryerson Ltd., Toronto

ISBN (clothbound edition): 0-8090-6933-4
ISBN (paperback edition): 0-8090-0120-9

Printed in the United States of America
Designed by Nancy Dale Muldoon

Library of Congress Cataloging in Publication Data

Gross, Robert A.
The minutemen and their world.

(American century series)
Includes bibliographical references and index.
1. Concord, Mass.—History—Revolution, 1775–1783.
2. Concord, Battle of, 1775. 3. Concord, Mass.—Social conditions. I. Title.
F74.C8G76 1976 974.2'72 75–46595
ISBN 0–8090–6933–4
ISBN 0–8090–0120–9 pbk.

To

my mother, my father,

and

Gary

PREFACE

A history of the town of Concord, were it tolerably, nay, badly executed, could not well be an *obscure* one. It must be either famous or infamous. . . . The annals of all our ancient towns and cities are of inestimable value, and will be faithfully preserved; but those of Concord,—old Concord, in connexion with very few others, are the pound of flesh nearest the heart of the Republic. He that should do justice to them, had reason to expect, and he had a right, as a man deserving well of his country, to enjoy, the gratitude of those he should serve.

—B. B. Thacher, "History of Concord,"
North American Review (1836)

The town of Concord has always occupied a special place in the minds of Americans, and naturally so. It was the starting point of the Revolution: the site of the battle of April 19, 1775, at the old North Bridge. And in the nineteenth century, as the home of Emerson and Thoreau, it became the intellectual capital of the new republic. Concord thus played a leading part in the achievement of our political and cultural independence as a people. In turn, the town has come to symbolize devotion to liberty, intellectual freedom, and the stubborn integrity of rural life.

Many writers have told Concord's story. For the most part, theirs have been tales of great events and great men—of the "embattled farmers" and the distinguished writers who have brought fame to the town. This book takes a different approach. It sets the Concord Fight, as it used to be known, in the context of the townspeople's ordinary lives, before and after April 19, 1775. It examines how the citizens farmed the land, raised their families, and carried on their politics at the end of the colonial period. Within this setting, it then asks what brought them to the bridge, and it shows how the peculiar tensions and social patterns of the town shaped both its response to revolution and what men did on April 19. Finally, it traces the townspeople through the Revolution and the war into the new republic and links the world of the Minutemen to that of Emerson and Thoreau. In this way, the Minutemen emerge as real people, with hopes and fears, ambitions and doubts, ideals and interests. Without such a connection between the soldiers at the bridge and the people of the town, it is difficult to comprehend the human meaning of the Revolution—to see it as a social force in men's lives, affecting what they would plant, where they would live, and what they could hope to achieve. Freedom, they knew, and we need to recall, is an intensely practical matter.

This study is part of the "new social history." It is based on a reconstruction of eighteenth-century Concord from such sources as vital records, genealogies, tax and assessment lists, wills, deeds, petitions, and the minutes of town meetings. Through the use of statistical methods and with the aid of a computer, such records can reveal the life of a whole community in surprisingly intimate detail. They allow one to write history "from the bottom up"—to tell the story of ordinary men and women who have left behind few of the diaries and letters on which historians have long relied. Unfortunately, quantitative social history can be dull and tedious work, and at times it requires technical knowledge and skills. In this book, I have chosen to relate Concord's response to revolution directly and simply, without flogging the evidence. The detailed support for my conclusions and the sometimes dry methodological issues of this research have been left to the notes. Social history, like any other branch of history, should be accessible to as wide an audience as possible, for it deals with everyday, fundamental experiences of human life—with work and play, with growing up and raising families, with growing old and facing death. It thereby provides us with our closest points of contact with men and women of the past. By seeing how earlier Americans have lived and struggled in their daily lives, we can come to recognize them as people like ourselves and gain a new understanding of our society and our heritage.

In the course of this project, I have acquired many debts. The bulk of my research was done at the Concord Free Public Library, which possesses an extraordinarily rich collection of manuscripts on all aspects of town life. Under the direction of Rose Marie Mitten, the library maintains a strong commitment to serious scholarship and to the preservation and use of the town's archives. I could not have written this work without the assistance of reference librarians Mrs. George Barker and Mrs. Norman Harris and most especially that of Mrs. William Henry Moss, head of the Reference Department. Mrs. Moss and her staff readily accepted my newcomer's interest in Concord history, graciously enduring my unending questions and requests. I am immensely grateful for all their kindness and help.

Other people and institutions in Concord have also facilitated my research. Robert F. Needham, chairman of the Town Records and Archives Committee, granted permission to use the official papers of the town. In the Town Hall, former Town Clerk Aljean Doty and former Town Treasurer Mary Sheehan guided me to the assessment lists in their care. The Minute Man National Historic Park and the Concord Antiquarian Museum assisted in gathering materials for the maps. And Mrs. Raymond Emerson kindly allowed me to use her transcripts of the diaries of William Emerson and Daniel Bliss.

Outside of Concord, I have drawn on the resources of many other institutions. This would have been a very different book if I had not consulted the Lemuel Shattuck Collection at the New England Historic Genealogical Society. For her cheerful assistance in my use of the Shattuck Collection as well as the Society's incomparable genealogical materials, I am grateful to Mary Leen. I also want to acknowledge the assistance of Leo and Helen Flaherty at the Massachusetts State Archives, Alan Fox and James Parla at the Massachusetts State Library, and Paul Sostek, Clerk of Courts for Middlesex County. Through the Genealogical Society of the Church of Jesus Christ of Latter-Day Saints, I was able to obtain microfilm copies of the Revolutionary War Pension Records at the National Archives; thanks are due to Robert Tarte for enabling me to use the microfilms at the Society's Boston Branch Library. Finally, over the last three years, I have been aided by the staffs of the American Antiquarian Society, the Boston Atheneum, and the Massachusetts Historical Society.

Large-scale projects in social history cannot be carried out alone. They are costly, and they involve the efforts of many people. This project was begun under a John and Louise K. Jay Fellowship from Columbia University; other early expenses were supported through the National Institute of Mental Health Training Program in Social History at Columbia. Through the auspices of Professor Donald E. Johnson, chairman of the Humanities Department, computer time was generously made available by Worcester Polytechnic Institute; programming services were provided by Edward Perkins and John Gabranski, former staff members of the Worcester Area College Computation Center. Connie Dionne did the keypunching.

Several people have assisted me in gathering data for the study. Debby London and Michael Baumrin, while undergraduates at Brandeis University, coded several assessment lists. Another Brandeis graduate, Alisa Belinkoff, contributed her friendship, her enthusiasm, and her impressive talents as a researcher throughout this project, coding assessment lists, inventorying sources, and compiling the file of Concord office-holders used in the political analysis of the town. I have gained, too, from the work of the "Concord Group" at Brandeis in 1972–73; the members—Marc Harris, James Kimenker, Susan Kurland, and Richard Weintraub—coordinated their research with my own while doing their senior honors theses under David Hackett Fischer. And from her research on Massachusetts officers in the French and Indian War, Nancy Voye, a graduate student at Boston University, generously supplied the service records of the Concord Minutemen.

This book has been long in coming, and I owe much to colleagues and friends for simply putting up with me during the years of research and writing. I have learned much about agriculture from Darwin Kelsey of Old Sturbridge Village and from Concordians Robert Flannery and Eleanor Snelling, who by their example have also taught me about the integrity of New England life. Douglas Hamar Jones and Linda Auwers Bissell have been hearing about and commenting on this work for so long that it seems almost redundant to thank them for their careful reading of the final manuscript. Thomas Conway's questions about Concord helped provoke the idea for this book; Richard Bushman criticized several early chapters.

Everyone who knows David Fischer is in awe of his remarkable energy, creativity, and willingness to share his work with other scholars. I have benefited greatly from his help; his comments on the manuscript have improved both style and substance considerably. To Stuart Bruchey, my sponsor at Columbia, I owe an enormous debt for his tolerance of my long delays and his confidence in the results. And I am grateful to Wendy Weil for her long encouragement and support and to Arthur Wang for being a model editor, patient and tactful as he persuades one to make valuable changes in the manuscript.

If Ann Gross successfully and wisely resisted becoming a research assistant, she has nonetheless had to listen to nearly every word of the manuscript, and most of the time she even did so cheerfully. Her sound judgment as an editor is reflected throughout this work. She also found the decoration for the title page and prepared the index. We have drawn closer together, I believe, by sharing in the creation of this book. Matthew Gross did nothing to help publish the book; indeed, he delayed completion of the manuscript. For that, I am most grateful. He took his father away from his work, gave him much pleasure and joy, and led him to realize what was truly important and what was not.

R.A.G.

Contents

Maps

The Minutemen and Their World

PROLOGUE

Winter Soldiers and Springtime Farmers

SPRING came early to New England in 1775, after one of the mildest winters in memory. Not once that year had the mercury dropped below zero, and most of the time it stood above freezing. The light snows of January and February scarcely muffled the sounds of Minutemen at drill. "Extraordinary Weather for warlike Preparations," Concord's fiery minister, William Emerson, called it. Men and women had gained a brief respite from what was usually a cheerless, idle time, when impassable roads kept them huddled close to home, repairing tools, spinning and weaving, reading Bibles, and mourning the always large number of winter dead. Now, in March, as the ground thawed and farmers drove their ox teams to the fields for the annual plowing, people in Concord were once again moving to the timeless rhythms of rural life.[1]

In rapidly expanding colonial America, Concord was an old town by 1775. It had once been Massachusetts's first frontier, the first settlement beyond the sight and smell of the sea. For six generations since 1635, its inhabitants had been getting a living from the soil and gradually increasing their numbers until they were some fifteen hundred persons (about 265 families) on the eve of the war. The Puritan founders, whose heroic achievements would inspire townsmen in the Revolutionary struggle against Britain, had been drawn to the site by its nine miles of river, rich in shad, salmon, and alewives, and by the abundant beaver and game that lived by the water and in the thick pine woods. Along the river lay an expanse of natural meadowland that promised plentiful fodder for cattle; bordering the grasslands were tracts of upland long since cleared by the Indians for corn fields. Each family received a share in these lands, which all agreed to farm in common, and built its house along the main road in the middle of town.[2]

Soon settlers scattered to other attractive areas. They and their descendants steadily hacked away at the woods so that by 1775 the landscape was more open than it is today and an invading army in the village center could be spotted easily from the northern heights two miles away. If a ne'er-do-well woodsman could still trap an occasional fox for its fur or shoot a rare wolf for the bounty, the ordinary farmer found little but squirrels, woodchucks, and raccoons for target practice. The salmon had long ago stopped running; as a conservation measure, the town made a monopoly of the "shad fishery." Men gave their attention to domestic animals; pigs ran at large through town, horses and cattle browsed along the public ways. Solid walls of stone, painfully dragged and shoved out of the fields, secured farmers' crops from destruction.[3]

A traveler in 1775 could reach the town by two main routes from Boston. He might, like the British spies who arrived that March to report on the Americans' military preparations, follow a roundabout, twenty-mile route, passing through the narrow Neck that linked peninsular Boston to Roxbury on the mainland and then cutting a northwesterly arc through Watertown and Weston to the Lincoln-Concord line. This was the road farmers preferred when they hauled wood or drove cattle to Boston market. But if he wanted to save a few miles, the traveler would go not by land but by sea and take an expensive ferry across the Charles River to Charlestown before proceeding, as directly as the winding Bay Road allowed, through Cambridge, Menotomy (now urban Arlington), Lexington, and Lincoln into Concord center. Between Lexington and Concord traveling was rugged, with the road at times dropping steeply into close passes through surrounding heights. The Redcoats took this road on April 19.[4]

A mile from Concord center, a glacial ridge rises abruptly from the plain to command the Bay Road. The original settlers had burrowed into the ridge during the first winter in 1636 while they

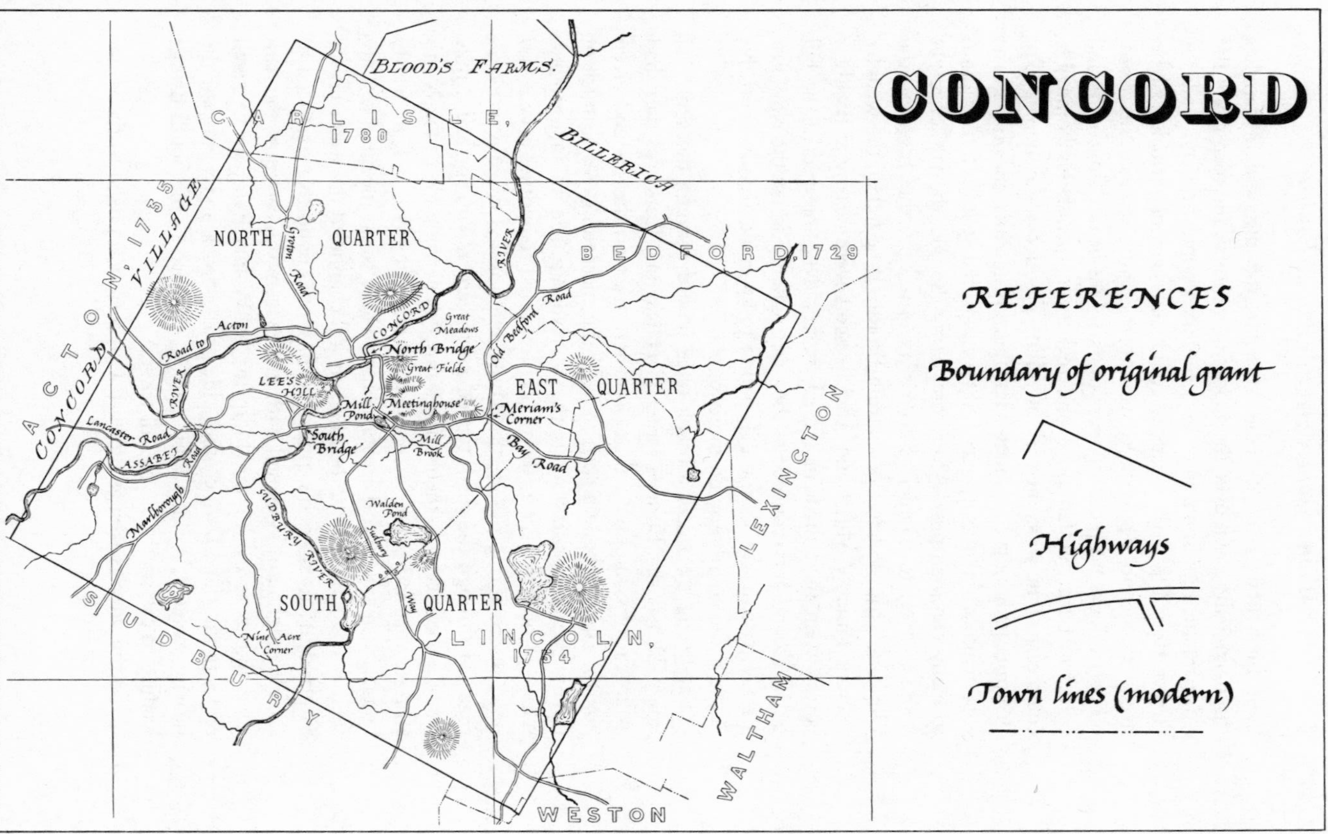

CONCORD
REFERENCES
Boundary of original grant
Highways
Town lines (modern)
BLOOD'S FARMS.
CARLISLE, 1780
BILLERICA
BEDFORD, 1729
CONCORD VILLAGE, 1735
ACTON
LEXINGTON
WALTHAM
WESTON
LINCOLN, 1754
SUDBURY
NORTH QUARTER
EAST QUARTER
SOUTH QUARTER
Groton Road
RIVER
Old Bedford Road
CONCORD
Great Meadows
North Bridge
Great Fields
Road to Acton
LEE'S HILL
Mill Pond
Meetinghouse
Meriam's Corner
South Bridge
Mill Brook
Bay Road
Lancaster Road
ASSABET
RIVER
Road
Marlborough
SUDBURY RIVER
Walden Pond
Sudbury Way
Nine Acre Corner

built their houses by its edge. Despite the dispersal of families throughout the town over the following century, the road along the ridge retained its importance as a center of population and trade. A farmer from the outlying areas could take care of virtually all his needs along the way: there were blacksmiths to shoe his oxen, tanners to cure his hides, coopers to barrel his beef, cordwainers and tailors to outfit his family, cabinetmakers to furnish his home. He could earn some welcome cash by selling produce at the shop of John Beatton, an honest Scotsman who figured accounts not only in the legal pounds, shillings, pence, and farthings, but split his farthing into so many common pins. After completing the sale, the farmer might wander over to Daniel Taylor's tavern, "by the Sign of the Elephant," for the latest news from Boston. If he fell ill, the wealthy doctors Timothy Minot and Abel Prescott were nearby to try their cures; when their medicine failed, he could be interred in the hill burial ground and mourned at the meetinghouse across the way. For a fee, Ephraim Wood, the 250-pound town clerk, would record his death at the courthouse on the common.[5]

Paralleling the ridge, a brook once flowed through the center of town. When the Puritan fathers had laid out Concord, they had awarded their minister a thirty-one-acre tract on the site and given him the right to build a corn mill. In the succeeding years, much of the ministerial plot reverted to the town for a public training ground, where in ordinary times the militia mustered four times a year and now, in the spring of '75, the Minutemen drilled twice a week. A road led through the field, turned northward to run for half a mile along a second ridge, then made a ninety-degree angle to the North Bridge, the battle site. Around the common stood a few private houses, a school, and the courthouse, where town meetings usually met. A few yards away, the milldam still channeled the water power to grind the townsmen's grain and formed a pond that extended to the meetinghouse. Widened with gravel from the common, the dam gave direct access to the highway to Watertown, which began opposite the ridge on the other side of the brook and went past the heavily wooded Walden Pond, and to the road to the South Bridge leading to the southern parts of town.[6]

To the west as well as the east, Concord was linked to the wider world. Beyond the North Bridge, the road led into the nearby towns of Acton, Littleton, and Groton before climbing upcountry into the hills of Worcester County and the wilds of New Hampshire; two hundred miles from Concord, it ended at Crown Point, the British citadel on Lake Champlain at the gateway to Quebec. Another road passed through Nine Acre Corner in the south part of town on its way to Deerfield in western Massachusetts. And just next door, in the town of Sudbury, was one of the principal highways of the colony: the road from Boston to Hartford and New Haven. Concord owed its importance to these roads. It was a hub of communications and one of the trading centers of the province. In all the old colonial wars against the Indians and the French, provincial military expeditions were frequently launched from the town. Concord served as a shire town, a meeting place for the Middlesex County courts. And when in 1752 and 1764 smallpox broke out in Boston, the province capital, Concord also became the temporary home of the colonial government. Good roads were thus a valuable resource. Without them, Concord would have been just another country town.[7]

The British spies dispatched to Concord that March had quickly noted the military advantages of the roads, the two bridges controlling the approaches from the north and southwest, and the hills commanding the view of the town. To the ordinary farmer in an outlying area, the topography imposed some everyday hardships. The wooden bridges were periodically washed out and the dirt roads blocked by snow or windfallen trees. Every spring he and his neighbors would work together to repair the ravages of the preceding season. Living four or five miles from the meetinghouse, on Sabbath mornings in the deep of winter he must have envied those fellow townsmen—nearly a third of the town—who had less than a mile's walk to church.[8]

Many people would have been on the road in April 1775. Spring was moving season, when families packed up their possessions for a fresh start in a different community and laborers searched for work to carry them through the coming harvest. Within towns, men went back and forth to their neighbors' farms—to borrow a team of oxen, buy a shoat, or rent the stud services of a bull. In May, Concord yeomen went upcountry on the annual cattle drive to summer pasture in northwestern Massachusetts or New Hampshire.[9] Normally, trade, too, would have picked up with the change of seasons. Farmers would have visited the stores to replenish their stocks of staples like salt and tea and to examine the latest manufactured goods from England. Peddlers would have made their way from house to house. But 1775 was not a normal year. The British had kept the port of Boston closed since June 1, 1774, in retaliation for the Tea Party, and the colonists had responded with a pledge to consume no British goods. Trade had come to a halt.

The movements of population reflected a regular adjustment of social life to the changing seasons. Men and women stirred at the deepest levels to nature's spring renewal. In the town clerk's register one reads the evidence: every year April through June was the most common time to conceive, as indicated by recorded births nine months later. During the hot summer of exhausting labor in the fields and the succeeding rush to harvest, conception fell to an annual low. It rose to a secondary peak in autumn when families could relax and enjoy the feeling of plenitude a good harvest brought; decline set in again during the long winter night. Marriage followed another rhythm, surging in May and in November and December, traditional months for Christian celebration. Death had its own seasons that mocked the promise of late autumn and spring. Infants were likely to enter the world during the periodic killing times: not only the bitter winters but also the summers when, as Concord's pastor Emerson noted in 1775, "Many were sick with dysentery—sickness continues and increases and in general prevails in this and other Colonies."[10]

Nature ordinarily ruled the timing of public events with equal rigor. Every March voters in Concord and throughout New England gathered in town meetings to elect their leaders and to plan another harvest year. Would the sheep be allowed on the common? Could hogs still run at large? A large part of local government was devoted to keeping one man's livestock out of another man's fields. Town meetings claimed jurisdiction over virtually all community life, but it usually took only two or three sessions a spring to do the necessary business for the year: electing officials, making laws, and voting money for schools, roads, and the poor. Every September, the judges of the county court would take advantage of the lull before harvest to hear cases in town. Magistrates, barristers, plaintiffs, defendants, and jurors from all parts of Middlesex County filled Concord's inns for a few days and provided public entertainment with their lawsuits and trials and after-hours political talk. Farming families added income from boarding or housing out-of-towners.

In 1775, however, the political calendar changed. The courts were closed: angry mobs, protesting judicial changes imposed by Parliament, refused to let them meet. Town politics became a year-round affair, with meetings throughout the winter to prepare for the expected assault by Redcoats.

The accelerating crisis disrupted not only the schedule of community life but its very substance. Ten years before, the town as a body seldom took notice of events beyond its borders. It elected a representative to the Massachusetts General Court, the provincial legislature, each May, but Concord bothered about colonial politics only once in a while—such as when a governor asked for towns' opinions on a proposed excise tax or when moves were made in the legislature to split Middlesex County in two, jeopardizing Concord's prized status as a shire town. County government caught Concord's notice more often, chiefly through its role in laying out highways. But now, on the eve of war, Concord busied itself with provincial affairs. In the meetinghouse a Provincial Congress assembled to direct the revolution in Massachusetts. In the courthouse delegates from all the Middlesex towns consolidated anti-government strategy in the county. Crowds gathered on the common to harass Tories. For a brief few months Concord emerged as the dramatic center of American resistance to Britain.

★1★
"Do Not Be Divided for So Small Matters"

CONCORD arrived at its strategic position in 1775 only after a good deal of foot-dragging. While Bostonians fulminated against British policies in the 1760s and early 1770s, the yeomen of Concord were squabbling among themselves in a series of increasingly bitter quarrels that threatened ultimately to divide the town into two warring parties. The local contentions had no relation to the colonial dispute with Britain; that subject came before the town only occasionally until 1774 and elicited only a mild response. Let others warm to arguments over the rights of the colonies and sound the alarm against a corrupt ministry in London and its lackeys at home. Concordians were more concerned over their roads and schools and meetinghouse.

★ ★ ★

When the eighteenth-century Yankee reflected on government, he thought first of his town. Through town meetings, he elected his officials, voted his taxes, and provided for the well-ordering of community affairs. The main business of the town concerned roads and bridges, schools, and the poor—the staples of local government even today. But the colonial New England town claimed authority over anything that happened within its borders. It hired a minister to preach in the town-built meetinghouse and compelled attendance at his sermons. It controlled public uses of private property, from the location of slaughterhouses and tanneries to the quality of bread sold at market. And it gave equal care to the moral conduct of its inhabitants, as Concord's William Hunt regretfully learned in 1764 when the selectmen took notice of his public tippling and idle "Loytring about from House to House Wasteing his time in a Sinfull maner" and advised innkeepers to shut their doors to his trade. No issue was in theory exempt from a town's action, even if in practice the provincial government occasionally intervened in local disputes and told the inhabitants how to run their lives.[1]

A remarkably broad segment of the population could join in this exercise of local power. To vote in Massachusetts town elections, one had to be a male, at least twenty-one years old, an inhabitant of a town for the past year, and owner of an estate that would rent for £3:6:8 a year in the local assessors' view. In a country town like Concord, most men could meet the property-holding requirement, which was the equivalent of a month's wages for a common laborer. In 1771 seven out of ten Concordians qualified. Those who could not were farmers' sons, only recently come of age, and day laborers and servants, dependent on others for their bread. In eighteenth-century Massachusetts, a citizen mattered politically only when his judgment was subject to no one else's whim and untempted by the financial inducements of designing men.[2]

With town government affecting so much of daily life, no New England community could escape political conflict. A road urgently needed by a man at the outskirts was often a wasteful expense to an inhabitant near the center, while one churchgoer's learned preacher was another's prideful sinner on the way to hell. Politics was, as ever, a contest over who got what of a community's scarce resources and whose values would prevail in local life. But provincial Yankees labored under a set of beliefs that made political activity as we know it impossible.

Eighteenth-century New Englanders demanded a great deal of their leaders. A magistrate, they held, was not a hired agent but a "father" to his people. He was raised up to rule as another Moses, a model of wisdom and righteousness, a lover of justice and champion of the people's rights. Like a good father, he was patient and gentle in guiding his subjects, but he could also be stern when necessary. He neither courted popular favor nor consulted private interest. He was ever-solicitous of the common good.[3]

The people of Concord sought such leaders among the well-born and the rich. Democracy and equality played no part in their view of the world. New Englanders believed that society was composed of "ranks and degrees," that just as the earth "has Mountains and Plains, Hills and Vallies," so "there are the Distinctions of Superiours and Inferiours, Rulers and Ruled, publick and private Orders of Men. . . ." The upper orders were to rule, the lower to follow. To place men of "low degree" in the council chamber would bring government into contempt. Magistrates must be distinguished men, known and respected by all. All authority—political, social, economic, and moral—was of a piece.[4]

By aristocratic English standards, Concord's governing class cut a minor figure in the world. A few leaders were country squires like Colonel John Cuming, a Harvard- and Edinburgh-trained doctor who oversaw a 250-acre farm in Concord and speculated in frontier lands in Massachusetts, New Hampshire, and Vermont. As a young man in his twenties, Cuming had fought in the old colonial wars against the French, in the course of which he received a musket ball in his hip—where it remained till his death—and was taken captive by Indians, beaten, and removed to Canada. He eventually won over his captors and gained release in a prisoner exchange. He returned home to build an extensive medical practice throughout Middlesex County and to become one of the town's leading men—the moderator of no fewer than ninety town meetings, justice of the peace, president-judge of the county Court of General Sessions. Concord often called on him to serve as its ambassador to the world. Cuming practiced the philanthropy his worldly status prescribed. It is said that he never charged for treating patients on the Sabbath. When Harvard Hall burned, he donated "two handsome brass branches for the use of the College chapel"; in 1771, he was awarded an honorary M.A. At his death in 1788, he left the College £300 sterling to establish a professorship of medicine. Together with other money, the bequest was used to start the Harvard School of Medicine.[5]

But most of Concord's leaders were substantial yeomen and

tradesmen with seventy-five to one hundred acres of land—twice the holding of the ordinary farmer. And while they engaged in trade more often than most inhabitants, it was business on the scale of Honest John Beatton, parceling out pins for change, and that of farmer-shoemaker Jonas Heywood, who every winter went from house to house in the countryside "whipping the cat"—boarding with his customers while he made and repaired enough shoes to last each family for the season. Still, hard-working, substantial men like Beatton and Heywood did stand out in a largely rural society, and they could afford to spend the typical selectman's four or five years in the public service. In the eyes of their neighbors, such men could rise to the standard of the public service.[6]

Ephraim Wood was another shoemaker-farmer who won the trust of the town. Born in 1733 and bred to his father's trade, Wood was a natural candidate for town leadership: he was the son of a selectman—as were nearly half the men Concord chose for this post. But Wood also commanded respect in his own right. At 250 pounds, he was an imposing figure; the calf of his leg was said to measure twenty-four inches around. He had a reputation for "a calm, considerate mind and sound judgment," and he so thrived in business that his name became synonymous with success. Once another shoemaker was complaining to a Scotsman about his bad luck and poor trade. "Oh," the Scotsman replied, "you have a very poor trade, but Ephraim Wood have a very good trade." In 1771, Wood succeeded Jonas Heywood as selectman and town clerk, and he served in these posts for the next twenty-five years. When he died in 1814, it was said that

> In him were united those qualities and virtues, which formed a character at once amiable, useful, respectable, and religious. Early in life he engaged in civil and public business, and by a judicious and faithful discharge of duty acquired confidence and reputation with his fellow citizens and the public. . . . The rights and liberties of his country were near his heart, and he was a warm and zealous defender of these against all encroachments. He was a true disciple of the great Washington, a friend to 'liberty with order.' . . . In domestic life, his disposition and example were highly amiable and worthy. As a Christian, he was devout and humble, sincere and ardent. Having lived the life, he died the death of the righteous.[7]

In the model commonwealth, public recognition flowed naturally to an Ephraim Wood. As he established himself in society and did his turns in a town's burdensome minor offices—posts like constable and surveyor of highways—men would notice his merits and soon elevate him to community-wide leadership. In Concord, high positions would normally come to a man by his mid-forties; the community desired leaders in their prime, not after retirement from active life. Ideally, a potential leader neither sought nor clung to office; were he to campaign openly, he would simply demonstrate his unfitness for public trust. Once elected, he would continue on the same conscientious course for the public good, heedless of his own popularity, the partial interests of powerful constituents, or the momentary wishes of a majority. Men would listen when he spoke and, whether they agreed or not, respectfully accept his judgments. So long as the magistrate upheld the fundamental liberties and interests of his community, no one questioned his fitness to rule.[8]

The ordinary citizen in this vision of politics had an equally virtuous code of conduct. When he joined in a town meeting, he would set the needs of the group before his own and strive to think as his neighbors thought. In the course of discussion, he might properly disagree with another speaker, but always reluctantly, with a spirit of accommodation in his heart. Never would he concert his opposition with others; such action was universally condemned as the work of "faction," of men in league against the common good. When the meeting came to a vote, the citizen would normally find himself in alignment with the prevailing trend; whatever doubts persisted would be curbed in the interests of harmony. To insist on a formal count of the yeas and nays or to demand a record of one's dissent in the minutes of a meeting was to subvert that perfect unanimity of minds that adorned the ideal community. Men believed, with Boston minister Jonathan Mayhew, that "Union was the source of public happiness."[9]

The New England town of men's deepest aspirations was a utopia: a corporate body free from power-seeking, from conflict, from hard bargaining among separate interests, from exploitation of the weak; free, in short, from politics. But there was no eliminating the facts of private ambition and group hostilities from social life. Colonial

Yankees strove instead to overcome them through their "precepts of peace" and, failing that, to escape them through a distinctive style of politics by denial. Men stood for office by renouncing ambitions, all the while discreetly publicizing their availability among friends. They feuded and squabbled over the same issues year after year; it was their opponents, they charged, who were violating the spirit of community. Often agreement could be reached only by compromising the ideal of town unity. And sometimes it could not be reached at all.[10]

Pre-Revolutionary Concord traced much of its political conflict to the growth of its population. From the very beginning, settlement was not confined to the village center; men took up choice spots across the river and formed distinct clusters whose existence was formally recognized in the three "quarters"—East, North, and South—the town established for the purpose of distributing land and apportioning taxes. But it was not until after the seventeenth century that much of Concord's land area was filled in; within its limits lay not only the present-day town but also all of the current town of Acton, to the west, and parts of Carlisle, Bedford, and Lincoln, to the north, northeast, and southeast. As the approximate number of inhabitants increased to 480 in 1679, 920 in 1706, 1,500 in 1725, the large estates of the original settlers were carved into smaller farms for succeeding generations. New communities took shape far from the village meetinghouse, with separate needs of their own and with a growing sense of separate identity.[11]

The "outlivers," as they were sometimes called, soon resented their subordination to the center. On Sabbath mornings families still had to travel five or six miles into town; during the week their children had to go back and forth across the river to the village grammar school. They were at a disadvantage, too, in town politics, for inhabitants in the center could pack special town meetings more easily than farmers on the outskirts.[12]

Samuel Kibby, who lived about three miles from the meetinghouse, had a special problem. His five daughters had trouble getting there on the Sabbath. They had to take turns riding the family's horse to Sunday meeting—"they were so heavy that only one could ride at once." But only a minority of families owned horses. When the town's leading men won permission to take common land for stables behind the meetinghouse, many voters must have suppressed a certain amount of bitterness; their wives and daughters had to walk into town in everyday stockings and shoes, then for the sake of appearances stop in a field and change into their go-to-meeting slippers. No wonder the residents of the remote northeast confessed that "in the extreme difficult seasons of heat and cold we were ready to say of the Sabbath, Behold what a weariness." [13]

Eventually, one section after another desired separate status as a town, either by itself or through union with outlying inhabitants in bordering communities. Concord's majority adamantly opposed these ambitions. Although the town let the pious residents of the northeast go in peace, it refused to approve any further secessions. There was a solid economic motive behind this resistance, since after a separation, each remaining taxpayer would have to bear a greater share of the minister's fixed salary. More important, loss of territory and population threatened Concord's proud position as one of the leading towns in Middlesex. In the face of this intransigence, the disaffected minorities appealed successfully to the General Court for relief. Acton was set off from Concord in 1735; another part of town joined Lincoln twenty years later.[14]

By 1765, when the colonial dispute with Britain first came before the town, sectional rivalry was a fixture of Concord's political life. Every spring, voters from the village marshaled their forces against the demands of outlying areas to make the grammar school "a moving school," which might travel through the town—six or seven weeks in one district, three weeks in another, and twelve weeks in the middle of town. For several years, the battle seesawed until in 1770 the townsmen wearied of the issue and handed the problem over to the selectmen. The grammar school stayed in the center.[15]

Delegating controversial issues to the selectmen proved to be no solution to strife. Indeed, the policy-making failures of town meeting simply intensified an ongoing struggle among sections to dominate the selectmen and through them decisions to lay out roads and locate district schoolhouses. In the 1750s and 1760s, the outcome of annual elections turned principally on which quarter of town could jam more inhabitants into the town hall. No section ever lacked representation on the five-man board of selectmen, but the North Quarter, with nearly 40 per cent of the population, controlled only 20 per cent of the seats. The real contest lay between East and South, with power continually changing hands. By 1771, however, everyone had tired of the annual fight: in a quiet compromise, never elaborated in the town records, the number of selectmen was reduced to three—one for each quarter. The inhabitants conceded the inevitability of separate interests in town life, in hopes of ending the contention they produced. Concord was, in effect, redefined as a confederacy of smaller communities.[16]

The factor of residence nonetheless continued to give some men disproportionate power in town affairs and to deny it to others. Although each quarter extended in a different direction from the town center to the outskirts, two thirds of the selectmen lived within a mile or so of the meetinghouse. So, too, did the town clerk and town treasurer. Officials could thus easily assemble for an evening's business over rum at one of the taverns in the center. Outlivers might wonder whether their interests were fully considered at such sessions.

Certainly the town had learned little from its previous failures to stop secession. In the 1760s and early 1770s, inhabitants in the northernmost part, four miles and more above the Concord River, pressed a bid for separation and, failing that, for some concessions to their special needs. The town meeting was in no mood for accommodation. Predictably, the town reasserted its refusal to let any territory go. But it also denied the petitioners' request for exemption from the minister's rate, so that they might hire their own preacher. No one seriously expected the remote northerners to attend the church regularly in town, especially when their only means of access, the North Bridge, was periodically washed out in winter. Still, membership in the community, even if it was forced membership, required support of the town minister. And if the outlivers did wish to go to meeting in town, they would get scant encouragement from the majority. Petitioners Joseph Taylor, Zaccheus Green, and others in the north part could not persuade the town to accept a proposed road enabling them "to go to the Public Worship and to market." Nor could they gain exemption from taxes for the undelivered services.[17]

It was thus after a decade's neglect for their needs that the northerly inhabitants neared the end of their patience. In 1772, "anxiosely Desirous if possable to obtain our Long Sought for Relief," they renewed their plea for separation or in-town status as a religious precinct. "We would still make use of Every Laudable means" to reach agreement with the town, they declared. Behind the outward deference to their townsmen's feelings lay the unmistakable suggestion that less than "Laudable means" had been promoted for breaking free. The majority ignored the hint and once more denied the request.[18]

The political conflicts created by sectionalism were not unique to Concord. Throughout the eighteenth century most long-settled Massachusetts towns contended with varying success against the ambitions of their outlying districts. In some places, separations were prevented by timely grants of precinct status or relocation of the meetinghouse; in others, by solutions imposed from the General Court. In places like Dedham, years of sectional sparring culminated in voting fraud, resort to muskets at town meetings, and "complete paralysis of the mechanisms of town government." Communities splintered on the inescapable consequences of social difference. Men had been raised to expect harmony in their affairs, and when all minds were not one, when separate interests fought for control, a New England town could become a hothouse of tensions and frustrations that threatened to tear the community apart.[19]

In Concord it was conflict within the established church rather than sectionalism that posed the most severe test of the integrity of the town in the generation before the Revolution. The troubles began back in 1738, when the town had to fire its minister of twenty years' standing, the Reverend John Whiting, because he drank too much. His successor, Daniel Bliss, was even more controversial. A twenty-five-year-old graduate of Yale College, Bliss took over the pulpit in admittedly unpleasant circumstances. Not only did the ousted parson, Whiting, remain in town, but he insisted upon occupying the ministerial pew on the Sabbath. Even so, Bliss's real problems were of his own making.[20]

In the 1730s and early 1740s, a wave of spiritual revivals spread throughout the colonies, and the new minister participated enthusiastically in this "Great Awakening" of religion. While at Yale, Bliss had felt the stirrings of God in his soul. A few years later, he was miraculously saved from drowning—an act of Providence he was still remembering in his diary after a quarter century. These events taught Bliss that men were utterly, irredeemably lost to sin and damnation without God's saving grace, and he carried the urgent tidings to Concord with a tireless emotional zeal. Without "conversion" by the Lord, he declared, nothing men did in this life mattered, and nothing would ease their pain in the afterlife: "When they shall have suffered as many millions of ages, as there shall have been moments from the beginning to the end of time, they will have arrived nothing nearer to an end of their torments . . . but will even then be beginning to make their beds in hell." With divine grace, they would be reborn—brought into a "new light"—and would walk among the elect of Christ.[21]

Bliss took his message to a decaying church. While everyone in Concord was expected to attend the preaching of the Word, church membership was restricted to an elite—to those who could testify to God's workings in their souls. It was the church members who enjoyed the fellowship of the communion table, the church members who ran the affairs of the church and who joined with the town meeting in hiring a minister. Indeed, the members *were* the church: the voluntary gathering of the Lord's chosen. But in the last difficult years of Whiting's ministry, fewer and fewer townspeople experienced saving grace. The church was dwindling to an aging, wealthy, and mostly female band of believers. Only thirty-three men—little more than a tenth of the adult males—belonged. The religious spirit of Concord had grown cold.[22]

Virtually overnight, Bliss revived the town. In two years, church membership went from eighty-three to nearly two hundred; the harvest of souls was greatest among teen-agers and young adults. For a time, religious meetings were held every day of the week. And in

October 1741, the great English evangelist George Whitfield came to town and preached to thousands in the open air. "The Lord is now gloriously at Work in this Town," Bliss exulted.[23]

But the Lord's "Enemies," as Bliss called his "Old Light" critics, were also active. To them, everything about Bliss was intolerable. He preached in other men's parishes without their consent. He let untrained laymen rant from his own pulpit. He undermined morality with his declarations that "it was as great a sin for a man to get an estate by honest labor, if he had not a single aim at the glory of God, as to get it by gaming at cards or dice." And his emotional sermons—the key to his success—were an outright disgrace:

> He began [wrote one outraged observer] in a low and moderate Strain, and went on for some Time in the same Manner; but towards the Close of the Sermon, as it was called, he began to raise his Voice, and to use many extravagant Gestures; and then began a considerable groaning amongst the Auditors, which as soon as he perceiv'd, he raised his Voice still higher, and then the Congregation were in the utmost Confusion, some crying out in the most doleful Accents, some laughing, and others huging, and Bliss still roaring to them to come to Christ, they answering, *I will, I will, I'm coming, I'm coming*.

Appalled by these excesses, Concord's Old Lights replied, "I will not."[24]

In the southeastern part of town, many inhabitants who had never before complained about the trip to the meetinghouse suddenly discovered that the Sabbath journey was long and hard. They successfully petitioned the General Court to incorporate them into a second parish, which in 1754 became part of the new town of Lincoln. Another group of dissidents, who represented at least a fifth of the town and included some of Concord's richest men but also some of its poorest, seceded from the church in 1745 and formed their own religious body. The West Church, as it was called, was never very strong; it never supported a regular minister, and since the town refused to let members use the meetinghouse for services, they had to worship in the Black Horse Tavern. Nevertheless, the venture lasted some fourteen years, long after the revival had waned. By 1760, a few dissidents were reconciled with Bliss. But most were attending church in Lincoln. They remained embittered against the pastor and the town, and their resentments were soon to disrupt Concord's politics again, down to the very eve of revolution.[25]

When twenty-two-year-old William Emerson assumed the Concord pulpit after Bliss's death in 1764, he inherited both the supporters and enemies of his predecessor. Emerson's selection was opposed by a third of the town in a vote that brought out nearly every eligible man in Concord. The contest was a re-enactment of the divisions under Bliss. According to Dr. Joseph Lee, a leader of the losing side, the youthful Emerson had been solicited as a ministerial candidate by church agent Jonathan Puffer in violation of explicit instructions to seek another. When challenged for his unauthorized action, Puffer unrepentantly told his critics that he had learned that "Billy Emerson was a converted man . . . and he was Detearmined that Concord should have a Converted man for their Minister Let it cost what it will." [26]

Lee, a former officer of the West Church, was furious. He and his followers had undoubtedly hoped that with the end of Bliss's pastorate, they might reunite with the town church. Now, they feared, another New Light preacher was being called into the pulpit. There were also more personal objections to young Emerson:

> Mr. Wm. Emerson come to my house [Lee recalled] to see me a certain day and we talked over all the matters relating to his coming into town and how he had spent his time since he Left [Harvard] Colledge, all as calm as a watch. He replyed that he was very senceable that he had fooled away his time and that he was very much to blame and ought to go back to Colledge and study Divinity two years before he undertook to supply a pulpit in any place. . . .

Lee and others were determined to make Emerson follow his own advice. After losing the fight against his selection, they whittled his annual salary down to £80 in hopes he would refuse the post. A few weeks later, Emerson's supporters succeeded in raising the figure to £100, whereupon nine former West Church members futilely asked the town to reconsider. By Emerson's ordination on New Year's Day, 1766, Lee was thoroughly alienated. The pastor's "introduction into the town," he wrote in a history of the dispute for his son, "was scandlous for it was done by Lying and deceit . . . and it laid a foundation for much Trouble, Contention, Confusion, and every evil work." [27]

As it turned out, Emerson proved something of a religious liberal. He cared little for theological niceties: if a man professed religious belief and was of good character, Emerson thought, he should be admitted into the church. An earnest preacher, the young minister memorized his sermons in advance and delivered them with eloquent grace. He also promoted a singing school among the young men to improve the Sabbath hymns. He liked good living and lively conversation; he was comfortable at Squire Cuming's table. Emerson also had a good deal of pride. "William," his minister father once rebuked him on the way to church, "you walk as if the earth was not good enough for you." "I did not know it, Sir," he replied. He could suddenly surrender to a moment's passion—at Harvard, he was once fined ten shillings for "throwing Bricks, Sticks, Ashes &c in at the Door of the Hebrew School"—and give vent to anger he would later regret. It was not long before the refractory Concordians gave him ample provocation.[28]

The chief instigator of contention was Dr. Joseph Lee. Within a month of Emerson's ordination, Lee applied for membership in the church and touched off the conflict that embroiled the town for the next six years. In 1766, Lee, age fifty, was the biggest landholder in town. From his home on Nashawtuc Hill in the South Quarter, he presided over a 350-acre domain, worked by his trusted slave Cato and an ever-changing crew of hired laborers. Besides managing the farm, Lee did part-time doctoring, rented out several houses, invested in western lands, put money out on loan, counseled his family of eight—and dabbled in Concord politics. As he looked out at the weathercock and belfry of the town hall from his hilltop a mile away, he must have occasionally chafed at his failure to obtain the respect due his high station in life. The town was quite willing to employ his talents as a surveyor of highways, viewer of fences, and sometime member of important ad hoc committees, but Lee still awaited election to the selectmen or to the General Court in Boston. His future prospects for political leadership were dim, for opportunities to achieve high town office were narrowing. The honor of serving in the General Court went to only two men from 1756 to 1775. The board of selectmen was filling up with the same familiar faces year after year. Thus, in the mid-1760s, Lee stood outside the political elite and, with the collapse of the West Church, outside the community's religious structure as well. Exclusion from the trust and fellowship of his townsmen bred in him an acute sensitivity to slights. Like Emerson, Lee was quick to anger and quicker to see any public criticism as an attack on his rights. Responding in kind, he was vitriolic in a fight.[29]

Like any other applicant for church membership, Lee had to undergo the scrutiny of all the elect, poor as well as rich. Under the usual procedure, a candidate was "propounded" to the congregation by the pastor. A period of probation followed, during which members could privately raise objections to the applicant. If any came forward, the minister and deacons would press the candidate to "give satisfaction" to his critics. Until reconciliation was achieved, the church officers would put off a vote; no one was admitted who was not at peace with his neighbors. When it was finally clear that a consensus had emerged, the candidate would stand before the congregation, read a relation of his faith and his experience of the Lord, and then, no objections being heard, proceed to accept the covenant and enter the fellowship of the church. Election to membership was thus a seal of one's moral acceptability to the community—a judgment few individuals faced lightly and fewer still contested publicly. But Joseph Lee was ready for confrontation.[30]

Within days of his candidacy, "Mr. Lee's Affair [was] in Agitation," as William Emerson noted in his diary. Mrs. Lydia Hodgman came before the church governing committee, composed of Emerson and the deacons, and charged Lee with "mal administration" of her late mother's estate—particularly, with taking a pocketbook and some notes and with unnecessarily recording deeds. Soon others were telling their stories of Lee's "opresing ye fatherless and widoes in long Delays in Settling his accompts and making Large and exorbetent Demands for his Services."[31]

The church elders urged Lee to make peace with his critics, but without success. He denied any wrongdoing as an executor and soon became "exasperated" at the delay. "Giveing way to pastion," he insulted the pastor and the deacons and demanded a public hearing. They refused. "It would not be for ye Glory of God or for ye Peace of ye Ch^{h}," they explained. Lee's aim, they suspected, was to drum up supporters and cause a division.[32]

Lee responded with fury. He scolded the church fathers: "They had wronged him through prejudis and yt was ye principell they acted upon and . . . they kept lying, durty drabs in their Ch^{h}." Later that evening, he encountered deacon Ephraim Brown and, according to one account, "threatened and bull raged him in a most vile manner openly in ye highway." Brown said simply, "I was fureously Assalted by him with great Threaitnings." [33]

Amid the rising acrimony—still confined to private exchanges but surely rumored throughout the small town—the character of the new minister came under public attack. In an anonymous broadside posted in the village taverns, the people of Concord were astonished to read that their minister had traveled to Maine alone with Miss Phebe Bliss, daughter of his late predecessor and soon to be Mrs. Emerson. Not surprisingly, suspicions centered on Lee as the author of the report. Emerson quickly lost whatever patience remained for the frustrating process of Christian conciliation.[34]

Lee eventually got his public hearing, but it did him no good. The church voted that Sister Hodgman's objections were indeed "a sufficient Bar to his being received into full Communion." Lee waited a year to renew his application, meanwhile lobbying for support. In August 1768, at Lee's request, the church reopened his case, reheard the arguments, and reaffirmed its original vote.[35]

It was time for a change of tactics. Lee requested the church to join him in calling on ministers from other towns to mediate. It took nearly another year of haggling before he got his way. By then the argument had long since transcended the original charges surrounding his conduct as an executor. To Lee, the case was now a civil liberties issue, eighteenth-century style. His character had been impugned, he objected, without any formal statement of charges; public testimony had been offered against him although he had not been present to respond. One of the judges in the case had taken the part of a prosecutor. As for William Emerson: "I complain of the Rev'd. Pastor many Imprudences, gross Blunders to say no worse and of his Breach of Promise by all which I apprehend he has rendered himself unworthy of the Sacred Character of a Minister of Jesus Christ." [36]

The council that finally convened in Concord in April 1769 offered all parties to the conflict a means of saving face. It cleared everyone of the most serious charges—Sister Hodgman of spite, Dr. Lee of "Fraud and Injustice," Reverend Emerson of immoral designs against Miss Phebe, and Miss Phebe of . . . —accepted apologies all around, and disbanded with a pious reminder that "where there is Contention, there is every evil work." [37]

But as soon as the outsiders were out of earshot, the Concordians went back to bickering more bitterly than ever. Lee again sought admission to communion and was again rejected, after word got around that forty members would leave the church upon a favorable vote. In response, eleven of Lee's friends, known as the "aggrieved brethren," dissented and forced a protracted replay of the previous three years' querulous proceedings. Even a "Day of Humiliation and Prayer" brought no more than twenty-four hours' peace. Finally, the aggrieved brethren called their own so-called party council of ministers, which the Church refused to recognize, won a predictably friendly result, and proudly had it published in the May 6, 1771, *Boston Gazette*, where everyone in the province could read that the Rev. William Emerson displayed "a criminal disregard to TRUTH." [38]

That was not all. The furor seized town politics. In tandem with the newspaper attack on Emerson, Joseph Lee ran for Concord's seat in the provincial House of Representatives against the three-term incumbent, Captain James Barrett, a staunch supporter of the pastor and the man who was emerging as the dominant political power in town. Barrett was a commercial farmer who raised large crops of rye and oats and fattened substantial herds of cattle on his 150 acres two miles northwest of the village. Age sixty in 1771, he was the senior officeholder in town. A former militia captain, selectman, and moderator of town meetings before moving up to the General Court, he was soon to acquire a reputation for being "as great a patriot as was then or perhaps ever in Concord." But in May 1771 he encountered the toughest and most bitter opposition of his public career. Although he had joined the church late in life, during a brief flurry of revivalism which parson Bliss inspired in the year before his death, Barrett and his family had long been supporters of the religious establishment. The representative himself took no active part in the church opposition to Lee. But his brother Thomas, a wealthy miller, was one of the church deacons, and his son James, Jr., testified against Lee at the council of April 1769. In this fight the Barretts were allied with Squire Cuming, selectmen John Flint and James Chandler, and the father of town clerk Wood, all of whom had been converted to the church in the 1740s, at the height of the Great Awakening. The old party lines were forming once again. But not completely: one leader of the Emerson-Barrett faction, Captain Jonathan Buttrick, was a former defector to the West Church.[39]

For his part, Lee had important friends in the social and political elite. Nearly all the aggrieved brethren stood in the upper reaches of the economic order. Three of them were serving as selectmen in the years the controversy over Lee was building to a pitch. Lee even commanded support from two of his opponent's kin: Lieutenant Humphrey Barrett, Captain Barrett's first cousin, and housewright Josiah Meriam, his son-in-law.[40]

Lee's campaign against Barrett left only a few traces in the town records. On the day of the election, so many voters crowded into the town house that they had to adjourn to the larger meetinghouse. And while citizens usually cast their votes in public, this time a secret ballot was taken; in the tense atmosphere, few townsmen were willing to declare their sympathies aloud. When the ballots were counted, Barrett had won "a great majority." According to Concord historian Lemuel Shattuck, who interviewed survivors of the Revolutionary era about the dispute and then tactfully said as little as possible about it, "About one third part of the town was in favor of Lee. The party spirit was violent."[41]

Factional strife probably determined the outcome of the earlier March elections for town officials, too. Two aggrieved brethren served among the five selectmen every year from 1767 to 1770, but after Lee's supporters withdrew from communion in late 1770, all general town offices went to known antagonists of Lee.

With so little record of the party conflict, one can only speculate as to who supported which side and why. Possibly, farmers and artisans distrusted grandees like Lee, who made money from others' misfortunes, tying up estates in probate and taking their time about prying them loose. In 1767 another executor came under challenge in a case very similar to Lee's. Ebenezer Hartshorn had settled the estate of John Hunt, deceased father of the pro-Emerson deacon Simon Hunt, and was now pressed to justify his conduct. In a letter to one of Lee's close friends, Hartshorn attributed two possible motives to his critics: "A Party Temper of mind, or Ignorance in the worth of the work I did. As to the first, it is a hard thing to charge. As to the Second, it is no Scandal to say that it is very Improbable they Should understand what I did, tho' very good men in their own business."[42]

If social resentment of legal finaglers did prompt popular hostility to Lee, it was, at best, a partial cause of conflict. The Barretts, Cuming, John Beatton, and their allies were no less landed and no less sophisticated about the world's business than Lee and his friends. For both sides of the elite—and probably for the rest of the town—religious divisions lay at the heart of the fight.

Lee undoubtedly drew the bulk of his following from the former West Church faithful, still sullenly outside the church but still compelled to pay for its minister. In rejecting Lee, the church had rejected the first bid by one of its prodigal sons to come home after Bliss's death. His application probably represented a test case to the dissidents. Would the church, which had driven them out, now welcome them back in peace? It mattered not that Lee was a controversial candidate. To his friends, the message was unmistakable: the majority was declaring the rift in the community permanent. Lee's West Church allies, in turn, would make no further attempt at reunion. And they would be heartened by the moral support of the aggrieved brethren.

Lee's campaign went beyond the matter of church admissions. After March 1771, Lee and his friends were not only outsiders in religion but out of political office as well. It was probably this exclusion from town leadership that inspired the newspaper attack on Emerson and the challenge to Barrett. Indeed, Lee may have expressed the resentment and frustrations of all those who felt somehow excluded from the community's rewards: the old West Church congregation, the inhabitants of the north part of town, and all of the politically ambitious outside the orbit of the Emerson-Barrett establishment.

All of this conflict was too much for some townsmen to bear. One participant drew up for himself some "Remarks on Several Events in Concord since ye Ordination" of William Emerson. He detailed the public slurs on the pastor's honor, the rejection of Lee, the convening of the mutual and party councils, and the uproar that followed. "The dreadfull Event," he wrote, referring to the party council's decision "Contrary to Rule or Reason," was "a Stumbling Block to many and grait offence to others while multitudes were Rejoyceing as if Bedlam was broke lose and all ye Labour and panes of Spreading that Result by Rideing and writeing Hundreds of Coppeys Sending them abrod far and neer, yeat all would not Satisfie untill addvertised in ye public prints." He was offended, too, by "the most Cruel and uncristion proseeding against Cap^{n} Barrit and others which ye like was never heard of in New England before." The product of all this contention within town and church was a people in disarray—"all Society and fammelyes in Confusetion." [43]

Eventually, the audible fighting within the church sputtered to a close. A mighty council of churches met in July 1772 and exonerated the conduct of the Concord congregation and its pastor throughout the Joseph Lee affair—but not without a scolding. "Brethren," the council sorrowfully declared, "we lament that you have suffered yourselves to be so divided for so small matters. . . ." A strong dissent was filed against the decision, but everyone was sick of the subject. There was, after all, nothing more to say. Joseph Lee remained unacceptable to the majority, notwithstanding the division in the church. And the aggrieved brethren remained away from the communion table.[44]

The factional lines persisted. Unable to remove dissenters from their midst, the beleaguered town majority refused them a legitimate place in community life. Lee and his friends, frozen out of the church and purged from office, retained the power to disrupt; at town meetings they would pose a permanent threat of opposition both to the town's majority and to the authority of its managers. Meanwhile, the dissidents in the north grew ever more alienated, joining in town affairs for the sole purpose of seceding from the town. Concordians—at least, those active in public affairs—were engaging in a rancorous, competitive politics that belied their public values. Theirs was a divided town that was rapidly losing its moral center. This failure of community, at its height in the early 1770s, would play a large role in shaping the town's response to revolution.

★2★
The Reluctant Revolutionaries

IN 1775, Concord, Massachusetts, was a very minor outpost of the far-flung British Empire. Its inhabitants produced none of the great staple exports—tobacco, rice, indigo, sugar—that enriched His Majesty's Treasury. As consumers of British manufactures, its 265 families were but a tiny part of the great aggregate of colonial demand. Had it not been for its few months of military fame, Concord might never have reached the notice of high British officials. Indeed, had they given a moment to its fractious affairs, imperial policy-makers would undoubtedly have regarded Concord as one more dangerous colonial democracy, full of unseemly conflict, run by men ill-fitted to rule, barely conscious of its subordination to the mother country. It was just the sort of community that men in London had been attempting, since the early 1760s, to bring under the tighter control of king and Parliament.

Between 1764 and 1774, Great Britain imposed on her American colonies a series of measures that plunged the empire into periodic and ever more serious crises until the armed confrontation of April 19, 1775. The main lines of the story are generally known: when Britain tried to tax her provinces without consent, they resisted under the banner of "No taxation without representation." First came the Sugar Act (1764), laying a fresh set of tariffs on colonial trade and curtailing Americans' longtime habit of smuggling sugar and molasses from the French West Indies. The next year a Stamp Act (1765) levied an unprecedented direct tax on virtually every piece of public paper in the colonies—newspapers, almanacs, diplomas, deeds, wills, customs documents. It even taxed tax receipts.

Under a storm of defiant American protests and under the pressures of a boycott of British imports, Parliament repealed the stamp duty, but not without announcing in the Declaratory Act (1766) its power to legislate for the colonies "in all cases whatsoever."

Soon the legislators were putting principle back into practice. In 1767, Parliament enacted Chancellor of the Exchequer Charles Townshend's duties on all lead, glass, paper, paint, and tea imported into the colonies. Once again American opposition mounted, not only to the taxes themselves but also to their enforcement provisions and to the intended use of the money to strengthen British influence over provincial governments. Although moderates dragged their feet, another intercolonial boycott of British goods was begun. In Boston—the "sewer" of America, to many conservatives—mobs rioted against Townshend's customs commissioners. In 1768, Britain stationed two regiments of troops in the town, but instead of keeping law and order, the presence of Redcoats provoked the so-called Boston Massacre two years later. Parliament again retreated, leaving only a symbolic tax on tea. Two years of quiet followed. But when the Tea Act (1773) allowed the British East India Company the unusual privilege of selling its dutied tea directly to America, the whole issue of British taxation revived. No provincial port would receive the tea; Bostonians threw it into the bay on the night of December 16, 1773, in the famous Tea Party. An outraged Parliament retaliated by closing the port of Boston to trade and revamping the government of Massachusetts, and in the process it touched off the events that led directly to Lexington and Concord.

Behind this simple catalogue of British action and American response lay a far more complex situation formed by divergent political and constitutional developments on both sides of the Atlantic. That Parliament had not taxed the colonies for revenue before 1764 reflected neither consistent policy nor principle; its reversal of course after that date was likewise expediency—a response to the staggering bills facing the British Treasury in the wake of the Seven Years War (in America, the French and Indian War). Still, freedom from direct Parliamentary taxation had become precedent to Americans. Moreover, since the early eighteenth century, the colonists had been periodically restless under the authority of royal ministers at home and in London, and their assemblies had taken advantage of the weapons at hand—notably, power of the purse—and of the slender British presence in North America to seize a high degree of self-government. Colonial legislators not surprisingly resented Parliament's invasion of their hard-won prerogatives. But the imperial dispute was more than a jurisdictional feud between rival legislative bodies. It involved a sustained argument over the fundamental concepts of eighteenth-century Anglo-American government.[1]

Devotion to constitutional principle alone did not push men straight into revolution. Indeed, it could and did prompt many colonists to condemn all violent opposition to British measures and to urge peaceful submission to law while more petitions were forwarded to Parliament. Political leadership was also needed to formulate strategy, to organize tactics, and, most important, to supply an energizing vision that would transform legalistic protests into a revolutionary movement. In almost every colony a small group of politicians, printers, and pamphleteers fulfilled these functions; particularly important was the coterie centered in Boston led by Samuel Adams, John Hancock, and James Otis. These radical leaders interpreted the ominous new imperial laws from a perspective known as the Real Whig tradition, a body of dissenting English political thought that assessed trends in the mother country in the most alarming light.[2]

English government, Real Whigs declaimed, had fallen away from virtue, austerity, and liberty. It had forgotten the principles of its Glorious Revolution against Stuart tyranny. Now, the executive, centered in the Crown and managed by royal ministers with Parliamentary seats, was not only corrupting members of both Lords and Commons with a host of pensions and places but even bribing supposedly independent British freeholders in a successful perversion of Parliamentary elections. None of the Real Whigs thought for a minute that these attempts to influence Parliament were innocent: all of human history revealed continuous assaults by the aggressive forces of power on the passive, frail figure of liberty. Power was the domain of the Crown, liberty of Parliament. Thus, when British legislators, at the urging of Crown-appointed ministers, began to tax the colonies, radicals were quick to smell a plot. Provincial Whigs initially put the blame exclusively on colonial placemen like Massachusetts Governor Francis Bernard, whom they accused of promoting the subjection of America for his own personal gain. But gradually they expanded their indictment to include the ministers of the government in London and ultimately, by the early 1770s, King George III himself. Seeing reform dead in England, they urged unflagging vigilance on behalf of American rights.

Not everyone was prepared for this challenge. In the 1760s and early 1770s, inhabitants of communities like Concord frequently failed to heed the radicals' warnings. Concord was no friend to the Stamp Act or to the other new taxes, but the townspeople were not ready to change their politics overnight. Through its representative to the legislature, the town was allied to the royal administration in Boston, and this association continued in the early years of the Revolutionary movement. Even after the town changed sides in the provincial arena, imperial issues made little difference in the town's political life. Before they could become the "embattled farmers" of history, the townspeople had to transcend their traditional immersion in local affairs and to transform their constitutional opposition to British policies into many personal commitments to resistance shared throughout the town. In mid-1774 this point was reached. Then, making up for lost time, Concordians marched with single-minded militancy into the front ranks of the Revolution.

★ ★ ★

The farmers and artisans of Concord were absorbed in their own religious affairs when the new imperial program went into effect. As news of the Sugar Act and a possible stamp duty reached Boston in mid-May 1764 they were burying their contentious pastor, Daniel Bliss, in an expensive style that was sure to increase local taxes. The parishioners entertained funeral attendants liberally with wine and spirits, bestowed gloves and rings on the pallbearers, and hired Ebenezer Hartshorn to fashion an elegant coffin. Hartshorn, a West Church communicant, sealed Bliss snugly for eternity with five hundred "jappaned black" nails and five hundred small white tacks. In all, the town's mourning cost more than £66. The inhabitants could expect to spend another £100 to induce a new minister to settle in their religiously divided community. That task, as we have seen, occupied more than a year, raising the townsmen to a pitch of political excitement and probably overshadowing the news that the stamp tax would be law by November 1, 1765.[3]

As with nearly all nonlocal matters, the voters of Concord dealt with the Stamp Act through their legislative representative. Every year, without fail, Concord sent a delegate to the General Court in Boston, where, as a member of the House of Representatives, he would join with the Council, the upper chamber of the legislature, and with the royal governor to make laws for the colony. In provincial affairs the town was more diligent than most; before the Revolutionary crisis, a majority of communities could spare neither the time nor the tax money for such regular representation. Concord's delegate usually acted at his own discretion. In accord with the prevailing view of the responsibilities of magistrates, he was expected to employ his judgment and integrity on his neighbors' behalf. The townsmen seldom instructed him on how to vote or required him to account for his conduct. Town meetings were simply not the forum for provincial and imperial issues. But in the unusual circumstances of the Stamp Act crisis, Concord departed from custom and directed its representative's vote.[4]

In the fall of 1765 the town of Boston called on the countryside to endorse its resistance to the new law. Like rural voters elsewhere, Concordians met to instruct their representative "about any Important affair that may be Transacted at the General Court Concerning the Stamp Act." Unfortunately, their decision was not recorded. After taking its vote, the meeting ordered town clerk Jonas Heywood to record the instructions in the "town book"—which he omitted to do, perhaps to avoid future trouble with provincial authorities. According to Lemuel Shattuck, the nineteenth-century Concord historian, the town had voted to oppose operation of the law and to seek its repeal by all constitutional means—substantially the same position as that announced in the Braintree Resolves, drafted by an obscure lawyer from the town of Braintree named John Adams and widely circulated in the press. More than forty communities adopted the Resolves as their own that fall. To judge from Shattuck's summary, Concord's voters were among them.[5]

The Braintree Resolves assailed the Stamp Act on both economic and constitutional grounds. It was a "burthensome tax," loading down ordinary economic life with unbearable charges and threatening to "drain the country of its cash, strip multitudes of their property, and reduce them to absolute beggary." But the law was more than a raid on property: it robbed Americans of their basic rights. "We have always understood it to be a grand and fundamental part of the constitution," the Resolves declared, "that no freeman should be subject to any tax to which he has not given his own consent, in person or by proxy." Since Americans were not represented in Parliament, the stamp duty was plainly unconstitutional. "The most grievous innovation of all," though, was the provision for enforcing the act through vice-admiralty courts. This endangered the right to impartial justice, for "in these courts, one judge presides alone! No juries have any concern there!" Once again the constitution and the Massachusetts Province Charter of 1691 were being breached.[6]

Given these violations of colonial rights, the Resolves enjoined Braintree's representative—and presumably that of Concord—to use every "lawful means, consistent with our allegiance to the King, and relation to Great Britain," to prevent implementation of the tax. "We further recommend," the instructions concluded, "the most clear and explicit assertion and vindication of our own rights and liberties to be entered on the public records, that the world may know . . . that we have a clear knowledge and a just sense of them, and with submission to Divine Providence, that we can never be slaves. . . ."

The Resolves put forward a very different conception of Anglo-American government from that prevailing in the mother country. In England, Parliament, embodying king, lord, and commons in their legislative capacities, was considered the supreme authority in government and the arbiter of all its powers. In theory, all citizens of Great Britain were "virtually" represented in Parliament, whether they elected its members or not (and most didn't); it was enough that they shared common interests with the lawmakers. "Parliament," said Edmund Burke, "is a *deliberative* assembly of *one* nation, with *one* interest, that of the whole, where, not local purposes, not local prejudices ought to guide, but the general good, resulting from the general reason of the whole." In effect, Parliament was *the* nation organized to make its own laws.[7]

But Americans, denying a natural identity of colonial and English interests, insisted that "no member can represent any but those by whom he hath been elected; if not elected, he cannot represent them, and of course not consent to anything in their behalf." And they proceeded to erect the constitution into a barrier against invasion of their rights by men they had not elected. By "constitution," eighteenth-century Anglo-American writers meant not a written document but the existing arrangements of government—laws, charters, customs, and institutions—together with the principles these incorporated. In 1765 provincial writers counted on the principles to restrain the conduct of the institutions; in succeeding years, they would come to define a constitution in the terms we have inherited: as a fixed plan specifying the rights of citizens and prescribing the powers of government.[8]

However much it diverged from English constitutional precedents, the Braintree document summarized more than a century's experience of self-government in communities like Concord, where voters gathered annually to elect every official, including the neighbors who served on juries, and to vote their own taxes. Representation to colonial Yankees was a direct relationship between magistrate and people: the representatives to the General Court were all chosen by specific towns. And as Concord's experience attests, even within a town selectmen were often spokesmen for smaller parts of the community. New Englanders, too, were continually writing what were, in effect, constitutions to carry out their social life. By formal covenants they had formed towns and embodied churches in the seventeenth century; now they covenanted as Concordians did, when they established any organization from proprietorships to regulate land use to singing schools to improve church music. The purposes of the organization were always set forth, together with the duties of members and the specific powers of any officials. New Englanders thus operated on an unspoken assumption that later generations of Americans would take to extremes: every institution must have its charter.[9]

Concord's instructions had their intended effect. In January 1766, in the only recorded roll call of the Stamp Act crisis, the town's representative, Charles Prescott, joined an overwhelming majority of the House in urging the opening of the province's courts for business without stamped paper—a direct defiance of the law. But his must have been a reluctant vote. Prescott, fifty-four years old and a veteran of six terms in the legislature, was a stalwart of the "Court Party," the faction centered in Governor Francis Bernard and cemented by the ample patronage that Lieutenant Governor Thomas Hutchinson efficiently distributed. A gentleman-farmer of considerable property, Prescott had been well rewarded for his regularity with prestigious appointments as justice of the peace and lieutenant colonel of the county militia. "The Office of a Justice of the Peace," John Adams complained in 1774, "is a great Acquisition in the Country, and such a Distinction to a Man among his Neighbours as is enough to purchase and corrupt allmost any Man." Prescott thus owed considerable loyalty to an extensive Crown-backed political machine, and his votes in the House on imperial issues reflected this debt as well as the opinions of his Concord constituents.[10]

Before receiving town instructions, Prescott had apparently backed Lieutenant Governor Hutchinson's every effort to qualify and dilute the province's opposition to the Stamp Act. The administration faction had packed the Massachusetts delegation to the intercolonial Stamp Act Congress with "fast friends of the government of Great Britain"; had come within a single vote of winning House support for "submission" to the duty; and had successfully blocked a move to conduct public affairs in disregard of the law until angry voters in the countryside forced the legislature's hand with the Braintree Resolves. In response, the Boston-led opposition, styling itself the "Popular party," determined to purge its conservative "Court" enemies from the General Court. In the spring of 1766, on the eve of new elections for the House and before news of the Stamp Act's repeal had reached America, the radicals inserted in the newspapers the names of thirty-two representatives whom they had singled out as friends of the Stamp Act. Concord's Charles Prescott was on the list.[11]

Without directly urging defeat of the thirty-two, the Bostonians stated the choice before their countrymen in terms no one would misunderstand. If the representatives had ardently defended "the rights and liberties of the people," suggested "J.R." in the *Boston Evening Post*, let them receive "those honors . . . they justly deserve."

> But if they have acted a part, the reverse of this: and in particular, if they have in any shape discovered an approbation of the *Stamp Act*, and manifested a willingness that it should take place in this province: Then, without doubt, they are justly to be accounted *enemies of their country;* and accordingly their names ought to be HUNG UP, and exposed to contempt . . . in every town of the province. Whoever contributes to enslave posterity, and bring a lasting ruin on his country, his name should descend, with all the marks of infamy, to the latest times.

Lest anyone miss his intent, the anonymous writer went on to observe bluntly that "*a general purgation,* and thorough reformation in *both houses,* is *of absolute necessity.*" [12]

The Boston opposition won its case. Nineteen of the thirty-two representatives were purged, and the Popular forces gained control of the House. "Several gentlemen of respectable characters, considerable property, and heretofore of uninterrupted authority [in] their towns were flung out and ignorant and low men elected in their stead," Governor Bernard commented in disgust. Next door to Concord, Lincoln representative Chambers Russell, a judge of the despised vice-admiralty courts, went down to defeat.

But the townspeople of Concord resisted the general retaliatory mood. Charles Prescott was re-elected to the House, keeping his constituents securely in the royal government's camp for two more years.

In returning Prescott, Concord voters opted for politics as usual in a province temporarily seized by ideological fervor. They were, of course, not alone. Many towns in remote western Massachusetts also stood aloof from the furor; they deferred, as they always did, to their traditional leaders—the "river gods" of the Connecticut Valley, who formed a solid bulwark for royal authority. Old habits remained strong. Taught over the years to respect independent, upper-class leaders, the voters of Concord could not easily cast aside a magistrate for reaching unpopular decisions. And besides, when he got his instructions, Prescott voted with his town.[13]

When news of the Stamp Act repeal reached Concord in July 1766 the townspeople rejoiced, and William Emerson offered their thanks to the Lord. The inhabitants were reassured by Britain's retreat. Over the next two years, Concord was more concerned with the local politics of Middlesex County than with the great issues of the British Empire. The town took little part in the protests against the Townshend acts in 1767 and 1768. While citizens in several dozen Massachusetts communities agreed to boycott a long list of British luxuries, the people of Concord did no more than pass a mild Boston-inspired resolution urging the promotion of "industry, oeconomy . . . Frugallity and Manufacturys at home." By contrast, when the General Court in 1767 considered proposals to relocate the Middlesex County courts, the townsmen were quick to pursue their interests.[14]

For years, farmers had complained of the long distances—up to forty or fifty miles—they had to travel to Cambridge or Charlestown in order to register a deed, prove a will, or appear in court. Now they were demanding that the county seat be relocated to a more convenient spot. Concord joined the movement. It formed a coalition with the towns of upper Middlesex County and sent Squire Cuming, Colonel Prescott, and Dr. Joseph Lee to appear at legislative hearings on the issue. Pleading the case of the "many Jurors and poor people" obliged to waste time and money in the conduct of legal affairs, the coalition urged the transfer of all county business to Concord.[15]

The majority of county justices, content to remain where they were, fought back with all the ammunition they could muster. Concord, they retorted, was no major market center like Cambridge or Charlestown. During its annual fall court sessions, its inns were overcrowded and overpriced, and there was nothing to do when court recessed. As a final shot, the justices remarked that "it is the general opinion that however healthy the Air in Concord may be to the Inhabitants . . . the Fogs arising from the River and low grounds there, are always prejudicial to the health of Strangers; and it seldom happens but some, and often many, are taken sick there during the term of the Court. . . ."

The cause of clean air prevailed. Although the legislative committee that heard these conflicting claims recommended a partial transfer of legal business to Concord, the measure was killed in the Council in

June 1768. It seems likely that Court Party counselors, though a minority of the upper chamber, played an important part in blocking Concord's ambitions, for the Bernard administration was adamantly opposed to bringing what it considered an already dangerously democratic government any closer to the people, as the relocation proposal would have done. If so, the Council decision must have reinforced the shift in Concord's political loyalties that had taken place in the recent spring elections to the General Court.[16]

In May 1768, Captain James Barrett replaced Colonel Prescott, his first cousin by marriage, as Concord's representative. One suspects that the colonel was forcibly replaced. The previous session of the House had seen a bitter fight by the Court Party to stop passage of the Massachusetts Circular Letter, a statement of constitutional objections to British taxation. Whig leaders had proposed to send the letter to all the other colonial assemblies in order to forge a united front against the Townshend duties. Government supporters temporarily succeeded in blocking the move. But the radical Whigs eventually prevailed and even wiped out the record of their earlier defeat from the journals of the House. Given his previous political record, Colonel Prescott undoubtedly backed the administration in this fight. Perhaps it was just coincidence that he did not return to the next session of the House. And perhaps it was also coincidence that, a few months later, Prescott was named a special judge of the Middlesex Court of Common Pleas. But one can surmise that Prescott was defeated for re-election in Concord and then rewarded for his loyalty by the Bernard administration.[17]

Whatever the case, Captain Barrett swung Concord to the opposition. On June 30, 1768, he became one of the famous "Massachusetts Ninety-two" when he joined in defying a British ultimatum that the House rescind the circular letter or be dissolved. Three months later, sealing Concord's antiadministration stance, he represented the town at an extralegal convention to protest the imminent landing of British troops in Boston. But Barrett was no radical. Nor were most of the country delegates to that convention. As the arrival of the British Regulars drew near, Boston boiled over with threats of armed resistance; Lieutenant Governor Hutchinson was even warned that he might be killed. Meeting in the tense atmosphere of Boston, Barrett and his fellow delegates disappointed the firebrands. The convention simply passed a petition to the king and a statement of protest; all talk of violence was ignored. A week later the Redcoats were in Boston. And soon after Captain James Barrett took a contract to feed the troops with oatmeal and other provisions from his farm. This arrangement continued until 1774.[18]

Although Concord, as a town, said little about the imperial issues of the day, undoubtedly many inhabitants followed closely the events in Boston. William Emerson was in the capital on March 8, 1770, the day of the funeral for four men killed in the Boston Massacre on March 5. The men were shot down when British troops fired into a crowd. Emerson was deeply moved by "ye awful & solemn [funeral] Procession"—he shared the common opinion that the victims were "Martyrs in ye glorious Cause of Liberty!" But the Concord parson also had a more personal perspective on the event. His wife's brothers, Theodore and Samuel Bliss, lived in Boston, and they had barely escaped the Regulars' fire. "I was almost overcome with a relation of the tragical Scene," Emerson wrote Phebe. "May it deeply impress our Minds." [19]

After 1768 provincial issues disappeared from Concord's agenda for four years. The inhabitants of neighboring Lincoln voted in 1770 to boycott any merchant who violated the province's nonimportation pact. Concordians did nothing. If their opinion were wanted, someone from the outside would have to ask, and no one did. Only James Barrett at the General Court would be called on to speak for the town. The inhabitants' silence may have reflected, in part, their absorption in the Joseph Lee affair, then building to a height, but it was typical of Massachusetts communities at the end of the 1760s. Opposition to British policies outside Boston was at best an intermittent event in the life of most towns. Men would mobilize only in the face of the most blatant outrages, and when these were lacking—as they were after Britain in 1770 repealed all the Townshend duties but the one on tea—they preferred to be left alone.[20]

★3★
A Well-ordered Revolution

THE transformation of Concord politics began in December 1772 when a messenger delivered a letter from Boston to the town. The letter told of an appalling new attack on liberty. The justices of Massachusetts's highest bench, the Superior Court of Judicature, would soon be paid their salaries by the Crown instead of the General Court, and thus must surrender their independence to corrupt paymasters across the sea. This was another sign, the letter declared, of the "constant, unremitted, uniform Aim to inslave us." As proof, enclosed with the letter was a long statement from the Boston town meeting, detailing, step by step, the progress of that plot. First, Parliament had taxed the colonies. Next it had sent a legion of unconstitutional officers to collect the revenue. Then, when colonial opposition mounted, it had stationed a standing army in Boston. And now came the move to buy up the judges of the province. If successful, it would "compleat our Slavery." "The plan of Despotism [is] rapidly hastening to Completion," the letter warned. It asked for Concord's sentiments and urged the town to stand firm against the new British design. Only immediate and united opposition by the towns could save the province.[1]

The letter was written by the newly formed Boston Committee of Correspondence, which sent the same message to all the other towns in the province. On the committee were twenty-one men. They included James Otis and Samuel Adams, Boston representatives to the legislature and the leading radicals in Massachusetts, plus two little-known doctors, Joseph Warren and Benjamin Church, the first of whom would become a hero in the Revolutionary movement and the other fall into public disgrace. Samuel Adams was the leader of the group, and the committee was his idea.[2]

Then age fifty, Adams had been a tireless opponent of British policies ever since the passage of the Sugar Act in 1764. The son of a wealthy brewer, Adams had neglected the family business and lost his fortune. He was likewise a failure as a Boston tax collector—his accounts ran far in arrears. But as a political manipulator and agitator, Adams was nonpareil. He was always on call—to attend a meeting, write a pamphlet, or work behind the scenes to organize a mob. Adams had played a major part in the turbulent events of the 1760s, and by 1772 he was certain that royal officials in Massachusetts and the Ministry in London meant the colonists no good. True, Governor Bernard was gone, driven out by the furies that had stormed at the time of the Boston Massacre. But in his place was Massachusetts-born Thomas Hutchinson, the arch-corrupter, in Adams's view, who was packing public offices with family and friends and perfecting the royal patronage machine. Worse still, Hutchinson had skillfully managed to quiet the province. The nonimportation movement had collapsed, now that all but one of the Townshend duties had been repealed. People were even drinking the dutied tea. Massachusetts was asleep to the steady assault on its rights. Adams proposed to awaken the province through the Boston Committee of Correspondence. The letter which Concord received in December 1772 was the committee's first attempt to carry out that task.[3]

To answer the letter, Concord named a committee of its most distinguished men. The group embraced all political factions in town. It included James Barrett and his allies—his brother Thomas, a wealthy miller and church deacon; selectman John Flint; Colonel Cuming; and Ephraim Wood. But Joseph Lee and his friend Captain Stephen Hosmer, a prominent land surveyor, were also given seats. Opponents of the royal administration were balanced with supporters of the "Court": Colonel Prescott had a place, along with Captain Barrett. As justices of the peace, Squires Cuming and Prescott were part of the governor's county patronage network. So was another member—Squire Daniel Bliss, thirty-two-year-old lawyer son of the late town minister. Bliss, a Harvard graduate, had just moved back to

Concord after several years of practicing law in Worcester County. Altogether, seven of the nine committeemen had served as selectmen; between them they controlled about 1,300 acres in town. Three were Old Lights in religion—one-time defectors to the West Church; the rest were bulwarks of the establishment. The committeemen were, in short, a cross section of the town elite. Only a few months before, the people of Concord were bitterly divided over the respective grievances of Joseph Lee and the church. Now, as they prepared to give their judgment on Britain's imperial policies, they tried deliberately to frame a community consensus. Concord wanted to speak to the world with a single voice.[4]

The committee composed a moderate but firm assertion of colonial rights. It was acceptable to nearly everyone in town, except the very conservative Daniel Bliss, who declined to sign the report. By a unanimous vote, the town meeting endorsed the committee's work, adopting its reply to the Boston letter and its set of instructions for representative Barrett. Neither document was particularly original—indeed, the former was a selective rewording of the Boston town vote on colonial grievances—but taken together, their emphases and omissions were revealing.[5]

The people of Concord began their statement, as had the Bostonians, with first principles—a declaration of "the Rights of the Colonists and of this Province in Perticular, as Men, as Christians, and as Subjects":

> . . . as men we have a right to Life, Liberty, and Property; and as Christians we in this Land (Blessed be God for it) have a right to worship God according to the Dictates of our own Consciences . . . (Papists Excepted) . . . and as Subjects we have a Right to Personal Security, Personal Liberty, and Private Property, these Principal Rights we have as Subjects of Great Briton, and have a right to enjoy them and No Power on Earth can agreeable to our Constitution take them from us or any Part of them without our Consent.

And they agreed with Boston on the main threats to liberty: Parliament's unconstitutional assumption of the power to legislate for the colonies, including the levying of revenue taxes; the assignment of officers "unknown of in the Royal Charter" to "extort" the colonists' money; the introduction of "fleets and armies . . . to Guard those unconstitutional officers"; and "the Like Instances of oppression we have been Groaning Several years." The separate instructions to Barrett noted with particular alarm the prospect of Crown salaries for judges and the passage of the little-known Dockyards Act, allowing the Crown to try alleged violators of the revenue acts wherever it pleased.

In the context of other town replies to the Boston committee, Concord stood near the middle of the provincial Whig spectrum. The townspeople shared with most colonists one fundamental assumption—that men held certain absolute, inalienable rights that no government could rightfully abridge. But they shied away from any innovation in political doctrine. Their town statement, drafted by current and former magistrates, ignored Boston's iconoclastic description of rulers as mere servants of the people, hired to administer justice and maintain popular rights; the instructions to Barrett spurned the notion held in some towns that judges should be dependent on the people rather than on the Crown. "Courts of Justice," Concord affirmed, "always Should be uninfluenced by any force but that of Law." The town's language was mild, its counsel of action cautious. A radical community like Attleborough might rattle sabers at Britain with biblical eloquence: "Fathers Provoke not your Children unto Wrath . . . Since there is no new Discovered America for us to flee unto, we are almost Ready to think that we will let go our Plow Shares and Pruning Hooks,—to be maliated upon the anvil." Concord simply urged "an Humble Remonstrance" from the colony to the Crown and "an adequate Support" for judges by the General Court.[6]

The townsmen had done their duty. If the past were any guide, they would now retreat to their old indifference to imperial issues. But events were pressing in upon them, and the Boston Committee of Correspondence kept them informed. In October 1773 the townspeople learned of a new threat—the passage of the Tea Act. On the surface the law seemed innocent enough. It was designed to help save the British East India Company, then on the verge of bankruptcy. Ordinarily, when the company shipped tea to America, it was required by English law to auction its goods to wholesale merchants. But it was now allowed to sell directly to the public through its own American agents. By eliminating the middlemen, the company would be able to reduce its prices and compete more effectively against smuggled Dutch tea. Of course, Parliament could also have lowered prices by repealing its duty on tea. The tax stayed—for "political reasons," as the new prime minister, Lord North, confessed. Although one member warned that "if [North] don't take off the duty they won't take the tea," Parliament gave little thought to the American reaction when it adopted the law. Unwittingly, it stirred up all the old issues of taxation without consent.[7]

Once again the Boston Committee of Correspondence prompted Concord to act on the new danger to colonial rights. On November 31 it sent out another circular letter, drafted this time in co-operation with several neighboring towns, which had followed Boston's lead and established committees of correspondence of their own. The letter warned that the Tea Act was a further step in the plot to make Americans slaves. By lowering the price of tea without removing the duty, Parliament was trying to trick the colonists into accepting the unconstitutional tax. This was a "crafty" plan, said the committee, and if it succeeded, worse oppressions would follow—all "to support the extravagance and vice of wretches whose vileness ought to banish them from the society of men."

The letter urged no specific course of resistance, but the Boston committee enclosed with it the report of an extralegal "Meeting of the People of Boston, and the neighbouring Towns," held in the city's Old South Meeting House on November 29. At that gathering, several thousand people vowed to prevent the sale of East India tea. They also pledged to boycott all British tea sold in America until the tax was removed. Without such a ban, it would be easy for unpatriotic sorts to buy the East India product and disguise it as another brand. With the ban, anyone found drinking tea could be labeled an "Enemy" of his country.[8]

The report from Boston drew a quick response. On December 15, Jonas Heywood, Joseph Hosmer, and nine of their neighbors asked the selectmen to call a special town meeting on the subject. "We Look upon [the Tea Act]," they said, "as unconstitutional and a

Burden." Their petition testified to the town's growing engagement in the Revolutionary debate. Just the year before, Concord had met on the first Boston letter at the instigation of the selectmen themselves. Now ordinary citizens were taking the initiative on provincial issues. Heywood, of course, was the former selectman and town clerk. And Hosmer, though never elected higher than constable, was a leader of the militia—lieutenant of Concord's troop of horse. But associated with them were men outside the town's governing class. A few—yeomen David Whittaker and David Wheeler, Jr., blacksmith Samuel Jones—filled the lesser posts of the town, taking their turns as constables, tithingmen, and fence viewers. Others never had and never would be called to play a public role. They were plain mechanics of modest property and standing: Nathaniel Stearns, a currier, and Oliver Wheeler, a goldsmith who was known to drink too much. All these men represented an emerging Revolutionary "constituency" in Concord. They followed the news of protests elsewhere and expected their town to take its part. If the selectmen delayed in calling a meeting—as perhaps they did in this case—involved inhabitants would oblige them to act.[9]

The town assembled on January 10, 1774, nearly a month after a band of men, thinly disguised as Mohawks, secretly boarded the tea ship *Dartmouth* in Boston harbor and dumped its 342 chests of tea into the bay. The session took decisive and once again unanimous action. The citizens promptly enlisted in the boycott of all British tea and then named selectmen Ephraim Wood, John Flint, and Timothy Wheeler to draw up a statement of the town's sentiments. The committee report, unanimously accepted two weeks later, expressed a growing radicalism in town. It reaffirmed Concord's long-standing position that "These Colonies have been and are Still illeagaly and unconstitutionaly Taxed by the British Parliament as they are not Realy or Virtualy Represented therein." But there was a new tone to the town statement. The year before, the inhabitants had been moderate and lawyerly. Now they, too, were alarmed by a conspiracy against liberty: the Tea Act was a snare "to catch us in those Chains that have Long been forged" for the colonies; ". . . Enemies of this as well as the Mother Country [are plotting] to Rob us of our enestimable Rights. . . ." And they took a harder line on tactics. Without mentioning the Tea Party by name, the townspeople associated themselves with the celebrated destruction of the tea, thanking Boston "for every Rattional measure they have taken for the Preserveation or Recovery of our Invaluable Rights and Liberty. . . ."[10]

Still, Concord's commitment to resistance was limited. The town declined to establish a committee of correspondence to keep in touch with protests elsewhere. And the inhabitants still hoped to reconcile their loyalty to the king with their determination to defend their rights. They declared that ". . . in Conjunction with our bretherin in America [we] will Resque our fortunes, and Even our Lives in Defence of his Majesty King George the third, his Person, Crown, and Dignity," and in the next breath they promised "to the utmost of our Power, [to] Defend all our Charter Rights Inviolate to the Latest Posterity." What they wanted, along with most colonists, was a new definition of the imperial relationship: Americans would control their internal affairs free from Parliamentary interference while paying allegiance with Englishmen to a common British sovereign. This was akin to the "dominion" status Canada would later gain in the Empire, but in the late eighteenth century it was unthinkable to most English political figures, including the king. Sovereignty, they maintained, could not be divided. After Parliament retaliated for Boston's destruction of the tea, the American position was politically untenable.[11]

In a vengeful mood, Parliament first imposed harsh economic sanctions on the contumacious Bostonians: all further trade through the port of Boston was banned until the town compensated the East India Company for its losses. Then the angry members set out to attack the "democracy" of New England—a move long sought by beleaguered Crown officials in the colony. The royal governor no longer had to work with an elective council, whose members were chosen annually by the legislature; it was replaced by a Crown-appointed body, the so-called Mandamus Council. And the governor obtained enormous new powers unmatched by executives in the other colonies. He could now name all judicial and other officials without even consulting the malleable, appointive Council. His arbitrary authority reached as well into local government: no town meeting could be held without his express approval except the annual spring election session. Local selection of juries was abolished; county sheriffs, holding office at the governor's pleasure, would summon veniremen on their own. In effect, Parliament contemptuously abrogated the Massachusetts Province Charter of 1691, which the inhabitants treasured as a sacred guarantee of their liberties. About the same time, an exhausted Thomas Hutchinson stepped down as governor, and a military man, General Thomas Gage, the commander in chief of the British Army in North America, was named to head the arbitrary new regime.[12]

But the lawmakers miscalculated. Far from strengthening British authority, their acts inflamed the countryside, united the thirteen colonies, and led to the sudden and total collapse of royal government in Massachusetts.

News of the Boston Port Act, arriving in spring 1774, several months before reports of the other reprisals, prompted Samuel Adams and his associates in the Boston Committee of Correspondence to seek a complete cessation of the colony's commercial relations with Britain. Faced with widespread merchant opposition to this plan, the radicals came up with the Solemn League and Covenant, by which citizens would pledge not to consume any British goods after August 31. With no demand for their goods, wholesalers would presumably be compelled to stop trading with Britain. As further pressure, subscribers to the covenant promised "to break off all trade, commerce and dealings whatever with all persons . . . who do import." They would likewise end "all commercial connexions" with all persons refusing to sign the covenant and would "publish their names to the world" as "contumacious importers." The nonconsumption agreement would remain in effect "until the port or harbour of Boston shall be opened, and we are fully restored to the free use of our constitutional and charter rights." [13]

The covenant, recalling a seventeenth-century compact against Charles I, upheld the commercial embargo as the only "alternitive between the horrors of Slavery, or the Carnage and Disolation of a Civil War." Many Bostonians were unimpressed; they declined to endorse the covenant in town meeting, calling instead for an intercolonial boycott agreement. But Adams and his friends were not to be stopped. Turning to the countryside for support, the Boston Committee of Correspondence took the unauthorized step of forwarding the covenant to the towns for approval. It was "the Yeomanry," Adams declared, "whose Virtue must finally save this Country." [14]

The Boston committee blundered badly in this appeal. In June 1774 the yeomen of Massachusetts were no more willing than town merchants to take hasty action in advance of an intercolonial agreement or to force nonconsumption on reluctant neighbors. As the District of Granville explained, the covenant would "breed a discord among the Inhabitants, and . . . a Discord of Sentiment may be destructive of the good effect proposed." [15]

The people of Concord shared these objections. But unlike most towns, they were still willing to adopt the nonconsumption pledge—with significant revisions. In their desire for unity, they watered down the sanctions of the pact, promising only to buy no British goods from "contumacious importers" and deleting the provision to expose nonsigners to the world; the latter measure must have evoked unpleasant memories of the recent libeling of William Emerson in the Boston press. Moreover, the agreement would be abandoned should the forthcoming First Continental Congress recommend other action. Concordians were even willing to settle for less than "full" restoration of their charter rights. Nonetheless, in notable contrast to the 1760s, the inhabitants now acted while men in other communities held back.[16]

Concord's enthusiasm for the nonconsumption covenant can be measured precisely. The document has survived intact, with the signatures of every subscriber, 280 in all, including even a few "Singal women." When it is set alongside contemporary tax lists, it affords an extraordinary insight into the support for the American cause a year before the war. Signing the covenant was a serious commitment. On June 27, 1774, Concord as a community endorsed the boycott. The next day town officials began going from house to house to offer the nonconsumption pledge to every adult male. Meanwhile, Governor Gage in Boston issued a proclamation denouncing the covenant and ordering the arrest of all who circulated or signed it. That didn't stop the boycott campaign in Concord. No doubt, the first subscribers acted before the edict became known. But it took a week to canvass the entire town. By the end of that time, nearly everyone who signed must have heard of the governor's threat. Perhaps some looked for safety in numbers. And as it turned out, the proclamation went unenforced. Still, each townsman had to consider that if he took the pledge, he might end up in jail.[17]

Most inhabitants were willing to take that risk. Support for the boycott was widespread: altogether, eight out of every ten adult males subscribed. And it cut across all economic ranks. The rich committed themselves as fully as did "middling" men. Even the laboring poor, who normally lacked the property to engage in town politics, contributed their proportionate numbers. High town officials signed in equal measure with ordinary citizens. And men in all parts of the town subscribed—the secessionists of the north as wholeheartedly as the contented residents of the village. No area was isolated from the protest. Concord had become a more unified political community than it had been since its earliest days.[18]

Still, 20 per cent of the townsmen had not endorsed the covenant, and they included some of the richest and most prominent people in town. Five of the nine committeemen who had drafted Concord's first statement on colonial rights did not sign: Squire Bliss, Colonel Cuming, Captain Hosmer, Dr. Lee, and Colonel Prescott. Neither did Captain Duncan Ingraham, a wealthy Boston merchant who had made his fortune in the Surinam trade before marrying a Concord widow in 1772 and settling in town. Nor did Honest John Beatton, nor gentleman Thomas Whiting, nor shoemaker Josiah Holdin, nor innkeepers Jonathan Heywood and Ephraim Jones. All these men (except Hosmer and Lee) shared a common bond: they held county appointments from the Crown. Heywood was a Middlesex County coroner, Holdin a deputy sheriff, and Jones kept the county jail in Concord. Prescott, of course, was a judge; the others were justices of the peace. All were part of that network of royal influence, reaching from Boston into every corner of the province, that Governor Hutchinson and his predecessors had labored to build. They were the men whom John Adams had once scorned—"if the Devil were

Governor, as for them and their Houses they would be Governor's Men." But Adams was unfair. Many were men of honor, bound by loyalty and oath to uphold the king's law.[19]

Not all nonsubscribers were "Governor's Men." Religion as well as politics shaped responses to the resistance movement. At least a dozen men who had defected to the West Church in the 1740s refused to sign. They were nearly half of the tiny remnant of dissenters from Daniel Bliss's church who were still in town and were now causing trouble for William Emerson. They were mostly old men, but age itself did not keep them from taking the pledge. Their contemporaries who had worshiped with Daniel Bliss did not show the same reluctance to boycott British goods. No, these nonsubscribers were still fighting the battles of the past. A generation before, they thought they had witnessed the breakdown of social order—uninvited preachers invading other men's parishes, ignorant farmhands challenging learned ministers, emotional ranters destroying the decorum of the Sabbath. That dreadful experience taught them what could happen when social controls were loosened and popular movements got out of hand. To be sure, these men were willing to question authority. They could, like Joseph Lee, challenge the town fathers—but in the belief that they themselves were the natural leaders of society, denied the deference they were due. And they could criticize Parliamentary taxation in mild statements of principle and humble requests for redress. But when they were called upon to defy the highest authorities of their political world, they remained true to their principles and refused. Ironically, they were joined by Squire Bliss, son of their late ministerial foe.[20]

In the late summer of 1774, conservatives—and moderate Whigs as well—had much cause for concern. Throughout the countryside, a once complacent people exploded in protest against the British assault on their rights. Except for the Stamp Act, previous Parliamentary infringements on colonial liberties had been indirect and avoidable: one did not, after all, have to drink tea. Now the prospect of slavery was imminent. Town government was under attack. In equal peril were the courts. Faced with these threats, the citizens of Concord rushed to defend their autonomy. Their militant resistance carried them outside the usual channels of local government and beyond the control of local officials. But not for long. They soon lined up again behind the men who had guided their affairs for the past decade. And they continued to act with impressive unity, ultimately overcoming the older conflicts that had divided the town.

Opposition to the Coercive Acts, as the new British measures became known, first took shape on a county-wide basis. Many communities hesitated to risk meeting without the governor's consent. Far more prudent, their inhabitants thought, to act through ad hoc political groups. Besides, since Governor Gage refused to call the legislature into special session, there was urgent need to co-ordinate protests between towns. County government, the one level of government not subject to popular control, was a natural target. Justices of the peace, appointed precisely because they were "well affected" to the administration, ran the court system that Parliament was attacking, and they held the authority to discipline towns for disobeying imperial laws. If the Popular movement were to succeed, the justices' power must be checked or overturned.[21]

In the 1760s, Concord had tried and failed to capture the county courts from Cambridge and Charlestown. Now, in an unexpected turn of circumstances, the town became the center of resistance to those same county institutions. On August 30, 1774, at Concord's invitation, some 150 delegates from all over Middlesex County gathered in town to plan a course of action. Concord was represented by veteran selectmen Ephraim Wood and John Flint and by a new colleague, Nathan Meriam. "Life and death, or what is more, freedom and slavery, are in a peculiar sense, now before us . . ." the convention warned the people of Middlesex. Their forefathers had left "a fair inheritance, purchased by a waste of blood and treasure." Their own children had a right to receive that legacy intact. If they would be true to their heritage, true to their posterity, true to themselves as men, they must resist. But resistance must be rational, "never degenerating into rage, passion and confusion." Accordingly, the delegates recommended limited defiance to illegal authority. No one who accepted a commission under the new regime should be obeyed. The county courts should be suspended rather than comply with the law. And a provincial congress was "absolutely necessary in our present unhappy situation." [22]

In Concord, two weeks later, a "Great Number of Freeholders and others" massed on the common to carry out the convention's will. The Court of General Sessions was scheduled to meet. The crowd was determined it should not. Ten justices arrived. Squire Bliss and Squire Ingraham were there, but Squires Beatton, Cuming, and Whiting chose not to appear. The Whig newspapers reported the crowd acted with restraint. The justices clearly feared for their lives. The crowd was at least a hundred strong, many of them armed. And it blocked the courthouse door. The men "utterly refused and peremptorily forbid and hindred" the justices from doing business. The justices, in their long robes and powdered wigs, turned around and went to consult at Ephraim Jones's inn. They soon proposed a compromise: they would open the court but do no business, then adjourn. The "Body of the People," as it was called, promised to reply in two hours. The justices sat in Jones's inn and waited—and waited and waited. Finally, "after the Setting of the Sun," a delegation arrived with the answer: the "Body" had rejected the offer. By then, there was no point to continuing the charade. The justices "made no other effort." The county court would not meet in Concord for another year.[23]

The most ardent defenders of the Popular cause were not content just to close the courts. They were determined to hunt down and punish active supporters of the government. No one was tarred and feathered with mud. Nobody was given a "Hillsborough treat"—the popular Boston practice of smearing an enemy's house with excrement. The crowds that assembled on Concord common asked only the public abasement of their opponents and pledges of future good behavior—in effect, the open conversion of their enemies, sincere or not. But the possibility of violence always hung in the background. Colonel Prescott aroused popular anger when he signed a statement praising his late patron, Thomas Hutchinson, on the eve of the governor's replacement by General Gage. Prescott was soon made "Sensible" of "the great Uneasiness" which his action had caused. "I am heartily sorry," the colonel told the angry citizens who called on him, "for I did it in haste, and I solemnly declare, that I detest those unconstitutional Acts and would not take any Post of Honor or Profit under the Same."[24]

Prescott was wise to apologize promptly. Other administration sympathizers had to run the gauntlet of popular disfavor at a mass meeting on the common. On September 19 the Body of the People was back in force, and "every person suspected of being a *tory* was compelled to pass the ordeal of a trial. If found guilty, he was compelled to endure such punishment as an excited multitude might inflict, which they called 'humbling the Tories.' " Their most prominent victim was Dr. Joseph Lee.[25]

Lee's encounter with the mob stemmed from his conduct on the night of September 1, as the people of Concord and their neighbors prepared to respond to the so-called Powder Alarm. In a surprise move, British Regulars in Boston had that day seized the provincial armories at Cambridge and Charlestown. Rumors quickly billowed through the countryside that royal warships were bombarding the capital and royal soldiers slaughtering the inhabitants. In a comic rehearsal for April 19, twenty thousand Yankees picked up their muskets and headed for Boston, only to find that the town was safe and the Redcoats back in camp.[26]

On Concord common, hundreds of people, some of them armed but many not, assembled for the march to Cambridge. One of their aims was to force the resignation of the Mandamus counsellors. The Middlesex County convention, which had just adjourned, had authorized this action and had named Ephraim Wood to a committee to press its demands on the royal appointees. As Wood's great-grandson told the story, the town clerk "went to his neighbor, Dr. Lee (supposing him to be a whig)" and invited him to assist the committee in carrying out its assignment. "My heart is with you," replied Lee, "but I cannot go." However, "immediately on his family retiring to bed, he started to inform the officers, and was seen in the morning fording the river above the South Bridge in great haste, with his long stockings down to his heels."

Two weeks later, Lee was hauled before the Body of the People and compelled to account for his nightwalking. He confessed that he had gone to see Council member Joseph Lee of Cambridge, his namesake but no relative, and had warned him of the impending descent of the countrymen, so "that he and others concerned might prepare themselves for the event, and with an avowed intention to deceive the people. . . ." This "imprudent conduct," Lee now recognized with regret, had exposed his fellow citizens "to the brutal rage of the soldiery, who had timely notice to have waylaid the roads, and fired on them while unarmed and defenceless in the dark." Facing a potentially unruly crowd, Lee brooked his temper and made apologies to his outraged neighbors:

> When I coolly reflect on my own imprudence, it fills my mind with the deepest anxiety. I deprecate the resentment of my injured country, humbly confess my errors, and implore the forgiveness of a generous and free people, solemnly declaring that for the future I will never convey any intelligence to any of the court party, neither directly nor indirectly, by which the designs of the people may be frustrated, in opposing the barbarous policy of an arbitrary, wicked and corrupt administration.

Lee's words saved him from anything worse than a public humiliation—for the time being.

There were undoubtedly many citizens who were glad to see Lee receive his due. But to the town's upper-class Whig leaders, the resistance movement was rapidly getting out of control. As Squire Ingraham and his wife rode through the village one day, the back of their chaise was adorned with a sheep's head and offal by contemptuous townsmen. One evening, while Ingraham was entertaining some British officers at home, "twenty or thirty rogues" assembled outside and "honored" the party with a serenade of tin pans and cracked instruments. Concord common was becoming a gathering point for every agitator in the neighborhood. The contagious spirit of mobbing was infecting the town, leading many in the lower orders to forget their places in the campaign to harass and humble suspected Tories like Ingraham and Lee. It was imperative, Concord's selectmen resolved, to clamp down on such spontaneous radicalism. They gladly seized on an opportunity provided by General Gage to bring their constituents into line. The governor had called a special session of the legislature to convene in Salem on October 5 and had authorized town meetings to elect representatives. The selectmen added a crowded backlog of town business to the agenda for the election session, the first meeting since all the Coercive Acts had taken effect. At the top of the list stood a measure to restore public order. It won speedy acceptance by the town. The citizens voted to form themselves into a Committee of Safety to "Suppress all Riots Tumults and Disorders . . . and to aid and assist all untainted magistrates . . . in the Execution of the Laws . . . upon all offenders against the Same." Captain and Mrs. Ingraham could henceforth proceed through town undisturbed.[27]

The people of Concord pursued a course of "well-ordered resistance" to tyranny, as the Middlesex County convention had prescribed. In defiance of the Massachusetts Government Act, the town met regularly without the governor's consent on a wide range of provincial business. It finally established its own committee of correspondence. As in earlier years, Concord frequently acted in response to outside initiative, but the Boston Committee of Correspondence was no longer its mentor. The Massachusetts Provincial Congress and the First Continental Congress now assumed the guiding roles.[28]

In early October the Provincial Congress took over the practical governing authority in Massachusetts after General Gage revoked his warrant for the special session of the legislature. Despite the governor's action, the representatives assembled at Salem at the appointed time. When the governor refused to deal with them, they resolved themselves into a congress and were joined by additional delegates whom most towns, anticipating such a convention, had already elected. The Congress sat first in the Concord meetinghouse from October 11 to 15. Ten years before, at the outset of the imperial dispute, the General Court had briefly come to Concord to escape smallpox in Boston. Now, thanks to its central location in the countryside, the town made an excellent meeting place for a revolution. And interestingly, Captain James Barrett sat in both bodies.

The presence of the Congress intensified Concord's attachment to the Popular movement. It also provided unexpected income to the innkeepers of the town. Parson Emerson opened the sessions of the Congress with prayer. Landless laborer Jeremiah Hunt served as the doorkeeper. The Congress soon adjourned to Cambridge but returned to Concord the following March for continuous sessions until the verge of war. Not surprisingly, then, the people of Concord responded promptly to the Congress's directives, as it dismantled royal authority in the province. In late November the town voted to turn over its provincial taxes to Henry Gardner of Stow, receiver-general of the Congress. Concord also followed the Congress's recommendations in making military preparations.[29]

Concord carried out the decisions of the First Continental Congress with equal dispatch. From September 5 to October 26, delegates from twelve colonies met in Philadelphia to consider the crisis of empire provoked by the Coercive Acts. Many had expected the Congress to be a moderate body, dominated by "a few Gentlemen of distinction and character," as one Tory put it, and genuinely interested in finding an accommodation between the mother country and her colonies. But those expectations were confounded. The Congress rallied to Massachusetts's side and adopted its own program of retaliation against Britain, known as the Continental Association. This provided for a staged escalation of economic warfare, beginning with nonimportation and nonconsumption, ending with a complete commercial embargo, and lasting until the mother country repealed virtually every one of her obnoxious laws.[30]

True to their word, the citizens of Concord repealed the Solemn League and Covenant and accepted the Association in its stead. Like the earlier covenant, the Association was offered to all the adult men and heads of household in town. The pact was stricter than the original covenant that the townsmen had weakened only the previous June, but they showed no reservations about adopting it—unanimously—in town meeting. They did go slowly, however, to enforce its sanctions, which included a complete cessation of commercial dealings with nonsigners along with their social ostracism "as [persons] unworthy of the rights of freemen, and as inimical to the liberties of their country." Before putting their neighbors beyond the pale, the townspeople extended the final deadline for subscription three times, the last only a month before the outbreak of war. This conciliatory policy worked. Whereas a fifth of the voters had declined to endorse the Solemn League, only three inhabitants adamantly refused to sign the Association. Joseph Lee was apparently one. But even his close ally Stephen Hosmer signed, though he stipulated one condition: he could buy "tea for his wife only."[31]

While Concord was dependent on outside leadership for some of its Revolutionary activity, its early preparations for war placed the town in the advance guard of the Popular movement. In late August, militia captain Jonas Minot, a former selectman, told Cambridge Tory William Brattle, in a report soon passed on to General Gage, that pressure had been building up for him "to warn his company to meet at one minutes warning equipt with arms and ammunition." He would soon have no choice but to accede. "If he did not gratify them," said Minot, who was widely suspected of Tory sympathies because he held land under a Crown grant, "he should be constrayned to quit his farms and land." As it turned out, three days later, during the Powder Alarm, Minot's men had their wish, and they fumbled the opportunity. By the time the country was ready to march, Gage's troops had already seized the weaponry at Cambridge and Charlestown and retired to their quarters on Boston Common. The militia companies had shown themselves ill-equipped to meet an emergency. It was hardly surprising: they embraced almost all the able-bodied men in town between sixteen and sixty. These citizen-soldiers, dispersed on distant farms and busy with everyday chores, could not readily be summoned together. A special force was needed to alarm the country. That force was the Minutemen, and Concord has as good a claim as any town to be their birthplace.[32]

On September 26, at the same meeting called to elect a representative to General Gage's short-lived legislative session and with no more rhetorical flourish than if they had decided to let the hogs run at large, the townsmen of Concord voted

> that there be one or more Companys Raised in this Town by Enlistment and that they Chuse their officers out of the Body So Inlisted and that Said Company or Companies Stand at a minutes warning in Case of an alarm and when said Company Should be Call^{d} for out of Town, in that Case the Town Pay said Company or Companies Reasonable wages for the time they were absent.

Only five days before, a Worcester County convention, thirty-five miles west of Concord, had done the same thing. The Worcester convention has been taken as a touchstone of Revolutionary radicalism in late 1774. Yet, Concord was not simply following its neighbor's lead. While that convention was voting, the selectmen placed the Minuteman proposal on the agenda for the September 26 meeting. In military affairs, the yeomen of Concord had become at least as militant as the angriest farmers of the countryside.[33]

The townsmen's martial spirit faded a bit when it came time for actual enlistments. It was several months before Concord raised a single soldier for ten months' service as a Minuteman. In the meantime, the Committee of Correspondence added large quantities of cannon, cannon balls, grape shot, and gunpowder to the town's armory. The town finally got around to signing men up in early January 1775. The Provincial Congress set a quota for the town of one hundred men—about one quarter of the men of military age. First enlistments fell far short of that number. A training day on January 12, at which William Emerson preached, was "unsuccessful." Another muster, two days later, netted only fifty or sixty. The problem was money. Potential soldiers were not attracted by the wages their frugal townsmen had offered: one shilling, four pence for drilling two half-days a week, at a time when a common laborer could earn two shillings a day. But the voters refused to bargain, instead ordering the town militia captains to lean on their men. Not until after the quota was filled at the end of the month did the town reward the Minutemen's sacrifice with an additional four pence a day.[34]

Taken together, the 104 officers and enlisted men of the two Minutemen companies formed a socially inclusive group. Under the province charter of 1691, militia officers had been commissioned by the royal governor. Now the Provincial Congress authorized enlisted men to elect their own leaders. The change—significant in theory for its expansion of popular power over government—had little immediate effect. The farmboys and mechanics who filled the ranks of the Minutemen chose the same sort of leaders as the royal governors had done. David Brown became captain of one company, Charles Miles the other. In age and status, the two men were alike: both in their forties and owners of one-hundred-acre farms. Brown had the advantage in political experience—he had been a selectman for four years. But Miles was no novice—he had held a commission as lieutenant in the militia since 1771. Most of the junior officers stood just below them in experience and wealth. The ordinary privates were younger men—most of them under twenty-five—just starting out in life. They were the "embattled farmers'" sons. Only the laboring poor had not enlisted in full force—perhaps because few had strong roots in the town or perhaps because men were expected to furnish their own muskets. As it was, the town had to lend weapons to fifteen of the Minutemen.[35]

In Concord, as we have seen, where you lived was often as important as what you owned in determining how you participated —if at all—in town affairs. The Minutemen, too, were influenced by this rule. Captain Brown lived in the North Quarter, and most of the men in his unit were his neighbors; the same held for Captain Miles of the South Quarter and his company. But the two companies reached out into nearly every neighborhood of the town. The whole purpose of the Minuteman organization was to alert the countryside to an emergency as quickly and as fully as possible. Consequently, a determined effort was made to enlist men in all the outlying parts. Only one neighborhood did not produce its fair share of Minutemen. That was the remote north, normally isolated from the town's collective life. The northerners organized a "minute" company of their own.[36]

Concord's Revolutionary mobilization overcame not only barriers of residence and wealth but also the bitter factional conflict that had long plagued the town: the fight between Joseph Lee and his supporters, on the one hand, and the town and church establishment, led by Captain Barrett, on the other. In their desire for a unified response to British oppression, the voters had placed Lee and Captain Stephen Hosmer on the committee to draft the town's first statement on colonial rights. And by early August 1774, Lee had sufficiently worked his way back into his neighbors' good graces that the split in the church was at long last about to be healed. The church brethren had offered to admit Lee into full communion if he would seek forgiveness for his "many hard speeches, and unjustifiable Reflections upon ye Pastor, Church and perticular Members." In exchange, the aggrieved brethren had announced that "ye Difficulty in their Minds was hereby removed" and had promised to return to the fellowship of the Lord's Table. With his impetuous trip to Cambridge on the early morning of September 2, Lee lost all these gains and more. His supporters included some of the most fiery Whigs in town. They now deserted him. The aggrieved brethren resumed their places in the celebration of communion, and they returned to important town offices after four years in the political wilderness. Meanwhile, Lee made his confessions to the mob instead of the church. On Sabbath days he walked several miles to Lincoln to hear a suspected fellow Tory preach the gospel.[37]

Not all the credit for bringing the town together belongs to the unhappy Dr. Lee. Successful mobilization of the community virtually required a reopening of important leadership positions to members of the dissident faction. The organization of a revolution was hard and heavy labor. The Minutemen had to be mustered. Supplies had to be stockpiled. The Association needed to be enforced. Industrious though they were, the small coterie of men who handled the chief tasks of government just before the Revolution—the three selectmen, the town treasurer, representative Barrett, and a few ad hoc committeemen—could not carry the new burdens alone. Consequently, opportunities for doing significant and prestigious town work, which had been shrinking over the past two decades, suddenly expanded greatly in 1774. Revolutionary committees needed members, and as long as a man had social status and solid Whig sentiments, no one with talent or experience would be excluded.

It was, above all, to men of experience that the townspeople turned in the political emergency of 1774–75. Thirteen current and former magistrates dominated Concord's Revolutionary committees. Behind them lay over seventy years of leadership as selectmen, representatives, and town treasurers. They had toiled for the town principally over the past decade, although a few were survivors from the 1750s, suddenly plucked from early political retirement. But the committeemen were not simply veterans of town government. In their ranks were influential elders of the community. Normally, men in their sixties seldom took an active hand in running the town; they now made up a quarter of the Revolutionary leaders. Captain Stephen Hosmer, age sixty-four, and Captain James Barrett, sixty-five, helped draw up the Minutemen's oath. Captain John Green, despite his sixty-seven years, carried the Association pledge from house to house in the north part of town, and Captain Thomas Davis, who was a year younger, aided in its enforcement. As the clutch of captains indicates, the committeemen, young as well as old, were persons of substance and social standing—a miniature of the prewar governing elite. Thus, faced with an unprecedented crisis in their community, the townspeople sought guidance from the same steady, moderate men they had long been accustomed to trust.[38]

Nonetheless, the Revolutionary movement was transforming the relations between magistrates and people. The traditional political philosophy that Concordians and other Yankees had heard from their ministers for over a century enjoined officeholders to "act, vote, and advise agreeable to the inward Sentiments of their Souls, in every Case; undaunted by Frowns on the one Hand, and Clamours on the other. . . ." But the townspeople were now starting to punish some men and reward others on the basis of their conformity to popular views. It had taken several years before the voters were finally ready to cast off Colonel Prescott for his Court Party ties in 1768—if that is what they did. It took only a few months, in the political explosion of 1774, for them to purge military and political officeholders suspected of "Toryism." The cautious Jonas Minot lost his captaincy. Colonel Prescott forfeited command of a regiment when militiamen replaced Crown-commissioned officers with men of their own choosing. (Ironically, James Barrett assumed the command as colonel of the Middlesex Regiment.) Even Squire Cuming went into political eclipse. From 1767 to mid-1774 he had been the invariable choice to preside over the increasingly contentious meetings, notwithstanding his friendship with William Emerson. But Cuming could not bring himself to sign the Solemn League and Covenant. Over the next nine months, he was chosen to moderate only one of the eight town meetings that preceded the outbreak of war.[39]

Agitation against British policies was, indeed, proving the key to political success. Samuel Whitney, a native of Marlborough, Massachusetts, moved to Concord from Boston in 1767 with his wife, Abigail, six children, and two slaves. He was a wealthy merchant; in 1770 his estate was the sixth largest in town, right behind Squire

Cuming's. On coming to town, he had bought a white stucco house behind a picket fence along the Bay Road. There he and Abigail produced nine more children over the next ten years. To the side of the house, he kept his store. As the conflict with Britain intensified, Whitney gained popularity as a "hot Whig," and although newcomers usually had a long waiting time before winning their neighbors' trust—if ever—he suddenly became, after June 1774, the busiest Revolutionary activist in town. He was moderator of town meetings, delegate to the First Provincial Congress, muster master of the Minutemen, and member of the Committee of Correspondence, Committee of Safety, and Committee of Inspection for the Continental Association. With the last post, his political progress came to an abrupt halt. His attachment to the town perhaps weakened in turn. After 1778, Whitney left town for Boston and later moved on to Castine, Maine. In Concord his mark would stand out on the town's vital records, but his role in politics was largely forgotten. He is remembered today chiefly as a man who once lived in The Wayside, Nathaniel Hawthorne's longtime Concord residence.[40]

Lieutenant Joseph Hosmer earned more enduring rewards for his exertions in the Revolutionary effort. At the Middlesex County convention, Hosmer, a thirty-nine-year-old cabinetmaker and farmer who had previously been an active supporter of Joseph Lee, emerged as a powerful exponent of provincial rights. Hosmer's moment came after Daniel Bliss, the Tory lawyer, delivered a sarcastic, urbane, and seemingly unanswerable speech on the folly of resistance to the mighty British Empire. For a long time, the audience sat in silence, crushed by the weight of Bliss's arguments. Then, as family tradition and Lemuel Shattuck's *History* have it:

> From the opposite corner a man rose, plainly dressed in a suit of 'butternut brown.' He commenced slowly and hesitatingly, but in a few moments his timidity vanished, and, in the language of Shattuck's history, 'he replied to Mr. Bliss in a strain of natural, unaffected eloquence, for which he was ever afterward distinguished, which at once attracted public attention and introduced him to public favor.' A Worcester lawyer, standing near Mr. Bliss, saw that he frowned, bit his lip, pounded with his boot-heel, and, in a word, showed marked discomposure. 'Who is this man?' 'Hosmer, a mechanic,' was the

> answer. 'Then how comes he to speak such pure English?' 'Because he has an old mother who sits in the chimney corner and reads English poetry all the day long; and I suppose it is "like mother like son." He is the most dangerous man in Concord. His influence over the young men is wonderful, and where he leads they will be sure to follow.'

Despite Bliss's sneer, Hosmer was by no means a humble mechanic. He came of a comfortable farming family, and he, in turn, was thriving as a furniture-maker and farmer. His wealth and social position entitled him to be considered for leadership in the town. But until 1774 he had served only single terms as a lowly hogreeve and a constable. Now in the wake of his popular triumph, he was starting to build a successful political career. "The most dangerous man" in Concord joined the committees of Correspondence and Inspection. He would soon be representing the town in the General Court.[41]

As common citizens assumed a more direct and influential role in town government, their Whiggish political principles began to change. The inhabitants, good Yankee farmers, did not waste words explaining their actions when work needed to be done. They had already declared in their first reply to the Boston Committee of Correspondence that Parliamentary taxation and the enforcement measures that came with it violated the colonists' inalienable rights "as Men, as Christians, and as Subjects." This was their bedrock position throughout the imperial dispute, from the Stamp Act crisis to the achievement of independence. But with the resistance to the Coercive Acts came a new emphasis on the accountability of government to the people. In 1773 the magistrates who wrote Concord's moderate defense of colonial rights had rejected the notion that judges should depend on either the Crown or the people. Now their selectmen, as delegates to the Middlesex County convention, endorsed a resolution "that there is no greater species of corruption, than when judicial and executive officers depend, for their existence and support, on a power independent of the people." The convention also denounced the Mandamus Council and the ban on town meetings as equally despicable assaults on popular power; indeed, the latter measure "cuts away the scaffolding of English freedom, and reduces us to a most abject state of vassalage and freedom."

Underlying these declarations were the fundamental assumptions of a republican state: government derives its just powers from the consent of the governed; laws must be made by representatives elected by the people; and the men who enact and execute those laws must be accountable for their actions. Public officials, in short, were servants of the people. To be sure, Concordians were still unready to forswear allegiance to the Crown, and the Minutemen took an oath to defend "to the utmost" King George III as well as "all and every of our Charter Rights, Libertyes and Privileges." But with the coming of war, the townsmen would announce themselves a proud and unyielding republican people.[42]

Concordians were republicans, *not* democrats. Despite the upsurge in popular power, they still regarded as illegitimate those values and practices we now consider essential to modern democratic politics. As Joseph Lee's failed challenge to representative Barrett demonstrated, organized competition for power between opposing candidates occasioned the most intense anxiety. Lee and his supporters, to many townsmen, were a "faction"—designing men in league against the common good. The voters simply could not accept that open expression of differences about men and measures that is required for full discovery of the majority will and its translation into public policy. Nor, as Lee's and Charles Prescott's forced submissions to "the Body" attested, would they tolerate active dissent from the community consensus. Indeed, faced with economic and social isolation for refusing to endorse the Association, nonconformists lacked even the right to remain silent. One was either a patriot or an enemy of the people—and, if the latter, "unworthy of the rights of freemen." The claims of self-governing communities overrode the civil liberties of private individuals. The townspeople of Concord demanded the appearance of unanimity, even if it was contrived under the threat of a mob.

But it was accommodation and not coercion that transformed Concord into "a united family of 'sons of liberty,' " as Lemuel Shattuck later put it with pardonable pride. The Revolutionary movement generated a drive for unity within all sectors of community life that was both cause and consequence of that unanimity so pointedly noted in the record of town votes against British policies. Internal conflicts, for one thing, were a disturbing distraction from the impending menace of slavery. When the inhabitants met in December 1772 to discuss the alarming Boston report of Crown salaries for judges, the indefatigable dissidents of the north insisted on taking up valuable time with another futile request to be set off from the town. It was imperative to remove the persisting sectional irritant from the political arena. The next May, the town set the northerners free from the ministerial rate as long as they hired a preacher of their own; the privilege was renewed the following year. The northerners temporarily dropped their secessionist campaign. Concessions were also extended, as we have seen, to the aggrieved brethren just a month before Joseph Lee's fateful trip to Cambridge. Conciliation was good policy. Under the leadership of Captain John Green, the northerners were more tightly integrated into the community-wide mobilization than they had been in any town effort for a long time. Lee's former supporters became major Revolutionary leaders.[43]

Pursuit of collective unity went beyond the need to rally the townsmen against outside attack. In January 1775 the brothers and sisters of the Concord Church suddenly moved to put the remaining divisions of the Great Awakening behind them. They invited back into their fellowship every one of their former communicants who had gone over to the West Church or who had left for any other reason and who still remained away from the Lord's Table. No questions would be asked, no new confessions of faith required. Only two families took up the offer, surely a disappointing response. Nevertheless, the church's overture, like the conciliation of the aggrieved brethren and the concessions to the northern inhabitants, reflected the inspiration of the resistance movement. In the successful drive to forge a united stand against British policies, many townspeople had glimpsed the possibility of transcending the tense divisions that had beset their community in the pre-Revolutionary period. Through their shared struggles and sacrifices in the defense of liberty, all Concordians—magistrates and subjects, Old Lights and New Lights, villagers and outlivers—might finally realize the trust, the fellowship, and the peace of the ideal New England town. Concord would become a harmonious Whig community—one that would meet the test of April 19 and the difficult long war that followed.[44]

★4★
A World of Scarcity

EARLY in 1775 plans for war dominated Concord. The previous November the Provincial Congress, now the de facto government of Massachusetts, had ordered an emergency stockpiling of arms and ammunition for use of the colonial militia, and the Congress's executive Committees of Safety and Supplies had quickly fastened on Concord as the principal arsenal of the Popular forces. Geography probably dictated the choice. Strategically located along the main routes to the west, accessible only by bridge from two directions, and commanded by surrounding hills, the town was well placed for defense in case the Regulars attacked.[1]

The narrow, winding roads from the seaboard to Concord were soon clogged with oxcarts supposedly carrying city products to the country. "Have seen twenty load [of military supplies] covered with dung go out of town myself," reported an observer in Boston, "but lately all carts have been searched by the [British] guards, and unluckily last Saturday evening a load of cartridges were seized pack'd in candle boxes. . . ." Weapons were bought, borrowed, or commandeered from every possible source. One daring band of Patriots even smuggled a British cannon out of Boston under the very eyes of its artillery company guard. Altogether, the Committees of Safety and Supplies achieved extraordinary success. It took a team of four oxen and a horse the better part of a day and a night simply to haul two cords of wood the twenty miles from Concord to Boston. Yet within a few months, despite shortages of arms in the colony, despite the need for secrecy, despite the muddiness of country roads during the winter thaw, the provincials managed to amass twenty thousand pounds of musket balls and cartridges, fifty reams of cartridge paper, loads of tents, pickaxes, spades, hatchets, and wheelbarrows, hundreds of barrels of flour and beef, tierces of rice, firkins of butter, and hogsheads of rum.[2]

James Barrett, now a colonel, took charge of military preparations in Concord. He distributed the provincial stores to some thirty private homes for safekeeping. To hide the supplies was surely treason to the Crown, yet men in all ranks of society accepted the risks, and those with the most to lose did far more than their fair share. The wealthy brewer Ebenezer Hubbard put barrels of flour in his malthouse, Captain Timothy Wheeler stored them at his grist mill, and landless laborer Daniel Cray kept barrels of beef at the house he rented from Tory Daniel Bliss.[3]

Other citizens manufactured supplies. Deacon Thomas Barrett and his son turned out firearms and gun carriages at their blacksmith shop in the town center. Housewright Josiah Melvin, Colonel Barrett's son-in-law, produced saltpeter; saddler Reuben Brown fashioned cartridge boxes, holsters, and belts. Even James Barrett's fifteen-year-old granddaughter, Meliscent, got into the act. In previous years a British commissary officer from Boston used to visit the Barrett homestead to buy provisions for the army. On one occasion he amused himself by talking loyalty to provoke Meliscent's rebel replies. How would the colonists ever resist Britain, he taunted, when they could not even make cartridges? She retorted that they would use powder horns and bullets—just as they shot bear. "That would be too barbarous," said the officer. "Give me a piece of pine and I will show you how." The spirited Meliscent learned quickly. On the eve of the battle, she was supervising the manufacture of cartridges by the young women of the town.[4]

Nearly all of local life took on a military cast. Guards were stationed around the clock at the North and South bridges, on the Bay Road, and in the village in order to protect the stores and alarm the countryside should the Regulars attack. Cannon were mounted in the town center. Minutemen trained twice a week on the common and carried their muskets everywhere, in the fields, in shops, even in church. Inevitably, there were citizens who shirked military duty, and Minuteman Captain Charles Miles asked the town to impose fines on all who missed militia drill. Still, when Provincial Congress delegate James Warren came to town in early spring, he found that "the people are ready and determine to defend this Country Inch by Inch."[5]

On March 13, the townspeople signaled their resolution to fight at a muster of all the armed forces in town. As fifes whistled and drums rolled, Concord's militiamen paraded in homespun breeches and hunting jackets and presented arms on the common to Colonel Barrett, commanding officer of their Third Middlesex Regiment. They were performing a familiar pageant in New England life. War had engaged nearly every generation of Yankees since the founding of Massachusetts in the 1630s. Concord itself had a long military tradition. Men of the town had walked into some of the bloodiest Indian ambushes on the continent, had starved during an abortive assault against Cuba in 1740, and had triumphed at the siege of Louisburg in Nova Scotia. In March 1775 there were many who carried muskets first fired in the French and Indian War. As a young private in 1755, Major John Buttrick, soon to be Colonel Barrett's second-in-command, had fought at Crown Point on Lake Champlain, where two years later the future Minuteman sergeant Amos Hosmer was reported among the sick and wounded. In all, over half of the thirteen Minuteman officers with a sergeant's rank or higher were veterans of expeditions to Canada against the French.[6]

As the troops filed by under the cloudy March sky, they presented a revealing portrait of the community. This was a citizen army of rural neighbors, in sharp contrast to the British Regulars, whose aristocratic officers commanded "the dregs of society," desperate men plucked from gaols and gin mills and other grim haunts of the English poor. The Concord militia included nearly everyone between the ages of sixteen and sixty: gentlemen, yeomen, shopkeepers, artisans, laborers, and teen-age apprentices. Only two groups were exempt—the young scholars of Harvard College (who even then had student deferments) and the town's dozen black slaves, whom the General Court, worried about possible rebellion, had denied the obligation to bear arms.[7]

The militiamen took their places according to their age or social rank. In the alarm list, a reserve unit assigned the lightest duties, one found the older men, mostly in their fifties and sixties. Not surprisingly, the two Minute companies, which were expected to furnish the first line of defense, were filled with vigorous young men, over half of them under twenty-five.[8] Most Concordians, though, marched in the town's three standing infantry companies or rode in a small volunteer troop of horse. At their head were officers drawn from the middle and upper classes, tested by years of service in peace and war. Even the lieutenants were over thirty.[9]

The muster was almost a family reunion. Fathers and sons, uncles and nephews, brothers, cousins, and in-laws often enlisted in the same units. All were joined together not so much by a chain of command as by a complex network of kinship. When Colonel Barrett issued general orders, they were transmitted through a son and son-in-law, both captains, to a second son and a brother, both ensigns, down to yet another son and a nephew, both corporals, and ultimately to several other nephews in the ranks. Major Buttrick commanded a son, a brother, five nephews, and an orphan who was his ward, all of them Minutemen. Indeed, the roster of the Minutemen made an intricate genealogical chart. The two companies embraced ten sets of brothers, ten of first cousins, ten of uncles and nephews, and at least four of brothers-in-law. Filial duty and family loyalty thus reinforced a soldier's obligation to follow orders. That obligation became even tighter in Minuteman James Cogswell's case. The nineteen-year-old youth was bound by an apprentice's oath to "gladly obey" the commands of his brother Emerson, an Ipswich-born tanner who was company sergeant.[10]

When the parade drill ended, Rev. William Emerson rose to preach a sermon.[11] It was almost ten years to the day since a divided town had called him to its ministry. He was then an untested young man just embarking upon adult life, like many of the Minutemen now before him. In the decades that followed, he had married Miss Phebe Bliss, fathered four children, built a graceful home, the Old Manse overlooking the North Bridge, and become an intimate of the town's leading men. He had taken his place in the world. In the process, he had been sorely tried and humbled by controversy. As he learned from sad experience to curb his temper, he had come to impress his parishioners with his sincere eloquence and patriotic zeal.

The Revolutionary crisis had brought a rare peace to his cantankerous flock. Now Emerson was expected to furnish spiritual guidance in his town's most difficult moment. He was ready for the task. He knew that his people's cause was the Lord's cause and that victory was certain if only they cleaved to their faith. And so he set out to rally his listeners against division and despair. They must stand in the days ahead as they did that afternoon: a united and well-ordered community.

Emerson took his text from the Book of Chronicles, "Behold, God himself is with us for our Captain," and he recounted how the army of Judah had vanquished a foe twice its size, thanks to "a firm and unshaken Reliance upon the God of Israel." Then he turned to his main theme: the character of the Christian soldier. Christianity, he remarked, obliged a man to "have right Aims and Views" when entering a military life. The good soldier did not enlist in order "to make a pompous Appearance . . . to look big, and to stalk proudly in Armor." He had a loftier purpose. ". . . What can this be," Emerson asked, "short of the Honour of God and the good of his Country?"

Yet high-minded motives were not enough. The Christian soldier must actively cultivate the talents appropriate to his calling. He must be hard-working, single-minded, and conscientious about details. He shunned "Intemperance, Luxury, [and] Idleness," on the one hand, and "Sloth, Security and overfondness for the present Life," on the other. He was careful to arm himself with the tools of his trade and to learn the discipline of military drill. Before entering battle, he donned "the whole Armor of God, that he may be fortified against the Enemies of the Mind: Fear, Distrust, Trembling, Cowardice, [and] Pusilanimity." And of the utmost importance, he obeyed orders precisely and instantly and guarded always against the slightest hint of "an ungovernable mutinous Spirit."

> . . . the Indulgence of such a Spirit is the worst of Plagues . . . that can invade an Army; it infects the Whole; it spreads like a Gangrene: it is cured by no Lenitives, and scarcely by the sharp corrosives of martial Discipline. Should such a Spirit be found among us at this Day, it would be one of the most dark and melancholy Omens upon

> the Face of our present Military Preparations that could ever pass before us!

These exhortations were directed to all of Emerson's listeners, young and old, rich and poor, master and servant alike. But the pastor recognized that men in different stations of life bore different responsibilities and were prone to different categories of vice. He thus singled out several of the groups before him for special words of counsel and prayer. He asked the Lord to inspire Colonel Barrett "with . . . Firmness and Fortitude" in his "double Capacity of a Statesman and a Soldier," and he called on the militia officers to "conduct [themselves] in such a Manner as to reflect Honour on the military Character . . . [and to] be a shining Example to the Soldiers under your Command. . . ." Finally it was the Minutemen's turn. Drawn from all ranks of society, many were still boys in their teens, whose knowledge of life came simply from their fathers' farms and the town's common schools. It was they, and more generally all members of the dependent social orders, who needed moral instruction most. Emerson gave it. He exhorted them "to conduct in your Place in such a Manner as to raise our Hopes . . . for if we see you transgress the divine Law, and stain the Camp of God's People with Intemperance, with Prophanity, with Violence, with a mutinous disorderly Spirit, you will, my Friends, dash all our hopes." Morality and patriotism were one.

Emerson spoke the traditional language of Puritan New England. His words had been intoned in seemingly limitless variations at nearly every public occasion in Massachusetts's 150-year history, but in the end they were no different from Governor John Winthrop's simple message to the founders of the colony as they sailed in 1630 for the New World: "God almightie in his most holy and wise providence hath soe disposed of the Condicion of mankinde, as in all times some must be rich some poore, some high and eminent in power and dignitie; others mean and in subjection." In Concord, as elsewhere, people were expected to know their place and to take their place in all of the community's affairs. When Concordians filed into the meetinghouse on Sabbath mornings, they went to assigned seats: men and women in separate sections, with the old and rich in front, young and poor in the rear, and blacks set off in an area of their own. Even the clothes men wore—gentlemen in silk and velvet, artisans in leather aprons—indicated their station.[12]

It was, then, a world of inequality and privilege but also of responsibility and duty that was on parade that March afternoon. War lay ahead, promising uncertainty and danger to lives and property, but as Concordians interpreted that prospect, there was to be no social revolution. Later generations of Americans liked to think, with the poet James Russell Lowell, that the British Regulars "came three thousand miles and died/To keep the Past upon its throne," but the provincials were looking backward, too—toward ancient ideals of peace, unanimity, and a fixed social order.[13] Yet even as Emerson spoke, the social basis for these ideals was slipping away. The problem was not simply that for at least two generations the townspeople had been quarreling almost constantly about the very nature of their community. No, the problem ran deeper, into the social and economic roots of their community life. For on the eve of the Revolution, Concord was a declining town facing a grim future of increasing poverty, economic stagnation, and even depopulation, a future that jeopardized the heretofore peaceful relations between social classes and that was already undermining traditional relations between parents and children. It was a future that was only temporarily obscured by the onset of war. As the Minutemen, their families, and neighbors listened to their minister and prepared to defend their land, many may have been driven to ask what sort of world they protected and what place it held out for them.

★ ★ ★

A month before the Boston Tea Party, while anti-British passions were stirring throughout Massachusetts, Stephen Barrett sat by the fire in his father's farmhouse practicing his school lessons. Though twenty-four years old, he was still going to school and still copying pious maxims ("A long Life has a lingering Death"; "Birds of a Feather Flock Togeather") and figuring the prices of cows and pigs in his workbook. "Stephen Barrett is my name and a very good rightor is my fame," he wrote, probably to relieve the boredom of his lessons. "So Style not this book for feir of Shame for in it is the onar's name." [14]

Within a year Barrett would make a very different sort of entry in his old book: his Minuteman's oath. But for the moment, politics were far from his mind. On long winter days, over a dreary seven weeks, he sat in a schoolmaster's house with twenty to thirty young people—some his age, most between eight and fifteen, a few as young as six—all waiting, no doubt restlessly, to recite their lessons. At night he puzzled over problems like this: "If you buy a Pasture Sufficient to Summer 15 oxen and 20 young creatures and give 700£ for it, how Long will it be before you make the money you gave, if you have 3£ per head for summering the creatures?" * This was the most schooling he was likely to receive in any year. Most of the time Stephen was too caught up in the endless, demanding round of farm chores to spend his days in a classroom. From early boyhood he had been working for his father and preparing to become a farmer himself, like his father, his brothers, and most other adult men he knew. Now he was ready to embark on his own. He was already managing a forty-acre farm—complete with a horse, two oxen, and two cows—that belonged to his father. Soon he would marry his second cousin Sarah Barrett and establish an independent household on the land.[15]

Stephen Barrett thus stood on the verge of adulthood, yet he remained in many respects a boy. One season he ran a farm on his own. The next he was subject to a harsh flogging from a threadbare schoolmaster only a few years his senior. On the eve of marriage, he still lacked legal title to his land and so depended on his father's good will—as he might continue to do for some years after the wedding. His semidependent status was shared by other young people in town. It was a traditional part of coming of age in New England, a way station in a gradual progress to full adulthood. This could be a frustrating time in a young man's life, when he pressed for independence although his family and society said to wait, and it was bound to cause at least occasional friction between fathers and sons. But in the past, young men had usually grumbled and resigned

*Answer: six years, eight months.

themselves to the wait, for as in Stephen Barrett's case, patience eventually had its rewards: he was sure to obtain his land someday from his father, Colonel James, and with it a secure place in the world as a scion of the most prestigious family in town.[16]

Times were now changing. The young men of Concord were no longer content to labor patiently on the farm until their fathers let them go. A silent struggle between the generations was under way, and the sons were gradually winning. Many fathers lacked the resources that James Barrett could employ to control his son's coming of age. And even Colonel Barrett would have to compromise with Stephen's desire for early independence. The slipping authority of the fathers reflected an inescapable dilemma in Concord's agricultural life: there were simply too many sons and not enough productive land for all. The problem was not new, but it had been getting worse and worse for a half century, ever since Colonel Barrett was himself a boy.[17]

Back in 1710, when James Barrett was born, Concord was a rough-hewn community, not too far removed from its frontier days as Massachusetts's first wilderness settlement. About a thousand people were scattered in small hamlets over an area more than sixty square miles. Much of the land was untouched by a plow. Thick stands of forest challenged the woodsman and supplied cover for wildcats and wolves whose cries rang out in the night. But the "howling wilderness," as the Puritans called it, was vanishing. Then, in its third generation, Concord was booming along with the rest of colonial America. Its vigorous inhabitants were doubling their numbers every twenty-five years and were rapidly carving out farms and building up sections that shortly clamored for township status of their own. Even with the successive separations of new towns, Concord continued to be the second largest and richest community in Middlesex County throughout the years that James Barrett was coming of age and starting his family. By 1750, when Stephen Barrett, his seventh child, was born (and before Lincoln was set off), about two thousand people lived there, in an area shrunk to nearly half its earlier size. By the standards of the past, Concord was getting crowded.[18]

The burgeoning population reflected the blessing of Providence on

New England: colonial families were fruitful, and they multiplied. James Barrett was one of eight children, and he and wife, Rebecca, produced nine of their own. Colonel and Mrs. Barrett were, however, unusually prolific. They had started their family early, when James was twenty-two and Rebecca Hubbard a girl of fifteen. But teen-age brides were uncommon. Ordinarily, women were married at twenty-one or twenty-two to men four or five years older, and the couples grew old together. By the end of the wife's childbearing years, they would have recorded seven children in the family Bible. And only once or twice would they endure the sorrow of having to insert death dates after the children's names. James and Rebecca Barrett were luckier: all of their children reached maturity.[19]

Other families suffered frightful losses in a single stroke. In 1744, Ephraim Stow watched his four children die within a fortnight, probably from the "throat distemper." His wife died a few weeks later. Stow was a poor yeoman, but his wealthy neighbors were no more secure against the terrible visitations of death. And as settlements increased in density, the fearsome threat of epidemics like throat distemper and dread smallpox grew worse. Still, though death struck cruelly and arbitrarily, it cut families down less often in New England than in Old. A Yankee patriarch could realistically hope to gather most of his children together at the end of his days.[20]

The expanding ranks of the young were eventually a cause for concern as well as pride. As one generation after another bent to the task of clearing woods, cultivating fields, and establishing its mark on the landscape, it became evident that Concord fathers presided over an ever-diminishing patrimony. In the mid-seventeenth century, Humphrey Barrett, founder of the Barrett clan, commanded an ample estate of 350 acres. He also held shares in the town's common meadows and pastures and owned rights to future grants out of Concord Village, a 9,800-acre tract that would become the adjoining town of Acton. These holdings could easily accommodate his several sons and grandsons, but by the time James Barrett came of age, nine great-grandsons required land and five great-granddaughters dowries. No one faced immediate poverty. Still, if the family domain were to be carved up among all the male heirs, no single one could enjoy the wealth and standing to which the Barretts were accustomed. The Barretts were better off than most. In the original distributions of town land, the typical family had received about 250 acres, which would have to provide for a longer line of progeny than Humphrey Barrett and his wife produced. Undistributed rights in Concord Village did serve as a partial hedge against the future, but only for a generation. With the allotment of the Village at the turn of the eighteenth century, the land bank ran out. Even the Great Meadows and the Great Fields were no longer common lands: they belonged to a distinct minority—descendants of the first settlers. Aspiring Concord farmers would thenceforth have to obtain land from their hard-pressed families or buy it on the open market. There was only one other possibility: becoming someone else's tenant. No one wanted that if he could help it.[21]

The impending shortage of land posed a fundamental threat to traditional family life. In seventeenth- and early eighteenth-century Concord, fathers effectively exploited their control of the land to delay the independence of their sons. Next to the land itself, a farmer's children were his basic resource. From sunup to sundown, throughout the year, and with only a few weeks off for winter school, his sons were with him on the farm, tilling his crops, building his income, easing his toil. No wonder, then, that farmers were reluctant to let their labor force go. James Barrett could start a family at age twenty-two only because his father had lost any say in the matter: Benjamin Barrett had died young, and his estate had passed early to his sons. Most young men had to wait to marry until their fathers willingly released control of land and enabled them to sustain households of their own. Yet marriage did not always break a father's hold on his sons. Often men obtained farms at marriage but no title to the land. Actual ownership came only with their fathers' deaths. Practical-minded Yankee farmers thereby ensured that, if necessary, their children would be a support as well as a comfort to their old age. But prolonged control of their sons worked only as long as fathers could promise substantial inheritances. As first James Barrett, and later Stephen, came of age, that promise wore increasingly thin.[22]

While land was scarce in Concord and in many other old towns in eastern Massachusetts, it abounded on the province's inland frontier.

So, as men were to do throughout American history, the Barretts and their neighbors began to look westward for an answer to their problems. If they could not provide farms for their sons in Concord or nearby, fathers would do the next best thing: give them a fresh start in a new community.

Beginning in the 1720s, land hunger dominated Concord, with ever-increasing intensity down to the eve of the Revolution. Buying and selling and moving to frontier lands caught up nearly every family in town, directly or indirectly, and it transformed the lives of those who stayed and those who moved away. Colonial New Englanders went west with a characteristic regard for order and regularity in their affairs. Concordians did not simply pack up their belongings and squat on unclaimed land far from civilization. They planned their moves with care. When their children were still young, Concord farmers bought into frontier townships in the broad, hilly region stretching southwest down to the Connecticut and Rhode Island borders and northwest into the mountain areas of New Hampshire. By modern standards, the frontier was close by, no more than twenty-five miles from Concord, but it had already taken the colonists nearly a century to advance even thirty miles above tidewater, and, in some areas, Indians remained a formidable threat. Settlement thus proceeded gradually—first, southwest into the safer areas of neighboring Worcester County, and then, with the removal of the French and Indian menace, at a faster pace into the wilds of New Hampshire. Many families had used these frontier lands as summer pasture for their dry cattle, and so, by the time they were ready to move, their sons already knew the countryside and could follow well-beaten trails into the wilderness.[23]

Although they felt less pressure on their resources than most families, the Barretts, too, were infected by western land fever. In the 1720s, brothers Benjamin and Joseph Barrett—Colonel James's father and uncle—engaged in several successful schemes to become proprietors of frontier townships. With one group of investors from Concord and neighboring towns, they won the General Court's permission to buy from the Indians what is now the township of Grafton in Worcester County, on the condition that the actual settlers of the town be "the petitioners or their posterity and no others." The territory was duly purchased for £2,500, and, when the land was distributed among the proprietors, Benjamin Barrett received 131 acres and his brother Joseph 121. But only one Barrett—Joseph, Jr.—settled in Grafton. In an even more blatant speculative venture, the Barretts were among a group of petitioners who obtained the township of Peterborough, New Hampshire, as a free grant from the Massachusetts General Court. The subscribers had explained that they were "without land for their posterity, and desirous that they should not remove from out of this Province, but settle together under the laws and liberties of this government where they were born." In fact, not one of the group ever moved to Peterborough. That was done by the Scotch-Irish immigrants who bought the land. If there were any casuists among them, the canny proprietors could later have justified themselves by remarking that Peterborough did eventually pass under New Hampshire control.[24]

These land speculations were not the work of eastern aristocrats raking an unearned profit off the needs of their fellow citizens. The Barretts were shrewd operators, to be sure. But they were attempting to deal with the same problem their neighbors faced: too many sons and not enough land. When Benjamin Barrett died in 1728, his estate could provide farms for only two of his sons, James and Thomas. But with the income from western lands, two younger sons were able to settle on farms in the Worcester County town of Paxton. Speculative investments were thus essential to maintaining the status of all the Barrett sons, whether they stayed in Concord or not. And in the next generation, thanks in part to profits from western lands, James Barrett could buy farms in Concord for sons Stephen and Nathan as well as settle his eldest and youngest on the family domain. In 1764, just before the Stamp Act crisis, James Barrett joined fifteen of the town's richest citizens in buying Berkshire County's "Township Number Four" at an auction held by the General Court. None of the investors moved there, nor did any of their posterity. In later years, the only link between Concord and the new town was its name—Cummington, after Colonel John Cuming, head of the speculators' group.[25]

Other ventures as well built the Barrett family fortunes. With a large farm and ample capital, Colonel Barrett was well placed to take advantage of new urban and overseas markets for farm produce. His 150 acres grew the oatmeal that fed the British Army in Boston and supplied beef to West Indian planters whose expanding demands had become essential to the prosperity of commercial farmers throughout the colonies. In 1771, Barrett devoted virtually all of his improved land to providing fodder for a herd of seventeen oxen, eighteen cows, and about twenty-five steers and heifers. Not all of the oxen were marked for immediate slaughter. Some were hired out to smaller farmers who could not afford to keep draft animals all year round. Barrett could profit, too, from his command of ready cash. On one occasion, he stood bond for £50 to guarantee a Littleton yeoman's appearance in Superior Court; if the defendant failed to show, Barrett would get his house and farm. (The defendant appeared.) But Barrett apparently abstained from one popular form of investment among Concord's upper class. Since there were no banks in colonial New England, many wealthy gentlemen put their money to work by lending funds at interest rates of 6 per cent or more. In all these ways, Concord's privileged elite solidified its position in town. Then as now, wealth generated more wealth.[26]

Behind the assurance, then, with which Stephen Barrett faced the future in 1775 lay two generations of careful planning, well-timed opportunism, and a bit of plain luck. While many families slipped downward in the social structure or had to move out, Colonel James Barrett had improved on his father's position and had achieved for himself the enviable status of a true patriarch: he could settle all his children around him. Yet Colonel Barrett chose to exercise his patriarchal powers with a light hand. Stephen received a farm by the time he was twenty-one, and he could look forward to obtaining title within a year or two of his marriage. His father had done the same for older brothers James, Jr., and Nathan, "in Consideration of my Love and good Will towards my Son/s/." The colonel's fatherly affections were undoubtedly genuine. But other sentiments probably figured as well in these grants of early independence to his sons.[27]

Colonel Barrett could no longer count automatically on his sons' willingness to wait indefinitely before coming into their own. During most of the colonial period, land was cheap on the frontier, and communities needed pioneers. If a young man tired of being on the family homestead and under the paternal eye, he could simply put relatives behind him and stake out a farm in a new town where no one knew his father and grandfather and great-grandfather before him. Not everyone, of course, could reap the advantages of a first settler. Nor did most men set out for the wilderness by themselves. As they did nearly everything, Concordians moved in family groups, planting little settlements of Barretts and Buttricks and Hosmers throughout the countryside. Still, the abundance of cheap frontier land, when combined with the scarcity of land at home, served to undermine fathers' traditional powers over their sons. Colonel Barrett's generation, the first to experience land shortage in Concord, had married earlier and emigrated more often than Benjamin Barrett's. Now his sons and the other young men of Concord were coming of age even faster. Stephen Barrett enjoyed the benefits of the westward movement without ever having to leave home. Thanks in part to his father's land speculations, Stephen could obtain a farm in Concord, and thanks to the emigration of so many of his schoolmates, he could realize an early independence on that land.[28]

On the eve of war and on the verge of adulthood, Stephen Barrett could confidently predict what his life held in store. He would live in his native town, farm as his father did, marry his cousin Sarah, and move in a world narrowly circumscribed by kin. His father, a former selectman and now longtime representative, was the most respected political figure in town. His uncle, the pious and mild-mannered deacon Thomas, wielded considerable economic power; to his mills near Colonel Barrett's homestead, farmers took their corn and rye to be ground and their logs to be cut into boards. In fact, all of the Barretts in town occupied positions at the top of the economic ladder. Through their marriages Stephen was connected to other prominent families: Minots, Prescotts, Hubbards, and Hunts. If he showed a liking and any talent for politics, he could expect to succeed, for pre-Revolutionary Concord chose one out of every two new selectmen from the families of political veterans; in addition, his well-placed relatives would help. And while his contemporaries would have to wait until their mid-forties to hold high office, Stephen, as a selectman's son, enjoyed a notable head start of six years. For all his newly gotten independence, Stephen Barrett would live much the same life as his father had lived. The rewards for staying in Concord were great, but they would not appeal to all. Such a well-charted life in the shadow of one's kin was likely to be confining and more than a little dull. Perhaps for that reason Stephen's cousin Charles Barrett—a son of deacon Thomas—turned his back on similar prospects and went pioneering in New Ipswich, New Hampshire, where he soon thrived and became a dominant personage on his own.[29]

★ ★ ★

When Colonel Barrett and his family went to town in 1775, they traveled the Groton Road, which passed near their home, winding southeasterly for nearly two miles to the North Bridge. Several hundred yards above the bridge, where the road bent to the left, a small red house stood with two adjacent barns on a twenty-acre lot. The colonel no doubt stopped by there often to discuss Concord's military preparations. It was the homestead of David Brown, the forty-two-year-old captain of a Minuteman company. Brown, too, had a son under his command, but, unlike Barrett, he could not assure the young man's future. Seventeen-year-old Purchase Brown had no place to go but down if he chose to spend his life in Concord.[30]

In the spring of '75, Purchase Brown was the oldest child in a household crammed with thirteen people. There were, of course, his father, Captain David, and his mother, Abigail, the Lexington-born daughter of a tavern-keeper who had settled in Concord. Purchase probably had to share a bed with an eleven-year-old brother and with uncle Elias Brown, who had been deemed "uncapable of managing any Business" for most of his forty-eight years. Four younger brothers and four sisters slept in two other rooms. Yet another sister arrived that April, whose birth David Brown understandably neglected to register amid the tense days before the battle. A year later the family was completed with a seventh son—the twelfth child in nineteen years, appropriately named Joseph. As the first-born, Purchase enjoyed important responsibilities in the household, helping his father with the farm and guiding his brothers at their chores. He probably welcomed this semiadult role, but living at such close quarters produced tensions and frustrations which a man could only temporarily escape in the privacy of the fields. As he neared maturity, the daily presence of so many brothers and sisters must have been an increasingly irritating reminder of an unhappy fact: Purchase would be forty years old before the youngest child came of age. There was no point in waiting around to take over the family farm.[31]

The Brown family was by no means of humble status. Purchase bore the name of a wealthy seventeenth-century ancestor who was pointedly described in the town's usually sparse death register as a "worthy gentleman." His great-grandfather had been town clerk for twenty years, his grandfather a selectman and militia captain, and his father was now in turn a respected town leader. Before his election as captain of Minutemen, David Brown had already served three terms as selectman and frequently managed the affairs of the Proprietors of the Great and Common Fields. He was a tall, good-looking man with a well-deserved reputation for vigor. It is said that the captain "never crossed alone the causeway to the 'North Bridge' after dark, on his way to and from market, without singing at the top of his lusty voice some good old psalm tune, that would ring out in the night, and wake many a sleeper in the village." With the approach of war, he was likely to play an increasingly important part in town life. Though no gentleman-farmer, David Brown had the economic standing required of pre-Revolutionary town leaders. His farm embraced not only the twenty-acre homestead but also another eighty acres scattered in several parcels throughout the North Quarter. This was a sizable estate, and with his father caught up in the Revolutionary crisis, Purchase Brown probably had to assume its active direction. But the farm and the status that went with it would never be his.[32]

When Purchase's grandfather died in 1750, the appraisers of the estate had warned against any splitting up of the family farm: it would "make but one Settlement without Spoiling the Whole." At one hundred acres it was nearly double the ordinary holding, but as with most farms, the bulk of the land lay in river meadow, pasture, forest, and swamp—all suited to livestock but unfit for human habitation. David Brown inherited the farm intact and, with a dozen children to support, was in no position to break it up. If Purchase were to be settled on a farm in Concord, his father would have to find another property.[33]

Captain Brown possessed the necessary means. He, too, had benefited from western land speculation, having inherited a small share in the township of Templeton and later joining in the Cummington purchase. In the late 1760s he had acquired through his mother's estate the fourteen-acre house lot just across the river that became the site of the Old Manse. He promptly sold the land to pastor Emerson for £240. Thus, the capital was available to buy Purchase a farm if David Brown had been willing to favor his eldest son over the rest of his numerous flock. This was increasingly the practice in middle-class Concord families faced with the problem of land scarcity. But Captain Brown did not do so, perhaps because, as he told another son years later, he felt "as much Love to one as the other and Love and Respect you all alike." Instead, he would provide a portion of his estate—in the form of money, preparation for a trade, or frontier land—to each of his children as they came of age. Only one, probably the youngest son, would get the Concord farm.[34]

There was, then, no certainty to Purchase Brown's future as there was to Stephen Barrett's. Purchase could not progress gradually from working his father's farm to running his own nearby, nor could he count on spending all his days in the same familiar surroundings. When he reached his early twenties, he would receive his portion and make his way on his own wherever he chose. He lacked the security of Stephen Barrett, but he gained a greater freedom to direct the course of his life.

The incentives to stay in Concord were modest at best, and meager by most expectations. Purchase need not necessarily remain landless. By delaying marriage, boarding at his father's house, and hiring out as a laborer, he might eventually, if he scrimped and saved, acquire a small farm of his own. On twenty to thirty acres, he could feed a family of six quite well, with ample daily supplies of milk, butter, bread, meat, beans, potatoes, and fresh fruits and green vegetables in season. This was substantial but monotonous fare. The bread was a coarse brown bread, made from home-grown rye and corn meal; wheat production had been ruined in eastern Massachusetts by plant disease, and only the rich—the "upper crust"—could afford to buy imported Pennsylvania wheat flour from the baker for use in white bread and on top of their pies. The meat was largely salt beef and salt pork, consumed day in and day out, even after it had grown "hard and often green within," as one early nineteenth-century inhabitant recalled with distaste. Most of the time Purchase's family would eat bread and milk for breakfast, meat and vegetable stews for noontime dinner, and bread and milk at the end of the day. By the late spring, when food stocks were normally low, the Browns might be reduced to a diet of milk and pumpkins.[35]

Purchase would enjoy little income to supplement his farm produce with store-bought goods. Nearly every acre of his farm would have to be pressed into service to secure a subsistence. A scant surplus would be available for market. Only by continuing to labor for other men could he obtain the money or credit for necessities like salt and sugar and, surprisingly, woolen and linen cloth: small farmers seldom kept sheep or raised flax, the source of linen fiber. And there would be shoemakers, blacksmiths, and physicians to pay, to say nothing of the inevitable tax collector. Purchase's family might simply have to do without such luxuries as tea or chocolate or rum. And there might be no hard cider for cold comfort, since many dirt farms lacked even an orchard.[36]

This was a hardscrabble existence Purchase Brown faced, and it was likely to get ever harder simply to stay even. For, as Purchase undoubtedly knew from working his father's farm, Concord land was wearing out. David Brown raised cattle for market on a more modest scale than Colonel Barrett. Every year he drove three or four cows and two oxen to deacon Brooks's slaughterhouse on the other side of town. This was still twice the herd an average farmer fattened for sale, and it supplied a valuable income. But the support of livestock required nearly all of Brown's cultivated land. His hay fields, scattered in the Great Meadows along the Concord River, grew substantial crops, but his pastures were depleted from decades of reckless overgrazing and undercultivation. In 1771, Captain Brown estimated that it took three and three-quarter acres just to sustain a single cow for a year. He was worse off than most farmers. Even so, he continued to overburden the land, stocking his forty-five acres of pasture with a bull, four oxen, seven cows, a few steers and heifers, a horse, and nine sheep. He could not afford to give the land a rest. Beef, wool, and perhaps mutton sales were necessary to maintain his family's accustomed standard of living. And he apparently lacked the upcountry pastures that some of his neighbors used to ease the pressure on their fields. Brown's grazing lands were thus certain to decline still further, forcing a conversion of even more of his farm into grass. His predicament was widely shared. On the eve of the Revolution, large stretches of the town were run-down pasture—a dilapidated landscape of brown and mottled green.[37]

Concord's grain fields, meadows, and orchards were no more flourishing. For generations, while land was plentiful and labor scarce, farmers had practiced an extensive agriculture, planting the same crops on their fields year after year until the soil was used up, then moving on to other fields, heedless of the future. The worn-out land would lie fallow for as long as a decade, to serve as meager pasture for livestock; when the soil recovered its fertility, the cycle of exploitation and exhaustion would resume. But as population soared and the average farm shrank to a lower limit of fifty to sixty acres, yeomen with large families, like David Brown, could no longer keep valuable land out of production. The period of fallow was reduced to a year or two. Crop yields inevitably declined, and hard-pressed farmers were forced to put more and more marginal land under the plow. For the time being, it was profitable to clear their forests and sell off the lumber for shipbuilding or firewood or even as charcoal or potash—the major ingredient in soapmaking—at the Boston market. In the long run, Concord faced a potential energy and food crisis.[38]

The solution was to cultivate the land intensively, plowing better, manuring more, weeding more thoroughly, and sowing forage crops like timothy and clover in their arable fields. On the eve of the Revolution, some farmers were already putting part of this program into practice and shifting over to English clovers, which improved the land by fixing nitrogen in the soil. Undoubtedly, smaller farms would have encouraged these reforms by requiring men to concentrate their efforts in order to survive. But Brown's townsmen generally clung to the careless habits of the past, often because of shortages of labor or capital. A substantial minority owned no oxen and had to borrow teams from relatives or neighbors or else hire a roving plowboy. And most farmers no longer commanded a docile, cheap labor force in their sons. So long as abundant, virgin soil could be had on the frontier, young men like Purchase Brown would choose to move rather than toil for their fathers or adopt new techniques on smaller farms. The emigrants left behind an economy of increasing scarcity in an environment of spreading blight.[39]

Yet, in the years before the Revolution, competition for frontier land was accelerating. Every decade from the mid-1740s on, one out of every four taxpayers moved out of Concord, thereby draining off the landless and the poor and keeping the town's population nearly constant. The same thing was happening in most of the other old towns of eastern Massachusetts. As a result, by the early 1770s emigrants had to seek cheap land farther and farther from home. Worcester County, in its second generation, was rapidly filling up; such New Hampshire settlements as New Ipswich and Jaffrey—little Concords on the frontier—had already distributed their best lands. Attention thus turned toward Maine, then a part of the Massachusetts Bay Province. In the late 1760s, Concord innkeeper Peter Heywood headed a small pioneer settlement in the interior of Maine on behalf of the Kennebec Land Company; for his efforts he was awarded four hundred acres of wild land. Soon other townsmen were following his lead.[40]

Perhaps Purchase Brown was thinking about joining them when the rush of events toward war temporarily distracted him from his plans for the future. On coming of age, he would probably receive a modest gift of cash from his father. This would be a useful start in the world, though no guarantee for the future. And unlike the prospect of a Concord farm, it would not keep him on the homestead for long. Indeed, the sooner he left, the better. Unless he gained a foothold in a pioneer settlement, Purchase would share the fate of most latecomers, paying more for less desirable land and falling behind in the contest for social place. Even if Captain Brown could offer him frontier land, Purchase would still be in a hurry to leave, to begin clearing a farm from the wilderness—an arduous, lifetime's work. The longer he waited, the harder his eventual task and the more resentment he would feel for the father who had held him back.

Powerful emotions as well as economic calculations underlay the contest between fathers and sons. The transition between generations is seldom easy, but in cramped households like the Browns', the distinctive tensions it produced in colonial New England smoldered beneath the daily routine, adding to the inevitable frictions of life at such close quarters. Families struggled to keep the peace: conflict at home was even more threatening then contention in the community. But by the 1770s, pressures were mounting on an increasingly fragile peace. With nearby farm opportunities declining and a longer journey to the frontier, sons had less reason than ever for patience with paternal restraints. Tensions must have flared in many households, and tempers have risen in turn.

No doubt most fathers seldom tried to extract more than an extra year or two of labor from their sons. And many, having themselves pressed against parental controls, gladly bestowed property upon their children and sent them forth into the world. For in the end, what young men like Purchase Brown wanted could hardly be denied: to be, like their fathers, independent householders on the land. There was no generation gap. Despite the tensions, young and old pursued traditional goals.

★ ★ ★

While militiamen paraded on Concord common that March, Ezekiel Brown was missing from the ranks. He languished in debtor's prison in Boston, unable to pay his bills. The thirty-one-year-old Ezekiel, a distant relative of Captain David Brown, belonged to a family that had lost its footing in Concord and wandered about Middlesex County in search of a home. In 1766 he had returned to his native town to seek a living in trade. With only a meager portion, he made his way as a small country storekeeper. But in an uncertain business climate he lacked the means to succeed. Freed from parental control, he was now subject to the whims of chance—to the arbitrary twists and turns of an impersonal imperial economy.[41]

In the early eighteenth century, Ezekiel's paternal grandfather, a prosperous weaver, ranked among Concord's wealthier men. But in the now familiar story, he had too many sons and not enough land.

And so, Ezekiel's father, burdened with a family of seven and without a farm of his own, moved on, first to Groton, then to Dunstable, back to Groton, and again, in a few years, to Dunstable. Although the Browns obtained land in Groton, they were probably dirt poor: "there being no evidence to the contrary," remarked the Victorian author of Ezekiel Brown's memoir, "one always assumes that a rolling stone is not gathering much moss." The town officials of Groton and Dunstable certainly did. Whenever the Browns came to town, a constable soon appeared on their doorstep and warned the family to get out of town.

"Warning out," as it was called, was an eighteenth-century way of keeping undesirables out of town and off the poor rates. Colonial Yankees looked strangers over with some care, for signs of idleness or drunkenness or poverty, and with good reason. Every community was expected to provide for its own when residents fell in need, through old age, ill health, or even their own fault. To admit as legal inhabitants potential paupers like the Browns was to risk burdening a town with their support. Thrifty citizens grumbled enough as it was about the costs of caring for the deserving, native-born poor. By officially forbidding newcomers to become inhabitants, a community could escape responsibility for helping them out.[42]

Occasionally, transients were physically removed from a town to their last known residence, only to be sent packing again and handed from constable to constable until they reached the end of the line—usually their birthplace. Home towns were seldom pleased at this return of their prodigal sons; reversing the process, they soon bounced the unfortunate travelers back toward the towns that had started the chain. More often newcomers were allowed to stay, whether or not they had been warned out. Those who were warned suffered a humiliation from which no family member was exempt. When the Browns arrived in Dunstable, the constable punctiliously warned out every one of them by name, starting with the parents and proceeding systematically from seventeen-year-old Ezekiel down to infant Hannah in her mother's arms. Sometimes the resentful objects of a warning spitefully suggested additions to the list: in Lexington, an angry mother reminded the constable that he had not warned out the cat![43] Landless families like the Browns were thus placed in a dilemma. If they stayed in their native town, they would sink into the ranks of the poor, but if they left in search of opportunity, they would forfeit what little security they had.

At the age of twenty-two, Ezekiel Brown came back to his native town, carrying his worldly goods over his shoulder, his portion in a purse, and his father's reputation before him. Concord promptly warned the young man out. Ezekiel was undaunted. Somewhere, in the course of his family's wanderings, he had picked up a decent schooling and learned to write a good hand. He now put this training to use as a scrivener, copying letters and keeping accounts, probably for a town merchant.[44] Within a few years he was able to branch out on his own. He bought a stock of goods and opened a store. The venture did well. He married in 1770; two years later he acquired a house, barn, and six acres in the center of town. It was a prime piece of real estate, and Ezekiel turned it to advantage. He mortgaged it for £133 to one group of creditors and gave a second mortgage for £70 to another. The money apparently went toward expanding his inventory. Clearly, Concord's officials had misjudged him: Ezekiel Brown was an industrious sort. And with a family and a thriving business, he seemed well on his way in the world.

Though it had warned Brown out, Concord soon made him part of the community. The town shunned paupers, not hard-working men, and throughout the eighteenth century it readily absorbed a steady stream of immigrants—day laborers, tradesmen, would-be farmers, servant girls—who came largely from the surrounding countryside, along with a predictable, small contingent from Boston. Most newcomers left within a decade or so, joining the ongoing exodus of natives from town, but while in Concord, they were inhabitants in all but the legal name. Ezekiel Brown participated more fully than most newcomers in town life. His store stood at the hub of the town, next to the old burying ground on the Bay Road, and it was surely, like most country stores, an important social center, where men traded gossip with their goods over plentiful glasses of rum. Ezekiel soon won the trust of his customers, many of whom had known him as a boy. Before the war, he was elected once as a fence viewer and three times as clerk of the market, charged with inspecting the quality of bread baked for sale. Dwelling amidst relatives and childhood friends and performing an important role in the local economy, he no doubt enjoyed a secure and respected place in a community for the first time in his peripatetic life.[45]

Yet his rising fortunes depended as much on gambler's luck as on solid assets or personal skill. Brown's business, like that of most country storekeepers, was built on an unsteady foundation of credit that could collapse at any time. Ezekiel financed his initial ventures in trade—and perhaps his purchase of the village property as well—largely with mortgage loans, and he expanded his business by ordering some £275 worth of supplies from a Boston import house. He, in turn, extended credit to his customers. Owing to a British ban on colonial paper money and to New England's unfavorable balance of trade with the mother country, hard cash was in short supply in rural towns like Concord. Indeed, from the wealthiest wholesale merchant in Boston to the laborers on Colonel Barrett's farm, men had to buy now in anticipation of paying later. Brown's patrons would ordinarily stretch out the settlement of their bills for years, periodically bringing in surplus produce or lumber to put on account; a final reckoning might not come until a customer's death, when anxious creditors gathered to learn if he was solvent. It was thus easy for Ezekiel Brown to overextend himself, especially since he was unlikely to balance his books at regular intervals. So long as times were good, he needn't worry: no one would press him to cover his orders all at once. But bad harvests at home or an international money crisis in London could touch off a general alarm, and each creditor would call in his obligations in a frantic scramble to stay afloat. With all his property mortgaged to his trade in a rickety stockpiling of debts, Ezekiel Brown was risking everything on his hopes.[46]

There was little ground for such confidence. Concord was, to be sure, one of the leading commercial centers of the province, with nearly as much business activity per capita as in the larger seaports of Essex County. Its six storekeepers bought and sold goods across a broad hinterland ranging from adjacent Acton deep into Middlesex and Worcester counties, and at least one merchant imported directly from England. Town artisans met a wide variety of local needs. Besides the usual millers, blacksmiths, carpenters, tailors, and shoemakers, there were coopers to barrel beef and tanners and curriers to process cowhides into leather. Gentlemen could call on the services of a wig-maker and furnish their tables at a goldsmith's shop. And both townspeople and travelers could find refreshment at any of nine inns. But in a largely rural society, the fate of all these trades hung ultimately on the prosperity of agriculture. On the eve of the Revolution, their immediate prospects were dim.[47]

Since the mid-1760s the all-important West Indian market for Yankee livestock, lumber, fish, and rum had been slackening, and Concordians, along with the rest of New England, inevitably felt the pinch of hard times. In addition to farming, about one townsman in six usually practiced a part-time profession or trade—a proportion that had increased only slightly over the eighteenth century. Now, in the early 1770s, some artisans were closing the doors of their shops. Throughout the town, property values were falling. Ezekiel Brown enjoyed only an artificial prosperity: with the collapse of the nonimportation movement against the Townshend duties, provincial consumers rushed to buy British goods after several years of enforced abstinence. The boom was sure to bust. And as Concord's newest storekeeper, with the least capital and the shortest line of credit in Boston, Brown would undoubtedly be squeezed out first.[48]

The rumblings of trouble may have sounded as early as 1772. Some time that year Brown was working as a "husbandman" in Kennebec, Maine, where he shortly obtained a grant of land. But he was soon back in Concord for the crash. In May 1773 his Boston supplier, the firm of Frazier and Geyer, sued Brown for his debt of £275. The defendant lost in Suffolk County Court and again on appeal to the province supreme court. Seven months later, a deputy sheriff, armed with a warrant to attach Brown's property, found nothing worth seizing and remanded him to a Boston jail. Ordinarily, imprisoned debtors were released within two or three months. But Brown's creditors chose to pay for his lodging and thereby keep him in jail as long as they wished—or until he settled his debt. It was, of course, an irrational situation: while he remained confined, Brown could earn nothing to put on account. Perhaps the creditors suspected him of planning to skip town and head for Maine.[49]

Whatever their purposes, Brown sat in jail while the Revolutionary crisis gathered to a head. It was his additional bad fortune to be held in Boston, the single area under firm royal control; elsewhere, as Popular forces closed the courts, preventing settlement of pending cases, debtors won release from jail. It was surely an added insult that one of his creditors, Frederick Geyer, was a well-known, wealthy Tory. Brown had good reason to be bitter. His strenuous efforts to raise himself in the world had failed. He was once again a man without a settled place. While he wasted in prison, his wife and two young children—one of whom was born during his confinement—faced certain poverty. And all because his creditors refused to wait longer than six months for payment! It was no wonder that most of his townsmen preferred to seek independence on the land rather than cast their lot wholly in trade. As one young man put it, after watching his merchant-brother go under, "A slave to property he alwais was, but he voluntarily made a bad exchange and became the Slave of Men—Such is the case of every man that is embarrassed by debts." Ezekiel Brown did not despair. While in prison he began studying medicine in preparation for a new career. It was to be an extended course: he would not win release until after General Washington liberated Boston in March 1776 and his Tory persecutor fled to England.[50]

★ ★ ★

Philip Barrett was not a Minuteman. Neither was Brister Cuming, nor Cato Ingraham, nor Caesar Minot, nor William Emerson's man Frank. So far as is known, none was a Tory, but Concord had no desire to enlist them for war. All were black slaves, the possessions of such notable citizens as Colonel Barrett, Squire Cuming, Duncan Ingraham, Captain George Minot, even the town pastor. Although they dwelled in the households of the great, the blacks were outsiders in Concord, men on the fringes of community life. Deprived of independence, denied the fruits of their labor, always subject to the will of others, they were living embodiments of what British "slavery" could mean—models that the whites of Concord now anxiously struggled to avoid.[51]

Slavery had existed in New England from almost the beginning of the Massachusetts Bay Colony, but except for a few areas, the institution had never taken deep root. It was the slave trade, not slavery itself, that helped to make New England's fortunes. During their transatlantic voyages, shrewd Yankee merchants plied the African coast to barter rum for slaves, and frequently, on the return voyage to West Indian waters, they sold the slaves for molasses, which would be distilled into more rum after they reached home, in order to lubricate the trade once again. The profits of slave dealing built the elegant mansions of some of Boston's and Salem's best families. Beyond the seaboard, only an occasional citizen such as Duncan Ingraham, who had trafficked heavily in slaves before retiring to Concord, had direct contact with the trade. Ingraham and his predecessors spread the practice of owning slaves throughout the countryside. Although Yankee farmers grew no plantation crops like tobacco or rice that required gangs of forced labor, a country gentleman could readily put one or two slaves to work on his farm or in his livery. Slaves were a badge of status, like an expensive horse and coach and a coat of arms, and in the early 1770s a dozen Concord families were proud to display them. Of slight importance to the economy, the blacks were an exotic transplant in a population grown for five generations from virtually the same English stock.[52]

The everyday life of a slave differed little from that of a white servant. Frank, William Emerson's man, did the heavy work of the farm, besides running errands for his master. He ate and prayed with the Emerson family and probably slept in a corner or garret of the Old Manse. In other households, male slaves might work as artisans by their masters' sides or perform personal service as valets; the few female slaves in town did whatever their mistresses wished. Even slaves were not without rights; unlike bond servants in the rest of the colonies, New England slaves could hold property, sue for freedom, and testify in court against both whites and other blacks. They could hire out their own time when not at their masters' command and keep all of their wages to themselves. And if they labored long and saved with care, they might even buy their own freedom.[53]

John Jack was one slave who did. An African native, Jack spent most of his adult life at a cobbler's bench, working for his shoemaker-master, Benjamin Barron, on the Bay Road. When

Barron died in 1754, Jack was appraised along with the livestock and furniture in the estate. He was worth a substantial £120. Yet within seven years he had earned the money to buy his freedom from the widow Barron. He was about forty-eight years old, a lifelong bachelor, and too old for a fresh start in a new town. Jack built a cabin in the Great Meadows, did odd jobs for farmers and cobbled in winter, and comforted himself with drink. His was a marginal place in the community, but it was nonetheless a real place. Jack belonged to the church, having been admitted during the religious fervor of the Great Awakening, and he soon gained a stake as a landowner in the town. He paid his taxes like any other citizen, although he was surely never allowed to vote in town meeting. By the time he died in 1773, Jack owned eight acres in the Great Fields and Great Meadows, "a good pair of oxen," a cow and a calf, some farming tools, a Bible and psalm book, and seven barrels of cider—all of which he bequeathed to Violet, an aged slave of his late master's daughter. He had probably done as well as a middle-aged freedman could expect.[54]

Still, slavery was slavery: a life a man could not call his own. John Jack, after all, had to buy a freedom that was the birthright of every white man in town. A slave couldn't move in search of opportunity, as could Purchase Brown, or even travel from Concord to Lincoln without his master's consent; if he were found on the streets at night, he would be flogged. He could marry, if his master permitted, but he, his wife, or children were liable to be wrenched at any time from familiar surroundings and sold off to another town; in 1772 young Stephen Barrett was already preparing this fate for his father's slave Philip, then eleven years old, in a copybook exercise. Perhaps worst of all, a slave was always subject to abuse against which there was no defense. If he struck a white man, he would be swiftly and harshly punished. One wintry Saturday, Samuel Whitney's slave Casey had to dodge one snowball after another from his master's son as he attempted to chop wood in the yard. Finally, his patience worn, Casey threw an ax at the boy. Young Whitney shouted in anger that "he was an ugly nigger and he must put him in jail." The next morning, Casey ran off and, to escape the pursuing neighbors, stood up to his neck in the freezing Concord River until nightfall. He stole his way back into the village after dark, got something to eat from a friendly townswoman, and then headed as far from Concord as he could. A moment's anger had risked his life. "We hear the names of the worthies of Concord—Squire Cuming and the rest," remarked Henry Thoreau, on hearing the story, "but the poor Casey seems to have lived a more adventurous life than any of them. Squire Cuming probably never had to run for his life on the plains of Concord." [55]

In the years just before the Revolution, opposition to slavery was growing. For thousands of years the institution had been accepted by men as a natural part of the social order. Then, in the mid-eighteenth century, Quakers became the first important group in colonial America to launch an antislavery crusade. Their influence was concentrated principally in Pennsylvania and New Jersey. But the Revolutionary movement drew new recruits everywhere to the cause. In New England, the exaggerated rhetoric about British "slavery" eventually hit close to home: the contradiction between the colonists' demand for natural rights for themselves and their apparent willingness to impose slavery on others was too painful or too embarrassing to be ignored. By the early 1770s, Samuel Adams and his friends were loudly denouncing the practice of slaveholding, and a group of Boston Negroes had pointedly told the General Court that blacks expected "great things from men who have made such a noble stand against the designs of their *fellow-men* to enslave them." In Concord, too, the issue was clearly posed. When John Jack was dying in December 1772 he appointed Daniel Bliss as his executor. Bliss was then in the midst of dissenting from Concord's statement of colonial rights. Not long after, he sat down to write his late client's epitaph, and the seeming moral hypocrisy of Concord's Whigs figured unmistakably in the elegant lines the Tory lawyer composed:

> God wills us free; man wills us slaves.
> I will as God wills; God's will be done.
> Here lies the body of
> JOHN JACK
> a native of Africa who died
> March 1773 aged about 60 years
> Tho' born in a land of slavery,
> He was born free.
> Tho' he lived in a land of liberty,

He lived a slave.
Till by his honest, tho' stolen labors,
He acquired the source of slavery,
Which gave him his freedom;
Tho' not long before
Death, the grand tyrant
Gave him his final emancipation,
And set him on a footing with kings.
Tho' a slave to vice,
He practised those virtues
Without which kings are but slaves.

Few Concordians would have missed the message.[56]

If moral argument failed, practical necessity might yet carry the antislavery case. During every colonial war in the eighteenth century, Americans had eventually been driven by manpower shortages to violate their own laws and enlist blacks into active military service. For many blacks, then as now, the Army provided an avenue of opportunity: slaves could win their freedom by fighting for king and country. In 1775, with more than enough whites ready to enlist, the provincials felt no need to call on slaves for help. Philip Barrett and his fellows were reduced to tending the parade grounds and cleaning their masters' boots. William Emerson never mentioned them in his sermon: blacks were, as usual, an unnoticed presence in the town. But as the militiamen marched on the common, the slaves may have recalled earlier wartime experiences and looked forward to better days ahead. In the approaching war for self-determination, Concord's least had most to gain.[57]

★ ★ ★

In another, more peaceful era, Lucy Hosmer would undoubtedly have enjoyed the spectacle on Concord common. Militia musters could be gay affairs, occasions for courting and dining and socializing as much as for parade-ground drill, and they provided the women of a town as well as the men with a welcome break from the monotony of rural life. But in March of '75 the thirty-two-year-old Lucy could only worry. Her husband, Joseph, was lieutenant of Concord's troop of horse, and just as he had led the way in political opposition to Britain, he would surely be in the front lines of battle in the event of war. It was thus her conflict, too, whether she liked it or not. She had married Joseph against her father's wishes and had left her home town of Marlborough to settle in Concord, fifteen miles away. Now, as a wife, Lucy was bound to follow her husband's lead. Although she joined him in managing a household, she would seldom, if ever, be consulted on affairs of the world. Joseph would act on his own, and Lucy would run the risk of widowhood with four small children and a farm and shop to direct by herself.[58]

Lucy Barnes had met her husband when she was a girl of thirteen and he a twenty-year-old cabinetmaker just starting out in trade. One autumn day in 1755, Joseph Hosmer delivered in Marlborough a load of furniture he had made to order for Lucy's father, a rich farmer and town clerk. As he prepared to leave, a thunderstorm erupted, and young Lucy grew worried. "Do not go tonight," she said, according to family tradition. "Please make him stay, Father. It is raining still, and Concord woods are very dark." "Since you ask me, I will," Joseph replied. Soon he was visiting often, and when Lucy was sixteen, he asked for her hand.

Jonathan Barnes flatly refused. For most of the eighteenth century, marriage was a hardheaded business proposition, not an affair of the heart: when a bride and groom took wedding vows, they not only bound themselves together for life but also united their families into social and political alliances. Barnes was determined to marry his daughter into a family as important and wealthy as his own. Joseph Hosmer didn't fit the bill. Hard worker and fine craftsman though he was, his prospects appeared dim:

> Concord plains are sandy [Barnes declared], Concord soil is poor; you have miserable farms there, and no fruit. There is little hope you will ever do better than your father, for you have both farm and shop to attend to, and *two trades spoil one.* Lucy had better marry her cousin John. His father will give him one of the best farms in the town, and Lucy shall match his land acre for acre. You must marry a Concord girl, who cannot tell good land from poor. As for Lucy, you must forget her.

Joseph Hosmer was a practical man. He returned to his worn-out land, built a house next to his father's place below the South Bridge, and installed his unmarried sister, Dinah, as housekeeper for himself and his apprentices. Meanwhile, Lucy exercised her right of veto—she refused her cousin John. Three years later, Hosmer was back in Marlborough, delivering furniture this time to his erstwhile rival, John, who had taken defeat in stride and found himself another bride. The Concord cabinetmaker seized his second chance. On his way home, he stopped by Jonathan Barnes's house and renewed an old acquaintance. This time around, Lucy's father did not object to the match.

Actually, Barnes had been robbed of his voice in the matter: Lucy was two months pregnant by the time she was wed. While the father hardly approved his daughter's conduct, he would not subject her—and himself—to public disgrace. Lucy's case was not unique. The young women of Concord were as rebellious as the young men and for the same reason. Many fathers could no longer command the resources to ensure their daughters' place in the world. In the pre-Revolutionary marriage market, a woman's stock depended very much on the dowry she could bring to a match, and few young women were as fortunate as Lucy Barnes. Indeed, in many hard-pressed families, at least one or two daughters faced the prospect of marrying downward on the social scale.

In these circumstances, many women chafed at paternal restraints regarding when and whom they could wed. Their spirit of independence spread even to upper-class girls like Lucy, who could have married her rich cousin John. Young people were in a hurry to grow up, to act as independent adults while they still remained in their parents' homes. In the course of their development, men and women in the late teens and early twenties naturally felt the stirrings of new physical drives, but in earlier generations they had resisted temptation. Now many seized control of their sexual lives. A worried William Emerson might preach sermons against fornication, but to no avail: in the twenty years before the Revolution, more than one out of every three firstborn children had been conceived out of wedlock. In the process, the young people subverted their parents' authority. Lucy Barnes and Joseph Hosmer got to marry by forcing her father's hand. In this contest between the generations, Lucy assumed the greater share of the risk. It was always possible that Hosmer would change his mind.[59]

If Jonathan Barnes could not stop the marriage, he could make his displeasure known. As an old woman, Lucy Hosmer still bristled with resentment as she recalled her wedding night, the Christmas Eve of 1761. When her brother Jonathan was married, a party of twenty couples on horseback had accompanied the newlyweds on the long way to their new home in New Hampshire, but there was no escort for Lucy and Joseph Hosmer on the short trip from Marlborough to Concord. "When your father and I were married," she told her children, "we came home alone through those dark Concord woods."

Gradually, Lucy's father became reconciled to the match and presented the couple with the income of a farm. By then, her husband was a figure of some substance. Joseph Hosmer farmed over sixty acres of land divided out of his comfortable father's estate and raised cattle for market. In the shop adjoining his house, he made furniture with the help of two apprentices. Hosmer's fine cherry and mahogany clock cases, desks, and chests were much in demand in the Concord area and now are collector's items. Politically and socially, too, as we have seen, he was a man of parts: militia officer, leading opponent of the Barretts, and, eventually, thanks to the Revolutionary movement, an active committeeman in the colonial cause. Lucy Barnes had married well for reasons of both head and heart. Well-established on the land, the Hosmers successfully declared the independence of their affections from parental control. Symbolically, they named their first child "Lovina."[60]

Even so, real social independence came to Lucy and Joseph Hosmer no more easily than to any other young couple in town. And for Lucy, as an individual, it never arrived at all. She and her husband lived in the direct shadow of her in-laws on land still owned by Joseph's father. In the everyday contacts between the two families, the younger Hosmers must have felt a constant, unspoken pressure to defer to the older ones on matters both large and small. Harmony was probably maintained but at a price: Lucy could not be complete mistress of her household while her mother-in-law looked over her shoulder. And if she was limited inside the home, Lucy had virtually no independent standing in society. In defying her father and marrying Hosmer, she had simply exchanged one master for another, for a married woman in eighteenth-century New England had even fewer legal rights than a slave. She was considered by the male-dominated courts to be "civilly dead," spoken for in the world by her husband. She could not vote, sue, make contracts, testify in court, or execute a will on her own. Whatever dowry she brought to her marriage was not hers, nor were any wages she earned: men succeeded to the property of their wives. No woman could effectively challenge this ordering of the world. A wife was bound by male law to obey her husband; if she did not, he could confine her to home or even administer a flogging. An unhappy woman had no recourse except in extreme cases of abuse. If a man strayed from the marriage bed, that was no ground for divorce. Adultery was only a woman's crime—a crime against property and the moral code. An enraged husband was entitled not only to divorce but also to monetary damages from the lover for lessening the value of his wife. Yankee women literally belonged to their men.[61]

These harsh provisions of the law were tempered by the actual realities of domestic life. Joseph Hosmer needed his wife's support as fully as Lucy needed his. While he labored in fields and shop, she saw to the family's immediate welfare. With the help of her daughters, she prepared meals at a blazing fireplace, baked bread and cakes in a brick oven, kept a vegetable garden and put up preserves, milked cows, churned butter, and made cheese. Her home was also a small-scale textile manufactory, devoted to spinning, dyeing, and weaving the clothes that she would later be continually mending, washing, and ironing. And, of course, the responsibilities of bearing, nursing, weaning, and caring for children—eventually, six in all—imposed their constant demands. A woman's work was, in truth, never done. But neither was a man's in this agrarian society. Joseph and Lucy Hosmer did what was necessary to sustain their family. On a practical level, they were partners in a common enterprise, although, in the end, only one was chairman of the board.[62]

If Lucy had any misgivings about her status, she need only look at her sister-in-law's situation in order to dismiss them. Dinah Hosmer was thirty-four years old in 1775, and she had not yet found a husband. She never would. The flight to the frontier had removed many more of Concord's sons than daughters, and in their wake, Dinah was left to join a growing company of permanent spinsters. As a single woman, she could be far more independent than Lucy Hosmer. She was free to move and work wherever she pleased, but in reality her opportunities were severely limited. The professions and colleges were reserved for men, while only a few women could earn a living by teaching school or keeping a tavern. With near certainty, Dinah would labor and live under someone else's roof and spend much of her time doing what the label spinster implied—spinning yarn in a tedious, endless round of days. Her social outlets—the church, friends, sewing and quilting bees—were no broader than those of a married woman. And if she ever acquired property, she would be subject to taxation without representation. Single women gained very little from their legal rights. And so, Dinah Hosmer could not expect much from life. If she had been of a poor or middling family, she would have gone straight into domestic service. As the daughter of a wealthy farmer, she would probably remain with her parents until they died, then enter her brother Joseph's household, to work under Lucy's direction and enjoy whatever satisfactions there were for a maiden aunt.[63]

The approaching war now threatened Lucy Hosmer with a position no better than Dinah's—that of a widow. Joseph Hosmer would not leave his wife and children without financial support. Lucy was legally entitled to the traditional widow's "third"—to inherit outright a third of her husband's personal estate and to receive a third of his real property for her "use and improvement" during the rest of her life. Hosmer could do even more to ensure her welfare. In his will he might direct his executor or one of his sons to furnish her with an incredibly detailed list of goods: with so many bushels of grain, barrels of cider, pounds of meat, tons of hay, and cords of firewood, to be delivered to her doorstep every year. If his instructions were violated, the son could lose his inheritance or the executor forfeit his bond in probate court. In this way many wealthy fathers controlled their children from beyond the grave. But Hosmer might die suddenly, without ever writing a will. Then Lucy would struggle to manage the farm with no great success. Forced to rely on one or two sons and perhaps a hired hand, widows reaped even less from Concord's run-down land than had their late husbands. And Lucy would not find it easy to attract a husband to help her out. The farm would ultimately revert to her sons, and few men wished to spend their days on land that would never be theirs and for the benefit of someone else's children. In any case, the exodus from town had dried up the pool of eligible males, and many widows never remarried. Some descended into the ranks of the town poor; others joined the army of transients, warned out from town to town. Revolution could radically change Lucy's life from a comfortable dependence on her husband to a risky existence on her own.[64]

Yet Lucy Hosmer did not just comply passively with decisions beyond her control. Though she could not vote, she doubtless held some political opinions, too; and if she were tenacious enough, she could succeed in making them heard, as had her aunt by marriage, Mrs. Stephen Hosmer, who insisted on having her tea. Indeed, a few single women, including two nieces of Colonel Barrett, had taken a public stand on the issues by signing the Solemn League and Covenant. But Lucy chose, along with virtually every other married woman, to exercise her influence traditionally and quietly through the home. Whether or not Joseph asked her opinion, there is little reason to assume that she differed with her husband. British policy, to Concordians, threatened their community and their homes. Lucy Hosmer had already rebelled once to win her place in the town; she was unlikely to give it up without a fight. In the days ahead she and many other women would, like their husbands, "go to extremes" to defend their fortunes and their lives.

★ ★ ★

"Gentlemen: In all Probability you will be called to real Service," William Emerson warned the assembled militiamen. "The clouds hang thick over our Heads. Indications of an approaching Storm of War and Bloodshed. The Enemies of our King, Robbers of our Constitution and of all our precious Privileges, are already in Arms against us." Not to resist would be an abject surrender of colonial rights and something worse: a personal betrayal of New England's Fathers. Emerson recalled for his parishioners the story of New England's founding, a legend that had been handed down from generation to generation. The first settlers had sought to escape the hand of tyranny by fleeing to "the American Wilderness." There, "like wise and provident Parents," the Founding Fathers had done everything possible "to screen us from the encroaching Arm of Unconstitutional Power"; most important of all, they had never acknowledged Parliament's right to govern the colonies. With these precautions, New England had flourished, "free from the Shackles of Slavery." But now, Emerson declared, the present generation was called to defend this legacy of freedom. ". . . We, the Descendants of such worthy Ancestors, are not willing, nay, dare not be guilty of such Edomitish Prophanity as to sell, or rather tamely resign our glorious Birthright into the bloody fangs of hungry Courtiers and greedy Placemen. . . ." Even in New England's darkest hour—indeed, most of all in her darkest hour—sons must follow in their fathers' ways.

Men go to war for many reasons. Some they proudly announce to the world, some they conceal, and some they scarcely imagine. The people of Concord said over and over again that they were fighting for the "rights of Englishmen"—the right to be ruled and taxed by representatives of their own choosing, the right to govern their own internal affairs. In 1775 they explicitly sought neither revolution nor independence. In matters of foreign policy and imperial trade, they willingly submitted to the wishes of the mother country and proclaimed repeated loyalty to their paternal king. This was a political resistance directed toward specific political ends.

Yet in the background of the townsmen's actions lay a deepening social and economic malaise. From mid-century onward, Concord was in the throes of a long, protracted decay to which the Barretts, the Browns, and the Hosmers adapted as best they could but which no one seemed able to stop. Signs of decline were everywhere: in the falling property values, in the worn-out land, in the goods that piled up in the shops after the French and Indian War, in the numerous vagabonds who tramped through town, and, most of all, in the steady exodus of the young.

There was no overwhelming economic crisis on the eve of the war. By exporting its youth to the frontier, Concord by mid-century had managed to work out a rough balance between numbers and resources and to escape the worst social consequences of overpopulation. Farms were not split up into smaller and smaller parcels. The proportion of the landless remained stable at about 30 per cent. The concentration of landholdings in the hands of big farmers actually lessened. And despite the slump in trade, people could still pay their taxes, and few owed staggering bills like that which put Ezekiel Brown in jail. There was, to be sure, a widening gap between rich and poor in the decade before the Revolution, but though an ominous portent for the future, the change was gradual and produced no apparent social conflict. Concord was thus rescued from stark class divisions by the frontier. In this case, the historian Frederick Jackson Turner was right: the west provided a safety valve for the pent-up pressures of an overcrowded civilization.[65]

Nevertheless, the people of Concord escaped economic crisis only at a heavy social and psychological price. In a world where, even in the best of times, whole families could be wiped out overnight and seven fat years followed by seven lean, there were now more uncertainty and insecurity than ever. Apart from the lucky children of the rich and fortunate eldest sons, many, perhaps most, of Concord's sons and daughters were being forced out of their native town—forced to head farther and farther back into the stony hills of New Hampshire or the pine woods of Maine, forced to drift about in the army of transients, warned out from town to town, forced to sink without a trace in the invisible Boston poor, or forced to become servants—dependents—for most of their adult lives. Even those who stayed in Concord had to take their chances: many would slip below their fathers' level on the social scale and would struggle ever harder to support a family on run-down farms. The terms of life were tightening. If some enjoyed a heady freedom in the opportunities for choice and gladly seized the chance to make their way on their own, others floundered without a settled social place. With their futures vague and their present without purpose, many lost their reasons for restraint, their reasons for deference to parents and to the old moral code. As the crowd of pregnant brides made unmistakably clear, young people were increasingly independent, but independent for what?

Members of the older generation had no answers. They had their own anxieties. They were failing as parents: failing to pass on their property and status to the next generation, failing to direct their children to their proper roles in life. They were failing as neighbors: fighting bitterly over one issue after another even as they invoked the values of community and peace. They were failing as farmers and failing in trade. And as they watched their children leave home, one by one, perhaps never to see them again, they may have wondered about their own futures, too. What would happen to them when they were old and in need of help?

Amid these circumstances, Britain moved to fix a new and stricter dependency on her American colonies. In the straitened economy, Concordians naturally resented new burdens on their purses, especially since they had not consented to their imposition. But the citizens were not simply tax shirkers, as English critics charged. Britain's imperial policy challenged the Yankees in a far more radical way. The colonists were already buffeted by a world of unstoppable social and economic change. Now, with the passage of the Intolerable Acts, they were losing control of their political lives as well. Against the rapid erosion of their traditional social world, the townspeople of Concord were in no mood to evaluate British policy coolly. "Hungry Courtiers and greedy Placemen," in William Emerson's fevered words, were descending upon them, to batten on the fruits of New England's labors.

The disturbing social and economic changes did not "cause" the townspeople's rebellion against the new British moves.[66] No doubt they would have risen against fundamental assaults on their autonomy at any time. But the continuing decay in their fortunes added special poignancy to their fears. Most Concord fathers could no longer pass on land to all of their children. And if British policy succeeded, they would soon lose even the ability to transmit the birthright of freedom that had been passed on from generation to generation since New England's founding.

Concordians did not move easily or quickly into armed rebellion. In a society where magistrates were spoken of as "fathers" and

England as a "tender parent," men did not reject established authority without long consideration, and only for the most serious cause. After all, many Patriots were themselves fathers under challenge in their own homes. And perhaps in their politics as well. It is striking that the "most dangerous man" in Concord, radical agitator Joseph Hosmer, was, at age thirty-seven, considered the leader of all the "young men" in town. But generational politics do not finally account for Concord's response to revolution. If young men had to prod their elders into a radical stance, there was ultimately no gap between fathers and sons: they shared the same Whiggish values and goals. Just as fathers eventually acceded to their sons' desires and set them up on the land, so they now responded to pressure and led the way to war. And the sons, having gotten their wishes, turned for guidance and wisdom to their elders. Revolution was a family affair.[67]

And so, William Emerson sent his parishioners off to fight a tribal war:

> As a friend of Righteousness, as a Priest of the Lord who is under the Gospel Dispensation, I must say, 'The Priests blow the Trumpets in Zion, stand fast, take the Helmet, Shield and Buckler and put on the Brigadine.'
> Arise my injured Countrymen, and plead even with the Sword, the Firelock and the Bayonet, plead with your Arms, the Birthright of Englishmen the dearly purchased Legacy left you by your never to be forgotten Ancestors, and if God does not help, it will be because your Sins testify against you, otherwise you may be assured.

Then he added a final word of caution:

> Let every single Step taken in this most intricate Affair, be upon the Defensive. God Forbid that we should give our Enemies the Opportunity of saying justly that we have brought a civil War upon ourselves, by the smallest offensive Action.

★5★
"The Regulars Are Coming Out!"

WHILE Americans were drilling throughout the countryside, General Thomas Gage was marking time in Boston. The fifty-six-year-old Gage, son of an English viscount, had not sought his post in Massachusetts, and he probably would have preferred to remain in England to enjoy the considerable fortune he had amassed during his years as commander in chief of the British Army in North America, an office he still retained. In fact, after nine months as governor of the Bay Colony, he was already "sick of his task." Parliamentary supremacy was more easily announced in England than enforced in the colonies.[1]

Although the man-of-war *Somerset* kept the port of Boston closed, Gage's power hardly extended beyond Boston Neck. The Massachusetts Government Act was a dead letter. To carry out the law, Gage would have to dissolve the Provincial Congress, arrest its leaders, and force the citizenry to accept the new regime. The governor was prepared to do the job, but he knew that would require a much larger army than the 3,500 soldiers he had under his command—perhaps as many as twenty thousand men. The Yankees were determined to fight. So, Gage urged his English superiors to make an overwhelming show of force. "A large force will terrify, and engage many to join you," he advised, "a midling one will encourage resistance, and gain no friends. The crisis is indeed an alarming one. . . ." Meanwhile, Gage hoped for reinforcements and tried to avoid provoking a clash of arms. He would not start a war on his own account without explicit instructions from authorities at home.[2]

As it turned out, the provincials were temporizing, too. Many

Whig leaders, including Samuel Adams and the members of the Boston Committee of Correspondence, knew that Massachusetts must remain on the defensive, an innocent victim of British wrath, if it wished to retain the support of the eleven other colonies represented in the First Continental Congress. Within occupied Boston, tensions were high, and street fights between townspeople and Regulars periodically threatened to burst into larger incidents. But local officials worked with General Gage to keep a fragile peace. Moderates were also in charge of the Provincial Congress. They successfully resisted demands by rural firebrands for an immediate evacuation of the capital and a full-scale assault on the British forces. In early winter they even put off a decision to raise a standing army, although the Committee of Safety continued accumulating military supplies. Most delegates were willing to fight, but only, as William Emerson counseled, in self-defense. No one of prominence wanted to fire the first shot.[3]

Despite complaints among rowdy troops that "Tommy" was little better than "an old woman," General Gage was in fact preparing for the war he knew could erupt at any moment. After the Powder Alarm, he had fortified the approaches to the capital as a precaution against provincial attack and had encamped his troops in barracks on Boston Common. The Regulars were kept in shape on long marches, some as far as eight miles into the countryside. Though closely monitored by the Americans, these excursions were never molested. They did not win the British any friends. One observer reported that "the troops . . . marched over the people's land—some where their grain was sown—and gardens; broke down their fences, walls, &c." [4]

Gage was also gathering intelligence about the Americans' military preparations. His spies journeyed to both Concord and Worcester, a secondary provincial depot, to map the roads and topography, take the political pulse of the countryside, and discover what they could about the Patriot armories. They relied on local Tories for help—with sometimes unexpected results. On March 20, Ensign Henry De Berniere, a veteran of Gage's old regiment, and another officer arrived in Concord and asked for directions to the home of Daniel Bliss, the well-known "friend to government." They stopped there for dinner and military information. Bliss gladly told what he knew. But he was unable to conceal the visitors from his neighbors' prying eyes. The townsmen soon sent word that Bliss would not leave town alive the following morning. Wisely, the Tory lawyer, who was William Emerson's brother-in-law, led the officers out of town that night and accompanied them all the way to Boston. He never returned home. "Verily our enemies are of our own household," lamented Emerson.

Bliss was not the only resident to suffer after helping the British spies. Just before he conducted his visitors from town, a terrified woman came to his house. She had innocently directed the officers to Bliss's earlier in the day, and now, she tearfully explained, "they [the people] swore if she did not leave the town, they would tar and feather her for directing Tories in their road." [5]

Another expedition to Concord was more successful. On April 11 there suddenly appeared in town a young man, dressed in a countryman's gray coat, leather breeches, and blue mixed stockings and claiming to be a Maine gunsmith looking for work. He was, in reality, a quick-thinking English civilian-spy named John Howe, who had just barely escaped the clutches of suspicious citizens in Marlborough. Howe quickly gained an introduction to Major Buttrick. "They said I was the very man they wanted to see, and would assist me all they could, and immediately went to hire a shop," the twenty-two-year-old Howe recorded in his journal. The young man was taken to a provincial storehouse and shown a variety of weapons. He also dined with several gentlemen and asked whether there were many Tories in town. "The answer was, they expected there were, but not openly." That evening, Howe took leave of the townsmen, ostensibly to retrieve his gunmaking tools in Maine. He spent the night with a sympathetic Tory in nearby Lincoln. In the morning his host rode into Concord and learned that Howe's ruse had worked. "They were very much pleased with the prospect of having an armory established there." [6]

When Howe returned to Boston on April 12, he delivered a report that may have shaped Gage's final decision to act. The young man strongly advised against sending troops to destroy the stores at Worcester, fifty miles from the capital. That town was too far away, reached only by winding, hilly roads, and the inhabitants in the surrounding countryside were "generally determined to be free or die. . . . If they should march ten thousand regulars and a train of artillery [there] . . . not one of them would get back alive." What about Concord, then, Gage asked? Howe answered with remarkable foresight. "I stated that I thought five hundred mounted men might go to Concord in the night and destroy the stores and return safe, but to go with one thousand foot . . . the country would be so alarmed, that the greater part of them would be killed or taken." Gage was impressed with the advice, but he was in no position to accept it all. He had no cavalry under his command. He would have to take his chances with soldiers on foot.[7]

Gage did not depend only on foreign spies. His secret agents were also operating deep within the American camp. One informant may have been a Concord resident. He passed along up-to-date lists of the exact hiding places of all the military supplies in town. Another spy was probably Dr. Benjamin Church, a trusted member of the Committee of Safety. Church was a zealous Boston Whig who also kept an expensive mistress; he chose passion over patriotism and entered Gage's pay. In the several weeks before the battle, Church—or else another insider in the top Whig leadership—filed regular reports on the changing political mood behind the closed doors of the Provincial Congress.[8]

When the Congress gathered in the Concord meetinghouse on March 22, the members were still divided over how and when to resist British moves. The most immediate problem was false alarms. Everyone expected the Regulars to march on Concord and, when on March 30 Gage's troops set out beyond Boston Neck for exercise, large numbers of edgy citizens flew to arms, only to watch the Redcoats "manfully [lay] siege to a certain swamp" and then return to camp. To control this volatile situation, the Congress advised its constituents that whenever five hundred Regulars advanced into the countryside with artillery and baggage train, "it ought to be deemed a design to carry into execution the late Acts of Parliament." The provincials should therefore sound the alarm and immediately form "an Army of Observation . . . to act solely on the defensive so long as it can be justified on the Principles of Reason and Self-Preservation and [no] longer."[9]

For the people of Concord, these tense weeks, as William Emerson later recalled, were a time of "dread Suspense." The citizens could do nothing but wait while their homes lay exposed to attack. Many in Concord and in the surrounding countryside grew impatient with the Provincial Congress's inaction. "The people without doors," Church wrote from Concord, "are clamorous for an immediate commencement of hostilities. . . ." But "the moderate-thinking people within" still resisted, and it was not until the second week of April that the Congress finally authorized the raising of an eighteen-thousand-man army, to be enlisted from all of the New England colonies. This was the furthest the majority would go toward war. A week later, on April 15, the Congress recessed for consultations with the other colonies and perhaps to ward off more radical steps. Massachusetts was left with only the Committee of Safety in charge. It was the perfect time to strike, Church advised. "A sudden blow struck now . . . would oversett all their plans." [10]

The spy's report was exactly what Gage needed to hear. Only the day before, H.M.S. *Nautilus* had sailed into Boston with "Secret Orders" for the governor. They contained the Ministry's long-awaited decision on a course of action. Massachusetts was "in open rebellion," wrote Lord Dartmouth, Secretary of State for America. "In such a situation, force should be repelled by force." Considerable reinforcements were on the way, Gage was told, and he was instructed to encourage the formation of a local corps of Tories. But the governor should not delay his moves until the additional support arrived. "The first and essential step" was "to arrest the principal actors and abettors in the Provincial Congress," even if that measure should trigger hostilities. "The violence committed by those, who have taken up arms in Massachusetts," Dartmouth explained, "have appeared to me as the acts of a rude rabble, without plan, without concert, without conduct, and therefore I think that a small force now, if put to the test, would be able to encounter them, with greater probability of success, than might be expected of a larger army, if the people should be suffered to form themselves upon a more regular plan. . . ." Dartmouth conceded that Gage would have to rely on his own judgment and discretion in carrying out these orders.

Nonetheless, there was no mistaking his message: a restive Ministry demanded action.[11]

The military blow Gage conceived was entirely predictable, given his political and strategic intelligence: a surprise pre-emptive strike to seize or destroy the ordnance and provisions at Concord. If the attempt succeeded, Gage would set back the provincial resistance for months, if not paralyze it for good. If it failed and the Americans took up arms against the British troops, they would bear the responsibility for starting the war. It is unclear whether the governor planned to arrest the top Whig leaders. In any case, all but Dr. Joseph Warren of the Committee of Safety were safely outside the capital. John Adams was at home with his wife, Abigail, in Braintree. Samuel Adams and John Hancock were lodging at Jonas Clarke's parsonage in Lexington, in close proximity to the political deliberations in Concord. Gage's plan was, as noted, what every well-informed colonist had been anticipating for weeks. The only question was *when* the governor would move, not *where*. But what neither side expected was the explosive combination of events that formed the so-called Battle of Lexington and Concord: an assault on unresisting militiamen at Lexington common, a military confrontation at Concord's North Bridge, and a classic guerrilla action by ill-disciplined provincials, drawing on Indian fighting experience to harry the British retreat to Charlestown on the bloody Battle Road.[12]

★ ★ ★

The British action was, from the first, plagued by miscalculations, leaks, and delays that helped to ensure its failure. On Saturday, April 15, Gage relieved his grenadiers and light infantry—the shock troops of eighteenth-century armies—from regular duties, on the pretext that they were to learn new exercises. No one was fooled. "This I suppose is by way of a blind," British Lieutenant John Barker remarked in his diary. "I dare say they have something to do." And when at midnight that day a fleet of boats was quietly launched from the warships in Boston harbor, men like silversmith Paul Revere, who kept a round-the-clock watch of British movements, grasped what was happening. That Sunday, at the direction of Whig leader Joseph

Warren, Revere hurried out to Lexington to warn Hancock and Adams of the impending British strike. On his way back, Revere arranged to signal friends in Charlestown whenever the Regulars marched. ". . . If the British went out by water," Revere later recalled, "we would shew two lanthorns in the North Church Steeple, and if by land, one, as a signal; for we were aprehensive it would be difficult to cross the Charles River, or git over Boston neck." [13]

By the time the seven to eight hundred Regulars did gather on Boston Common at 10 P.M. on April 18, the expedition was doomed to failure. For on the previous day the Committee of Safety had ordered the dispersal of the stores at Concord into the surrounding towns. As the Redcoats prepared to march, men and women in Concord were working through the night to remove the arms and ammunition by ox team to new hiding places in Acton, Stow, and Harvard and in the woods and outskirts of their own town.

Gage, unaware of the American activities, continued to operate in what he thought was the utmost secrecy. On the afternoon of the eighteenth, Lieutenant Colonel Francis Smith received orders to lead an expedition that night, but was told neither his assignment nor his destination until he was ready to depart. That night the troops were led to their rendezvous, as a deserter told the Americans, "by the sergeants putting their hands on them, and whispering gently to them, and were even conducted by a back way out of the barracks, without knowledge of their comrades, and without observation of their sentries." The men silently tramped to the foot of the common (at the present Charles Street) and boarded transport at 11 P.M. to Phip's Farm (now Lechmere Point) in East Cambridge. As the boats were launched, two lanterns appeared in the North Church steeple, Paul Revere began the first part of his midnight ride in a rowboat to Charlestown, and William Dawes—the "forgotten" express rider whom Joseph Warren had dispatched along with Revere—slipped through a British guard post, crossed narrow Boston Neck to Roxbury on the mainland, and stole his way to Lexington.[14]

Revere and Dawes were not the only couriers in the night. Other suspicious provincials had already carried the news to Lexington that a group of ten armed British officers was making its way westward that evening instead of returning to base. The officers were, ironically, sentries dispatched by Gage to intercept anyone seeking to alarm the people of Concord. So when Revere galloped up to Jonas Clarke's at midnight on his exhausted mount, he found militiamen posted outside to safeguard the persons—and the good night's sleep—of Adams and Hancock. The Clarke household, Revere was told, had asked not to be disturbed by any noise about the house. "Noise!" Revere exclaimed. "You'll have noise enough before long. The regulars are coming out!" [15]

The alarm bells sounded, militiamen grabbed their firelocks and hurried in the night to Lexington common, and Revere and the soon arriving Dawes hastened toward Concord. They were accompanied by Concord's young Dr. Samuel Prescott, who had been out late courting his Lexington girl friend. The twenty-three-year-old physician came from conservative stock—his father, Dr. Abel Prescott, was a wealthy money lender and land speculator, his uncle Charles was the former "Governor's man"—but he himself was an ardent Patriot, glad of the opportunity to warn his neighbors and friends. It was fortunate that Prescott turned up. Near the Lexington-Lincoln line, British sentries halted the progress of the night riders. Prescott jumped his horse over a stone wall and escaped through familiar fields and back roads. Revere and Dawes had to turn back, but not before Revere misled his captors with a story that five hundred men were on their way to Lexington.[16]

About 130 men had gathered by 2 A.M. on Lexington green under the command of Captain John Parker, a forty-five-year-old veteran of Rogers's Rangers in the French and Indian War. They talked over the situation, Parker later said, and "concluded not to be discovered, nor meddle, or make with said regular troops . . . unless they should insult or molest us. . . ." They would form the recommended "Army of Observation." Then they waited in the chill night air. None of the scouts Parker had dispatched returned with fresh information; all had been intercepted. Meanwhile, the British column, two hours behind schedule, lumbered through the night. As it advanced, church bells sounded and signal guns fired in the dark. Realizing his expedition had been discovered, Colonel Smith sent back to General Gage for reinforcements.[17]

Parker's men, tired of standing in the cold, disbanded, some to homes, many to nearby Buckman Tavern for a warming glass of rum. Finally, near daybreak, Thaddeus Bowman, the last scout Parker had sent out, raced into town with the news that the Regulars were near. While Hancock and Adams made a hasty retreat through the woods toward Woburn, Parker's drummer beat out the alarm. Seventy men—nearly half of Lexington's adult males—turned out. Parker lined them up in double file on the green and renewed his command to "let the troops pass by, and don't molest them, without the[y] begin first." Nearby on the common stood forty unarmed spectators.[18]

The approaching troops—an advance guard of six companies under Major John Pitcairn—primed and loaded their guns before entering the village fifteen minutes later. Thanks to Revere and several other Americans whom they had seized on the road, the Regulars were expecting to encounter an armed force of five hundred to a thousand men. Like his counterpart Parker, Pitcairn ordered his men "on no account to fire, nor even to attempt it without Orders." As the Regulars advanced, Pitcairn rode behind the Americans and commanded them to surrender their arms. For his part, Captain Parker, concerned for the safety of his men, told them to disperse peacefully. Some did, while others like old Jonas Parker, in his sixties, calmly prepared to make a stand. No one dropped his gun.[19]

What happened next is in dispute. Parker contended that the British "made their appearance, and rushing furiously on, fired upon and killed eight of our party, without receiving any provocation therefor from us." The other American witnesses agreed. Several officers came toward the provincials: "Ye villans, ye Rebels, disperse; Damn you, disperse!" "Lay down your arms, Damn you, why don't you lay down your arms!" Pitcairn denied, until his death at Bunker Hill two months later, that he or his officers had issued the command to fire. He was turning toward his men, he said, when a musket behind a stone wall flashed in the pan, several shots rang out, and the Regulars fired a volley.[20]

There is no doubt that Pitcairn's men raged out of control. They were "so wild," reported Lieutenant Barker, "they cou'd hear no orders," and they ignored their commander, uselessly cutting the air with his sword as the signal to cease firing. A few Americans returned the fire. Finally, Pitcairn called for a drum roll, and order was restored, as the major body of troops under Colonel Smith reached town. Eight Americans lay dead, most of them shot in the back; old Jonas Parker was first hit by a lead ball and then killed with a bayonet. Another nine were wounded.[21]

The British, having spent no more than half an hour in Lexington, soon departed with a traditional victory salute.

★ ★ ★

A little after 1 A.M. the bell atop the Concord town house rang out in the night. Samuel Prescott had arrived with the alarm. Half a mile away, in the Old Manse, parson Emerson heeded the warning and hurried into the village. He was the first to answer the call, so impressing the guard stationed at the town house that he later named his two sons William and Emerson.

Soon Minutemen and militiamen were streaming into the center from all parts of the town. The soldiers assembled at the Wright Tavern, the appointed rendezvous, under the command of Major Buttrick, the senior officer present. Buttrick dispatched saddler Reuben Brown to Lexington for further information on the Regulars' progress. Then he assigned some of his men to help in removing military stores from the village. The rest were dispersed, with orders not to return home. About 4 A.M. a company of Lincoln Minutemen joined their Concord neighbors in arms to wait in the cold.[22]

Meanwhile, the alarm was spreading into "every Middlesex village and farm" and beyond, into Worcester and Hampshire counties, to the west, and up into New Hampshire and Maine. According to tradition, Samuel Prescott rode west to Acton and Stow, while his younger brother, Abel, carried the news south to Sudbury and Framingham. The roads began to fill with men advancing on Concord from all directions. In neighboring Bedford, Minutemen gathered at Fitch's Tavern for some early morning refreshments before they marched. "It is a cold breakfast, boys," said their captain, "but we will give the British a hot dinner. We'll have every dog of them before night." In Acton a company of militiamen assembled at the farm of their captain, gunsmith Isaac Davis. He was then thirty years old, the father of four young children, all of whom lay ill. "My husband said but little that morning," his widow recalled years later. ". . . As he led the company from the house, he turned himself round, and seemed to have something to communicate. He only said, 'Take good care of the children,' and was soon out of sight." [23]

The Acton and Bedford men were marching to defend relatives and friends in the town to which they had once belonged. So, too, were Minutemen from much farther away. Fifteen of the ninety-eight-man company that answered the alarm from New Ipswich, New Hampshire, were one-time Concordians, returning to the homes they had only recently left behind. For some, the battle would be not only a fight for American rights but also a home-town reunion.[24]

By daybreak about 150 men stood around Concord common, waiting for news. At long last, Reuben Brown galloped into town with an eye-witness report of the firing at Lexington. Were they shooting bullets? asked Major Buttrick. "I do not know," Brown cautiously replied, "but think it probable." In his haste to report back home, Brown had not paused to determine the outcome of the confrontation on Lexington green. The Concord militiamen would consequently face the Redcoat invasion without knowing for certain whether blood had already been shed or if their fellow Americans had yet begun to fight. As far as they could tell, war or peace still hung in the balance.[25]

The provincials assembled, facing the meetinghouse, atop the ridge dominating the Bay Road. Some of the Minutemen decided to go forth to meet the British. "We marched down towards L[exington] about a mild or mild [and a] half," Amos Barrett, Stephen's first cousin, recalled in later years, "and we see them acomming, we halted and stayd till they got within about 100 Rods then we was orded to the about face and marched before them with our Drums and fifes agoing and also the B[ritish]. We had grand musick." Nineteen-year-old militiaman Thaddeus Blood was equally impressed with the spectacle. "The sun was rising and shined on their arms, and they made a noble appearance in their red coats and glistening arms." [26]

As the Redcoats entered the town, the provincials retreated to higher ground, somewhat beyond the center, and held a hasty council. Conflicting reports were heard of the number of the British troops and of what had happened at Lexington common. Then the militiamen noticed that six companies of Redcoats were heading toward the North Bridge. The ever-impetuous William Emerson urged an immediate stand: "If we die, let us die here." More prudent and militarily experienced minds prevailed. Colonel Barrett, who had arrived on the scene a short while before, ordered a withdrawal to the heights above the bridge, a mile or so from town.[27]

Barrett returned to his farmhouse to complete the removal of military stores to the surrounding fields and woods. The provincials retreated under the command of Major Buttrick and of Lieutenant Joseph Hosmer, who was reluctantly serving as Buttrick's adjutant—his executive officer—for the day. When Buttrick had asked him to take the post, Hosmer had protested that he was the only officer present in his troop of horse and could not abandon his men. Buttrick disagreed. If the company had to be left leaderless, "it must be so then. You must go." There was no time for argument. The provincials crossed the river to the high ground of Buttrick's own farm only minutes before the Redcoats reached the North Bridge.[28]

In the village center, the British forces encountered a near-deserted scene. Most of the inhabitants had fled in fear to farms on the outskirts or to the woods. A small group of women and children huddled for protection at the Old Manse, where the report of the Redcoat invasion had already caused a fright. According to a granddaughter, Phebe Emerson learned of the British entrance into town from the black slave Frank, "who rushed up into her room with his axe in his hand, saying 'The Red Coats have come!' She fainted; she was always delicate." But the parson's wife quickly recovered and saw to the needs of her guests, all the while resenting her husband's frequent absences. "Grandmama told me herself," said another descendant, "that she felt hurt because he did not stay more with her, and once when he was feeding the women and children with bread and cheese she knocked on the window and said to him that she thought she needed him as much as the others."[29]

The British commander, Colonel Smith, moved swiftly to accomplish his goal: the destruction of the colonists' military stores. Of the six companies dispatched to take the North Bridge, three went ahead under Captain Lawrence Parsons to search the Barrett farmhouse for weapons. From the center of town, another company proceeded to guard the South Bridge and investigate the surrounding neighborhood. Everywhere the British knew exactly what they were looking for and where. Their spy had furnished a map of the hiding places of all the supplies.[30]

The search-and-destroy operation was largely conducted with restraint—perhaps because British officers, appalled by the breakdown of discipline and by the bloodshed at Lexington common, were determined to avoid further incidents. In the town center an officer demanded admission to Timothy Wheeler's storehouse, where numerous casks of provincial flour lay. Wheeler readily let him in. Playing the ever-cooperative country bumpkin, Wheeler put his hand on one of his own barrels and explained, "This is my flour. I am a miller, Sir. Yonder stands my mill. I get my living by it . . . this . . . is *my* flour; this is *my* wheat; this is *my* rye; this is mine." "Well," he was told, "we do not injure private property." Many Regulars were equally conscientious when they entered private homes. Famished after their long night's march, they asked for refreshments and generally insisted on paying their hosts. Colonel Barrett's wife, Rebecca, at first refused compensation: "We are commanded to feed our enemies." But when the British officers threw money into her lap, she sourly accepted it. "This is the price of blood," she said.[31]

Not all officers were so gentle. Ephraim Jones, innkeeper and town jailor, tried to block Major Pitcairn from entering his tavern; in the adjoining jailyard, three cannon were hidden. Pitcairn shoved Jones to the ground and stormed at him with threats and curses. Pitcairn got the cannon, then returned to the inn and sat down to breakfast, for which he punctiliously paid the bill.[32]

At least Pitcairn was honest. A good many of his troops ignored orders against looting and removed nearly £275 worth of private property from town. Reuben Brown was the biggest loser, to the amount of £90; from his shop were seized saddles, bridles, stirrups, cartridge boxes, and a chaise commandeered to carry wounded officers back to Boston. The Regulars stole with scholarly zeal. They filched a "quilt and letterd" Bible in two volumes from the meetinghouse, *Ward's Mathematics* from the schoolhouse, and volumes on *Fevers*, *Liberty of the Will*, and *The Affections* from Dr. Timothy Minot. They took anything they could lay their hands on. Mrs. Ezekiel Brown later reported the theft of a wide variety of goods: a cotton shirt, a pair of shoes, an ax, a quart pot, pewter plates, a pewter basin, an iron spider, a glass of salt, two brushes, and some silver buttons. The goods were worth a little more than a pound, but in her tight circumstances it was a sum Mrs. Brown could ill afford.[33]

Thanks to Concord's quick-witted women, a good deal of the provincial stores were saved from destruction. Investigating Amos Wood's house near the South Bridge, an officer noticed that one room was locked. Were any women within? he asked Mrs. Wood. Avoiding a direct reply, she concealed a roomful of supplies behind a grave look of concern. "I forbid anyone entering this room!" the officer gallantly declared. At Ephraim Jones's tavern, a servant girl named Hannah Barnes deflected a British search with equal aplomb. When the officers demanded admission into one room of the inn, she protested that it was her apartment and held only her own property. After considerable argument, the British gave up. Inside the room stood the chest of Henry Gardner, treasurer of the Provincial Congress.[34]

The British came prepared to arrest those responsible for hiding the military supplies. But they had even worse luck seizing persons than property. Town clerk Ephraim Wood narrowly eluded capture. That morning the Regulars arrived at his house near the South Bridge and announced their intention to take him prisoner. Wood was not around; he was engaged in dispersing the stores. Not long after, the 250-pound Wood was heading home with a keg of powder on his back when he came in sight of the Redcoats stationed at the bridge. He immediately ran down to the river, got in a boat, and crossed to the other side just as the Regulars were reaching the opposite bank. Four miles to the north, Stephen Barrett, having guided approaching Minutemen from Harvard and Stow onto safe routes into town, returned to his father's farmhouse. The British demanded his name. Hearing "Barrett," they grabbed him by the collar, kicked him, and exclaimed, "Now we have got you. You must go to Boston with us, and be sent to England for trial." Mrs. Barrett quickly explained that he was her son, "not the master of the house." A bit later the officers missed their chance to arrest the colonel. They passed by him on their way back to the North Bridge. Dressed in an old coat, a flapped hat, and a leather apron, Colonel Barrett aroused no suspicion.[35]

The British search was not completely unsuccessful. The Regulars threw five hundred pounds of musket balls into the mill pond, broke open sixty barrels of flour, knocked the trunnions off the jailyard cannon, and, to add insult to injury, made a bonfire of the town's liberty pole. The fire spread to the roof of the nearby courthouse. Observing the danger, Martha Moulton, an aged widow who kept house for Dr. Timothy Minot on the green, mustered up all her courage, "put her life, as it were, in her hand, and ventured to beg of the officers to send some of their men to put out the fire. But," she told the General Court in a petition for a reward for her bravery, "they took no notice, only sneered." She persisted, only to be told, 'O mother, we won't do you any harm!" Still she continued her pathetic pleas, and eventually, as he put it, "under divine Providence, she was an instrument of saving the Court House, and how many more [houses] is not certain . . . at the great risk of her life." The fire was quickly extinguished, but its billowing smoke alarmed the Minutemen on the heights overlooking the town.[36]

As the provincials waited above the North Bridge, many grew increasingly unhappy about their long inaction. Reinforcements from Acton, Littleton, and other nearby towns had expanded their number to about four hundred. Down at the bridge, British Captain Walter Laurie commanded fewer than a hundred men. He had already sent Colonel Smith an urgent call for help. For a long time the two sides did nothing but stare at each other across the eight hundred yards separating them. The wait was so tedious that one Lincoln militiaman, "who was an Englishman and a droll fellow and a fine singer," handed his musket to a friend and went down to talk with the Redcoats. After a while, "he came back and took his gun and said he was going home. . . ." Finally, the ascending smoke from the town center precipitated a crisis.[37]

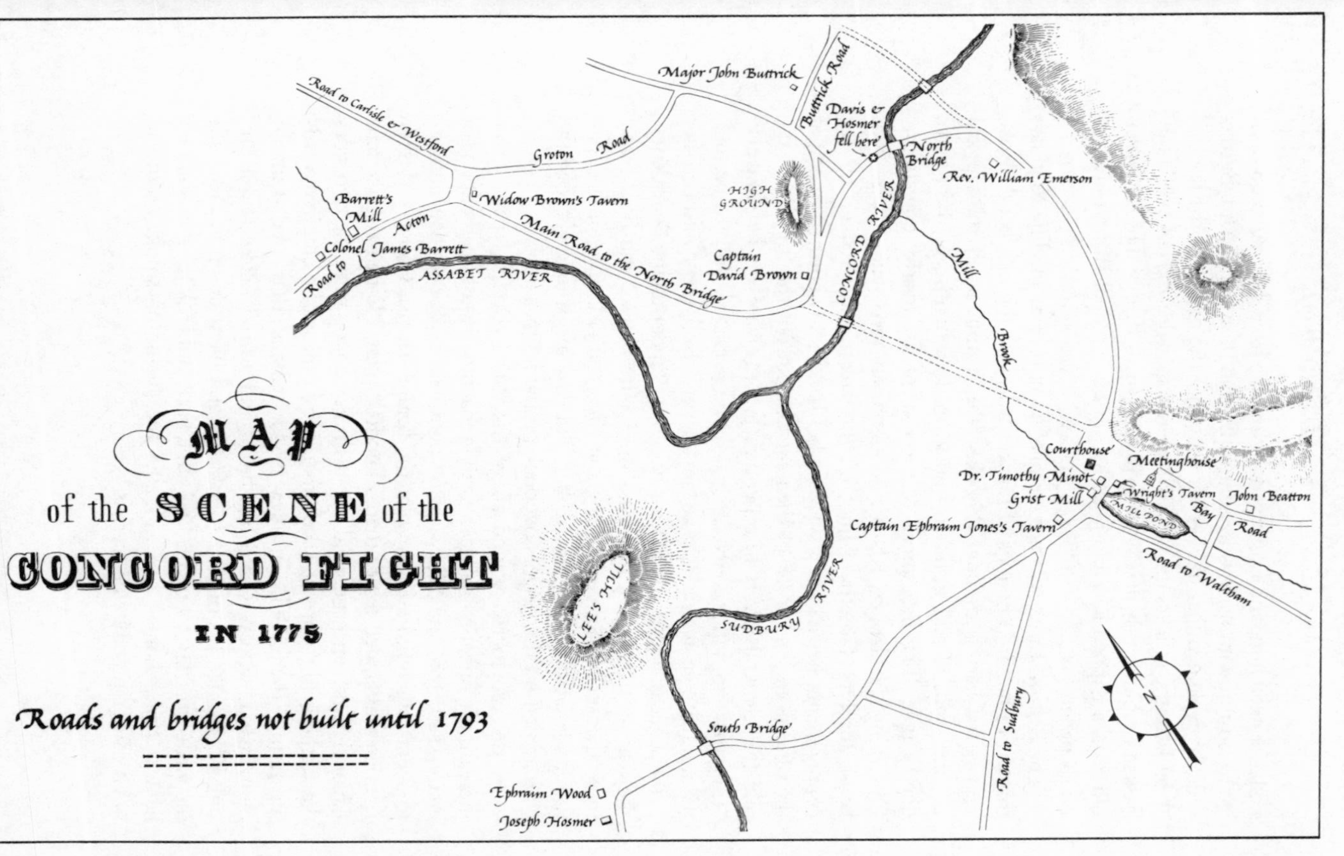

MAP
of the SCENE of the
CONCORD FIGHT
IN 1775
Roads and bridges not built until 1793
Road to Carlisle & Westford
Groton Road
Major John Buttrick
Buttrick Road
Davis & Hosmer fell here
North Bridge
Rev. William Emerson
Barrett's Mill
Widow Brown's Tavern
HIGH GROUND
Acton
Road to
Colonel James Barrett
Main Road to the North Bridge
Captain David Brown
ASSABET RIVER
CONCORD RIVER
Mill Brook
Courthouse
Meetinghouse
Dr. Timothy Minot
Grist Mill
Wright's Tavern
John Beatton
Bay Road
MILL POND
Captain Ephraim Jones's Tavern
Road to Waltham
LEE'S HILL
SUDBURY RIVER
South Bridge
Road to Sudbury
Ephraim Wood
Joseph Hosmer
N

Lieutenant Joseph Hosmer launched into another of his memorable speeches. "I have often heard it said that the British have boasted that they could march through our country, laying waste our hamlets and villages and we would not oppose them," Hosmer declared, in words that one listener vividly recalled years later. "And *I begin to think it is true.*" Then, pointing dramatically to the rising smoke, he turned to Major Buttrick. "Will you let them burn the town down?" Once again Hosmer was challenging the town's established leadership. Colonel Barrett immediately held a brief council. The decision was unanimous. They "resolved to march into the middle of the town to defend their homes, or die in the attempt." Barrett ordered the men, as his nephew Amos recalled, "not to fire till they fired first, then to fire as fast as we could." Then they marched. Concord's internal politics had forced the issue.[38]

To the fife strains of "The White Cockade," the provincials proceeded, in double file, toward the bridge—with the same solemnity, Captain Charles Miles said, as in going to church. Isaac Davis's Acton company was in the front line, followed by the Minuteman units of David Brown and Captain Miles. As they marched, David Brown, along with Purchase, passed right by his own house, where earlier his feeble-minded uncle Elias had spent the morning drawing cider for the Redcoats ("They were," he later remembered, "the prettiest men he ever saw"). The house was now deserted. In that remarkably warm spring, the grain already stood green in his fields. And the apple trees were beginning to blossom. All that Brown defended lay about him: the British were trespassing on his home. Every one of the Minutemen could have said the same.[39]

As the Americans advanced, the three British companies hastily crowded at the east end of the bridge. Some Redcoats tried briefly to pull up the planks. When the Americans grew near, the British fired a few warning shots, then a direct volley. "Their Balls," said Amos Barrett, "whistled well." Isaac Davis and his company's young fifer, Abner Hosmer, fell dead. Major Buttrick leaped into the air, shouting, "Fire, fellow soldiers, for God's sake, fire." The cry of "Fire! Fire!" flew through the ranks from front to rear. The resulting discharge wounded nearly a dozen of the enemy, three of them mortally. The provincials pressed on to cross the bridge; the British, jammed together at the end, panicked and ran, unpursued, toward town. The Concord fight—"the shot heard round the world"—had taken two to three minutes.[40]

After the shooting, about two hundred provincials crossed the bridge to the main road, then stationed themselves in a hilly pasture on the opposite side. Taking positions behind a stone wall, they watched and waited as the scattered Regulars tried to regroup. A detachment under Colonel Smith was laboriously making its way toward the bridge in belated response to Captain Laurie's earlier call for help. The reinforcements had been delayed by the Colonel himself, "a very fat heavy Man," as the acerbic Lieutenant Barker remarked, who "wou'd not have reached the Bridge in half an hour tho' it was not half a mile to it." As the British stood about the road, the provincials held their fire. "I beleave we could [have] kill'd all most every officseer thair was in the front," Amos Barrett recalled, "but we had no orders to fire. . . ." The Concordians and their neighbors were still fighting only in self-defense. Soon the Regulars marched back to town, and the militiamen dispersed.[41]

That was the end of American discipline for the day. Some militiamen had already returned to the Buttrick farm with their wounded and dead. Others simply went home. One man was spotted abandoning his company by his captain's wife, Mrs. Nathan Barrett. As the soldier passed by her house, she later told her young son, she called out to ask "where he was a going. He says, I am a going home; I am very sick. She says to him, you must not take your gun with you. Yes, he says, I shall. No, stop, I must have it, but no, so off he went upon the run and she after him, but he got away and she gave up the chas." Many others did not give up the fight. They raced across the Great Fields to the East Quarter of town and lay in wait for the retreating Redcoats. But there was no co-ordinated strategy. Colonel Barrett, Major Buttrick, Lieutenant Hosmer were left without their men. "Every man," said Thaddeus Blood, "was his own commander."[42]

One incident marred the Yankee triumph at the bridge. Captain Parson's detachment was still at the Barrett farmhouse when the battle began. Hearing the distant report of guns, the men abandoned their search for matériel and hurried back to the bridge. They encountered a deserted battle scene, strewn with the bodies of their fallen comrades. Among the dead lay a corpse with a bloodied, mangled head. The Americans, it appeared, had been scalping! As the story spread, further atrocities were added. British Ensign Jeremy Lister reported that four men had been "scalped, their Eyes goug'd, their Noses and Ears cut off; such barbarity exercis'd upon the Corps could scarcely be paralleld by the most uncivilized Savages." The episode became a staple of anti-American propaganda.[43]

The true story was less gruesome. William Emerson learned that a country youth, on his way to join the provincial forces, was approaching the battle site with hatchet in hand when a dying Redcoat stirred. Frightened, the young man—a twenty-one-year-old Minuteman named Ammi White—struck the soldier with his ax. "The poor object lived an hour or two before he died," Emerson reported. In the nineteenth century the incident became widely known when Nathaniel Hawthorne, living and writing in the Old Manse, brooded over young White's fate:

> Oftentimes, as an intellectual and moral exercise, I have sought to follow that poor youth through his subsequent career, and observe how his soul was tortured by the blood stain, contracted as it had been before the long custom of war had robbed human life of its sanctity, and while it still seemed murderous to slay a brother man. This one circumstance has borne more fruit for me than all that history tells us of the fight.

New evidence sets White's deed in a more favorable light. Mrs. Peter Barrett, the colonel's daughter-in-law, told a nineteenth-century interviewer that the Redcoat was "lying in a puddle of water so much in distress that he was trying to drown himself and begged someone to kill him." Young White put the soldier out of his misery. If this account is true, White could have lived out his life with a clear conscience.[44]

★ ★ ★

You know the rest. In the books you have read,
How the British Regulars fired and fled,—
How the farmers gave them ball for ball,
From behind each fence and farm-yard wall,
Chasing the red-coats down the lane,
Then crossing the fields to emerge again
Under the tree at the turn of the road,
And only pausing to fire and load.
—From Henry Wadsworth Longfellow, "Paul Revere's Ride" [45]

Back in the village Colonel Smith once again made a fatal delay. With the countryside in arms, his worn and hungry men should have marched back to Boston as fast as they could. Instead, the slow-moving Smith vacillated on his course. ". . . Ye Enemy," William Emerson observed, "by their Marches and counter Marches discovered great Ficklness & Inconstancy of Mind, sometimes advancing, sometimes returning to their former Posts. . . ." Smith was waiting, in part, for his wounded officers to be treated by Dr. Timothy Minot and Dr. John Cuming, who, appropriately enough, was using Daniel Bliss's abandoned home for a hospital. But no doubt the British commander was hoping desperately for the arrival of reinforcements from Boston. As they lingered in the center, the Regulars continued to pillage nearby homes and to outrage the local population. In Wright Tavern, Major Pitcairn supposedly stirred a "bloody finger" in a glass of brandy and declared "he hoped he should stir the damned yankee blood so before night." Finally, about noon, the Redcoats began their retreat, leaving several of their wounded and a long legacy of bitterness behind them. They had been in Concord for four hours.[46]

The British left the way they came, along the Bay Road, but this time without fife and drums. They were unaware they were walking into a trap. Above them, beyond the ridge which runs beside the road, the militiamen who had raced across the Great Fields poised to head off the Regulars' retreat. Ahead, at Meriam's Corner, about a mile from town, where the ridge dies away and the road forks, the provincials lay in wait. Additional Minutemen from Reading and Billerica were approaching from the north and a force of East Sudbury men from the south. The provincials now numbered more than eleven hundred men. They took cover behind the houses and barns of selectman Nathan Meriam and his East Quarter neighbors and in the surrounding hills and woods. "Silence reigned on both sides," said one Reading man. At the Corner, the road narrowed for a bridge over a small brook. As the British crossed, the shooting started. Reports differ on who fired first. But the Americans, though no marksmen and often beyond effective musket range, blasted the poor, weary Englishmen in the road. When the smoke cleared, "a grait many [British] lay dead," Amos Barrett wrote, "and the Road was bloddy." [47]

The fighting grew fiercer and bloodier after the Redcoats left Concord. This was war as provincial Indian fighters had long known it: every man for himself. To the British, accustomed to open field fighting, it was the action of "rascals" and "concealed villains," as one put it, "making the cowardly disposition . . . to murder us all." [48]

British flankers at first managed to keep their assailants at a distance, but not for long. As the road wound its way up and down hills and over brooks, the Redcoats were forced into indefensible natural traps. Outnumbered by an elusive, ever-increasing enemy and peppered by incessant fire, the beleaguered British used up their ammunition in often aimless shooting. They were exhausted after a virtually uninterrupted fifteen hours' march. Near Fiske Hill in Lexington, they began to break ranks and run in confusion. The rout ended beyond Lexington village, reported a British ensign, after "the officers got to the front and presented their bayonets, and told the men that if they advanced they should die. . . ." [49]

By then, the nine-hundred-man armored First Brigade, dispatched that morning in response to Colonel Smith's message to Gage, had finally arrived in Lexington. The retreating troops fled to safety behind the brigade lines and then fell to the ground, lying prone, like dogs with protruding tongues, according to a contemporary British historian. "I had the happiness," Lord Percy, the brigade commander, remarked, "of saving them from inevitable destruction." [50]

It was Percy who inflicted the heaviest damage of the day upon the Americans, using cannon effectively to disperse approaching provincials and sending his men into houses from which sniper fire came, with orders to kill those within. In Lexington center, the British burned several houses in order to deny the provincials cover while Smith's weary forces took time to rest. By the end of the day, Lexington's property losses would total over £1,700.[51]

Not surprisingly, innocent civilians were caught in the fire between Redcoats and snipers. In Menotomy (now Arlington), where the fighting reached its pitch, two well-known topers lingered at Cooper's Tavern outside which eighty-year-old Samuel Whittemore was taking fire at passing Regulars. "Let us finish the mug," said one, "they won't come yet." They did, and after leaving a wounded Whittemore for dead—he recovered to live nearly twenty years more—they finished off the drinkers. And in what became one of the favorite atrocity stories in the American post-battle propaganda, the Regulars forced Hannah Adams from child-bed with her eighteen-day-old infant. "One of said soldiers," she testified, "immediately opened my curtains with his bayonet fixed, pointing the same to my breast. I immediately cried out 'for the Lord's sake do not kill me'; he replied, 'damn you.' One that stood near said, 'we will not hurt the woman, if she will go out of the house, but we will surely burn it.' "[52]

The British finally forced their way through to safety in Charlestown, encamping on Bunker Hill, in a position they foolishly abandoned several days later. Seventy-three Redcoats were dead, 174 wounded, and twenty-six missing—a casualty rate of close to 20 per cent. The comparable rate for the nearly four thousand American participants was only 2 or 3 per cent: forty-nine dead, thirty-nine wounded, four missing. No longer would Redcoats who knew Americans doubt their will to fight.[53]

★ ★ ★

Concord was saved with only slight losses to the town. Throughout the long day, no townsman had died, and only four were wounded. Minuteman Jonas Brown, the twenty-two-year-old nephew of Captain David Brown, was grazed by a musket ball—a Redcoat warning shot—on the provincial march to the bridge. He shrugged off the injury with a quip. "Ah, Jonas," his mother dolefully advised him when she saw the wound, "if it had gone a little more towards your neck, it would have killed you!" "Oh, yes, mother," he replied, "but if it had gone a little further t'other way, *'t wouldn't touched me!*" Captain Nathan Barrett was wounded on the chase to Charlestown, along with Captain Charles Miles. Young Abel Prescott, who had carried the alarm to Sudbury and Framingham, was shot in the side just after he returned home and was watching the Regulars retreat. No one was very seriously hurt.[54]

The damage to property was also surprisingly light. The townspeople had kept most of the stores out of British hands, and the next day they were able to salvage a good deal of what the Redcoats had seized. From the mill pond they fished out iron cannon balls, lead musket balls, and barrels of flour. Even some private property was recovered. During the British retreat, Lieutenant Joseph Hayward, an old Indian fighter in his sixties, recaptured the two chaises taken earlier from Reuben Brown and John Beatton after killing an enemy soldier in each. The town also gained reparations of a sort when militiamen Nathan Barrett and Henry Flint returned home with Major John Pitcairn's horse, which had bolted under fire. The Provincial Congress later gave pastor Emerson use of the horse.[55]

There was a moral satisfaction, too, in the defection of a number of British soldiers to the provincial side. Of eight wounded left behind with Dr. Cuming, seven survived, never to return to the Regular camp. A Sergeant Cooper, who had been denied a glass of liquor while searching the Barrett farmhouse, married Cuming's servant girl. He was often heard grumbling that "he could not forgive Mrs. Barrett for not giving him some spirit that day." Cooper soon moved on. A permanent migrant was Samuel Lee, a British officer who was captured early in the morning between Lexington and Concord and would later boast that he was "the first prisoner in the Revolution." He married a Concord widow and settled down to carry on the tailor's trade for the rest of his life.[56]

For the next few days, the townspeople feared British revenge. On the twentieth, Joseph Lee recorded in his diary that "we were alarmed with a report that 200 were come to town to burn all ye Houses and many moved their goods to out places for safety." Another citizen later recalled that he had carried "a load of women" out of town. The people of Concord reacted with calm. Similar false rumors of a British descent on the countryside were creating panic throughout coastal Essex County. "The great Ipswich fright" began with stories that Redcoats had been landed from cutters in the Ipswich River and were already carving a bloody path toward the village. Within an hour the townspeople of Beverly heard that Ipswich's population had been decimated. Someone broke into a town meeting at Newbury with the news: "Turn out, for God's sake, or you will all be killed. The regulars are marching on us; they are at Ipswich now, cutting and slashing all before them." [57]

The panic soon died down. From Rhode Island, Connecticut, New Hampshire, and Maine a steady stream of militiamen was arriving to join the Massachusetts forces already encamped in the fields of Charlestown and Cambridge. The siege of Boston had begun. As the scene of action shifted from Concord, the townspeople could relax briefly and consider their day in battle. David Brown noted the "squirmish" in his diary, as did Dr. Joseph Lee, who, despite his Tory reputation, identified with "our people" and not the Regulars. At the end of April, William Emerson would observe that "this Month [is] remarkable for the greatest Events taking Place in the present Age." [58]

There was not much time for reflection. In later years Concordians would polish up their stories of April 19 and no doubt improve them in the telling. The events of the war would be overshadowed by the heroics of a single day. For now, much work had to be done. The town still had to guard the military stores and keep a dozen British prisoners under watch as well. Men had to be recruited for the Yankee army and the whole community mobilized for conflict. Concord Fight was an incident in a wider war.

★6★
"This Bleeding Land"

WHEN the shots were fired on April 19, Concord was already a wartime community. For several months the townspeople had been gearing their lives to the demands of raising and drilling troops, storing supplies, and watching out for Tories and spies. Now they redoubled their efforts. No one expected a long struggle. A siege of Boston, a thrust against Canada: quick, aggressive action would force the British Ministry to terms.[1] Instead, the eight exhausting years that followed the clash at the bridge would mark the longest conflict in American history until Vietnam. The War for Independence imposed heavy sacrifices on nearly every family in Concord and unprecedented burdens on local government as well. This was something more than a costly military contest: it was revolution, a great popular movement for self-determination that unleashed powerful liberating currents in a declining provincial society. The people of Concord had set out only to defend their traditional community life. Now they had to face the consequences of their fervent Whig insistence on the people's right to rule.

Concord's mobilization formed an integral part of a wider war effort. First the Provincial Congress and then the General Court directed military activities in Massachusetts, relying on the towns to execute their orders. Throughout the war local communities were responsible for furnishing men and matériel to the central authorities. Hometowns helped equip their troops, often paid their wages, and supported the needy families of men away at war. They were occasionally called on to intern prisoners of war and to hunt for internal enemies. The General Court even required every town to establish a committee of correspondence, inspection, and safety as a general agency in charge of war. In every case, Concord complied with these instructions. Where town meetings before the Revolutionary crisis had seldom noticed the outside world, after 1775 they often subordinated local needs to broad concerns of state. In the process of fighting the British assault on their autonomy, the townspeople allowed state government to assume extraordinary power over their lives.[2]

In the first years of the war, Concord had to cope with the new military demands amid a major population boom. As the siege of British-held Boston began, thousands of city inhabitants were evacuated from the capital, which became an enclave of Tories and Redcoats, and scattered into the countryside. The Provincial Congress ordered the nearby towns to provide for many of the Boston poor. Concord's quota was sixty-six—the third highest in Middlesex County—but the town eventually admitted and supported eighty-two poverty-stricken Bostonians, all of whom it would promptly have warned out only a few months before. So many refugees of all social classes crowded into town that they held a Boston town meeting there in July 1775 to elect legislative representatives of their own. The Bostonians were soon followed by displaced persons from Charlestown, whose homes had been burned by Redcoats during the Battle of Bunker Hill.[3]

Concord's most impressive newcomers were the students and faculty of Harvard College. The school's buildings in Cambridge were serving as barracks for the American troops, and as a result the college had to relocate for the 1775–76 academic year. Concord was chosen over several other towns in a decision that surely enhanced the community's prestige. About one hundred students and faculty found lodgings throughout the town—a dozen boarded at Dr. Joseph Lee's—and walked into the village for classes at the courthouse, the meetinghouse, and the grammar school. The presence of the college enlivened social life, but the students were bored with their country setting and unhappy at their inability to use the school's scientific apparatus, which had been left behind in Cambridge. As soon as the siege of Boston was over, Harvard officials would cite "the prevailing

Discontent" among the students and hurry back to their permanent quarters on the Charles.[4]

By mid-March of 1776, some nineteen hundred persons were concentrated in Concord, representing an increase of over 25 per cent in little more than a year. Not all of the growth came from newcomers. The outburst of war had put a temporary brake on emigration, as young men stayed in their native town in order to join the fight.[5] With the rapid build-up of numbers, the community's resources underwent serious strain. The mild winter and early spring of 1775 had given way to the worst summer drought in decades, reducing the harvest at the very time that the Army outside Boston added to the civilian demand for provisions. Inevitably, shortages appeared. Meanwhile, the public health was threatened by the close conditions in town. That summer—always a dangerous season—an epidemic of dysentery flared; it was followed by an eruption of "Distemper." By early September, William Emerson was preaching from the text, "If thou wilt diligently hearken to the voice of the Lord . . . I will put none of these diseases upon thee which I have brought upon the Egyptians, for I am the Lord that healeth thee." That same day, Emerson noted, a few people recovered; a week later, the sickness had abated, leaving several dead in its wake.[6]

Despite these pressures, Concord responded energetically to the early demands of war. Raising troops posed no problem at all. On the day after the battle in Concord, at least sixty townsmen enlisted for eight months in the Massachusetts Army laying siege to Boston. Within their two companies were nearly half of the Minutemen, whose units were apparently dissolved right after they had completed their assignment on April 19.[7] One Concord company took the brunt of the first two British assaults at Bunker Hill and suffered three dead, the town's first losses in the war. Not long after, along with the rest of the Massachusetts forces, both companies were incorporated into the Continental Army of the United Colonies, under the command of General George Washington. By July 4, 1776, the town had raised 190 men—half of its males over sixteen years old—for service on the Massachusetts coast, in Benedict Arnold's fatal expedition against Quebec, and on the New York frontier. Recruits were naturally the younger men, drawn from all social ranks, but virtually every able-bodied man under forty must have taken up arms for at least a few days, since the entire militia was called out for the Battle of Dorchester Heights in March 1776 when the Americans finally maneuvered the Redcoats into abandoning Boston.[8]

The most popular campaign of the entire war was an expedition to Fort Ticonderoga in northern New York, the former British citadel along Lake Champlain that commanded the approach to Canada. In August 1776, Captain Charles Miles led sixty-one of his neighbors on the 250-mile journey through New Hampshire and Vermont to the same region where many Concordians had been stationed in the French and Indian War. William Emerson accompanied them as chaplain. The townsmen's enthusiasm for the campaign had both strategic and personal roots. British troops were descending from Canada, and if they succeeded in recapturing the fortress, they would be well placed to attack New England from the west. In addition, the Massachusetts expedition was to be commanded by one of Concord's own, Colonel John Cuming. But a month before the men departed, Emerson found his friend Cuming "very low in Spirits & exceedingly cast down." Mrs. Cuming, remembering her husband's tales of captivity in the French and Indian War, was steadfast against his going off again to fight. Two weeks later, Emerson was stunned to learn that *"Colonel Cuming resigned his Commission!!!!"*[9]

The parson's alarm reflected in part his own difficult conflict between family and duty. Just nine days before he was to leave, Mrs. Emerson gave birth to a baby girl, the couple's fifth child. "Through mercy [I] have got out of the bounds of Concord . . ." Emerson wrote his wife after he had forced himself to go. " 'Tis harder parting with my Family and Flock than perhaps you are aware of." He was never to see them again. After a two-week trip along clay roads that suddenly turned into treacherous swamps during heavy rains, Emerson caught "a Sort of mongrell Feaver & Ague" in the American camp. He was discharged from service after two weeks but died at a fellow minister's house in Vermont on the way home. "I desire to leave You and our dear little Ones, to a kind and gracious Providence," he told Phebe in his final letter. "My dear, strive for

Patience, let not a murmuring Thought, and sure not a murmuring Word drop from your Lips." [10]

Those who stayed behind in Concord often performed important war-related work. Militiamen were assigned to guard the military stores and to keep watch over prisoners of war in the county jail. Deacon Thomas Barrett and his son Samuel established a gunshop at their millsite and experimented with the use of water power for boring, grinding, and polishing muskets. Many women also assembled supplies, knitting stockings and sewing shirts to fill provincial requisitions. Right after the Battle of Bunker Hill, the "patriotic ladies" of the town donated a chest of clothing and other articles for the wounded to the military hospital in Cambridge. "This instance of their humanity and public spirit," remarked one newspaper, "does honor to the town, and will, we hope, induce others to imitate so good an example." [11]

This outpouring of men and money was greatly facilitated by the absence of an active Tory opposition. In only a few Yankee families was the American Revolution ever an internal civil war. While William Emerson was preaching ardent patriotic sermons, his wife's brothers—the Blisses—divided sharply in their loyalties: attorney Daniel and his merchant brother Samuel had already fled to General Gage's Boston and then to Canada, there to serve as officers in the British Army; Thomas Theodore, a captain in the Massachusetts forces, was taken prisoner during Benedict Arnold's expedition against Quebec in the winter of 1775–76 and spent the rest of the war being shifted about from one British jail to another; the youngest, Joseph, was an eighteen-year-old clerk in Henry Knox's bookstore in Boston when war began, and he was shortly serving in his employer's famous artillery regiment, rising to the rank of paymaster in the Continental Army. [12]

There were undoubtedly others who harbored doubts about the American resistance but were unwilling to break with family and friends. For the time being they laid low rather than risk the reprisals which Concord's Patriots handed out to suspected Loyalists. Former selectman John Flint was overheard declaring that "For myself I think I shall be neutral in these times," and his name was later stricken from the jury lists. [13] Dr. Joseph Lee, who already had a good many enemies, was a particular target of retaliation. On the night of April 23, 1775, he was "seized for a Tory while in bed," hustled off to deacon Thomas Barrett's farm, and tried by the committee of correspondence for his political sins. The committee, on which his old rival's son, James Barrett, Jr., sat, ordered Lee confined to his farm on Nashawtuc Hill: ". . . if he should presume to go beyond the bounds and should be killed, his blood be upon his own head." For Lee, the first year of the war was a miserable time. Despite the committee of correspondence's urging that he be left unmolested, a group of thirty or forty soldiers fired on his house; a musket ball barely missed the frightened doctor. He also had to endure humiliating snubs. One day William Emerson passed by the farm. "I spoke to him civilly," Lee confided to his diary, "he kept along and made no answer." And there were poignant moments. From his hilltop he watched forlornly as the funeral train of Mrs. Stephen Hosmer made its way into town. With "a heavy heart and a Shaking hand" he apologized to his old friend Hosmer for not being among the mourners:

> You will excuse me for not shewing the Last respect to my Dear friend, by following her Corps to ye Grave when I tell you I could not Conveniently [go] but I advised my wife to Go. She Said She Should be Glad to Go and would Go with all her heart if her Husband might Go with her but to Go herself and Leave him at home Confined . . . she could not think of it but Chose rather to tarry at home and Suffer with her Husband. . . . Which made me think of the Famouse Roman Lady Portia who Could not be content untill She Suffered with her Husband.

To occupy his time, Lee compiled a family genealogy, rehashed his quarrel with William Emerson, and enjoyed the company of his boarders from Harvard College. (His son Samuel was a member of the class of 1776.) Finally, after numerous petitions from Lee, the committee of correspondence set him free in June of 1776.[14]

With so few obstacles in their path, the people of Concord moved easily toward separation from Great Britain. In the summer of 1775, on the advice of the Continental Congress, the Massachusetts General Court reconvened in Watertown and resumed its powers of government under the province charter of 1691, which Parliament had revoked. Declaring the governor's chair vacant, the legislature instructed the council to exercise executive authority. Formally, the province remained loyal to the king. So, too, did the Concord selectmen, who were prudently issuing warrants for town meetings "In his Majesties Name" as late as March 1776. But these tokens of allegiance to the royal sovereign made little sense when the citizens were killing his troops. Even before the Continental Congress acted, people like Captain Joseph Butler were making their own symbolic break with Britain by naming their sons for George Washington. As the first anniversary of the battle in Concord approached, William Emerson preached from the text, "Be ye not again entangled in ye Yoke of Bondage." And on April 19, 1776, Emerson commemorated the day with an effusive oration on independence:

> Woe to thee, O Brittain! O Brittain how art thou fallen! For thy King is a Child and thy Princes through unbounded avarice and inhuman pride have robbed thee of thy brightest Glory. . . . Thy Colonies are irrevocably lost and thou art become weak as other nations. . . . America and all her Sons justly disdain thy Power and nobly scorn that iron Yoke, that chafed her fair Neck. . . . [Britain will] sway her iron Sceptre over this new World no more. . . .

One listener, a Harvard minister with whom the volatile Emerson had feuded, was unimpressed. Rev. Caleb Gannett called the lecture "a flat, insipid thing . . . performed in a miserable manner." But no matter; Emerson expressed his people's convictions.[15]

In mid-July, acting on an order from the Massachusetts Council, Emerson read the Declaration of Independence from his pulpit, and Ephraim Wood inscribed it for a "permanent memorial" in the town book, to be read by future generations as they paged through minutes of town meetings about roads and schools and pigs. Soon the town was holding its meetings "In the Name of the Government and People of the Massachusetts Bay."[16]

★ ★ ★

Even as the colonies were boldly embarking on new careers as self-governing states, the practical problems of sustaining and winning the fight for independence were mounting. No end to the war lay in sight. The day the American Congress in Philadelphia was endorsing independence, thousands of British troops were landing unopposed on Staten Island for their successful occupation of New York City. They would soon be pursuing George Washington's Continentals across New Jersey. From the Canadian north the enemy was picking off one fort after another on its march toward Ticonderoga. On the seaboard British forces would be based in Newport, Rhode Island by the end of the year, in position to threaten the Massachusetts coast. The military situation improved in 1777 with the American victory at Saratoga, which led to the formal French alliance and eliminated the "Canadian dagger" at New England's back. Thereafter, the news was nearly all bad. In the desperate winter of 1777–78, Washington's soldiers at Valley Forge shivered and starved—and deserted. In the succeeding years, as the war shifted to the South, the king's troops kept the rebels on the run. Still, the conflict remained a costly stalemate. The Redcoats could seize territory but not hold it. The Americans would be defeated, only to rise again. The war ground on relentlessly.[17]

The darkening military outlook was accompanied by an increasingly desperate financial situation. At the start of the contest in 1775, the Continental Congress faced a dilemma: it had taken charge of the sixteen-thousand-man army outside Boston, but it had no cash to pay the troops and no power to raise any through taxes. The only solution was to turn to the printing press and issue paper money of its own. Congress took the plunge—again and again and again. Meanwhile, every state government was doing the same. And that was not all. Other forms of currency were added to the flood: the interest-bearing bonds that both Congress and states gave in exchange for private loans; the "I.O.U.'s" that Army commissary officers forced on reluctant farmers for supplies; and the counterfeit bills that British agents spread in order to disrupt the American war effort. Until late 1776 this infusion of money, combined with the Army demand for provisions, pumped new life into the state economies and brought good prices and prosperity to town and country alike. But no one bets on a likely loser without demanding higher and higher odds. As American military fortunes deteriorated, paper money inevitably sank in value, and prices and wages soared. Beef cost $.04 a pound in 1777; three years later, it stood at $1.69 and was still rising. Paper money had become simply that—a piece of paper and "not worth a Continental." In 1780, Congress conceded the obvious: through a drastic devaluation of the dollar, it effectively repudiated its money in which no one believed. Even that didn't work. The new bills it issued sank in value almost as soon as they came off the press.[18]

People in Concord drowned in paper along with everyone else. Runaway inflation disordered the finances of the town and claimed its classic victims: the poor, wage laborers, and all who lived on fixed incomes. Common soldiers suffered especially in their country's service. But even ministers of the gospel struggled to stay afloat. Rev. Ezra Ripley, who spent his senior year in Concord as a member of Harvard's class of 1776, returned two years later as William Emerson's successor. Before accepting the call to the ministry, Ripley shrewdly negotiated a contract that would protect him against the ravages of inflation. His annual salary of £100 was pegged to specific commodity prices and so would rise and fall with changes in the cost of grain and meat. But the arrangement failed to work. Despite the good will of his parishioners, they could not collect the ministerial tax fast enough to catch up with the ever-increasing prices. By October 1779, Ripley's salary had already dropped in real value to some £85; when he received it the following May, it was worth but £41. To get by, he had to take in students and do his own manual labor; even so, he weathered the financial crisis only with a long line of credit at deacon John White's store. Concord eventually made good Ripley's loss, but years later he was still lamenting his "loss in ministerial studies and acquirements."[19]

The skyrocketing prices of food and fuel benefited those farmers who could raise large surpluses for market and satisfy many of their own consumer needs. Self-sufficiency, of course, was never fully possible except at the rudest standard of living. But the war stimulated household industries and thereby saved money that had previously been drained away to the country stores and from there to Boston and beyond the sea. Before the Revolution many families had grown accustomed to buying the latest in imported English and European finery. Now that trade with Britain was proscribed, homespun clothing became the patriotic fashion of the day and women at the loom heroines of the Revolution. On Concord farms, flocks of sheep were once again expanding after several decades of neglect. To be sure, many substitutes for English goods could not be made at home. But skilled country artisans rushed in to fill the void, and they, too, thrived on soaring prices in a captive market. For both farmers and artisans, inflation carried an added advantage. It was easy to pay off old debts by stuffing a creditor's pockets full of paper—that is, if you could catch him.[20]

Yet, for most people in Concord, these were not prosperous times. Many lesser yeomen lacked room to expand; at best, they could drive a few head of cattle a year to market. And even substantial commercial farmers like the Barretts were limited in their ability to reap the harvest of inflated prices.[21] Throughout the war years farm labor was scarce. In this preindustrial society, war, like other human activities, conformed to the changing seasons. Armies normally campaigned during the warmer months, then retired to winter quarters. Men were thus called away to the fields of battle at the very time they were urgently needed in the fields at home. Military quotas remained heavy in Concord through 1778 and were often unpredictable. A sudden alarm could disrupt the farming schedule at its most vulnerable moments: in 1776 men were drafted for White Plains in the middle of the corn harvest. But the manpower shortage did not end after the war moved south. The removal of the British threat to the New England interior released a new wave of migration to the west. At least a fifth of the Concord Minutemen left home between the Battle of Saratoga and the final declaration of peace. Once again farms were exporting their youth to the frontier.[22]

It was not just human labor that was drained away from the land. Stocks of draft animals were depleted, too, as farmers sold off large numbers of horses and oxen to pull teams in the Army or to be slaughtered for meat. Farms consequently continued to deteriorate: with fewer field hands and work animals available, men plowed more shallowly, manured more thinly, and cultivated more carelessly than they had done even before the war. Crop returns fell to new lows, at the same time as the area under tillage contracted. More and more land was put into permanent pasture, which required less labor and helped accommodate the expanding flocks of sheep. But grazing lands were wearing out fast. Men estimated in 1780 that it now took over five acres of pasture to keep a single cow for a year.[23]

Army demands and farming problems led to real scarcities of food, further fueling the raging inflation. The hardships bore with particular severity on women, who often had to run farms while their men were away at war. Mrs. Phebe Bliss, widow of the minister, was left with only a daughter at home when her sons went their separate ways. To make ends meet she took in boarders—among them, British prisoners of war. Ensign Thomas Hughes came to her house in May 1778 and found the mistress to be "the genteelest woman I have met with in New England." But after several months Hughes was compelled to seek new lodgings. Mrs. Bliss could no longer keep up the boardinghouse, "as she had no man to hunt after provisions which are scarce." But even after the men came home, farm families had to make sacrifices. From October 1780 to July 1781, Concord was called upon to furnish 42,779 pounds of beef for the Army—the equivalent of at least a hundred head of mature cattle. Such animals were not quickly replaced. By 1784 Concord's holdings of oxen, cows, and swine were well below prewar levels. To feed the Army, the townspeople had to take food from their own mouths. "They ate poorer food," said the son of one Revolutionary veteran, and "wore less comfortable clothing."[24]

The uncertainties of war and economic change disrupted basic patterns of social life. This was no time to start a family or plan for the future. Those who did marry waited several years longer than was customary. Because of the declining number of marriages and also because military call-ups took husbands from the home, Concord's birth rate plummeted during the period of most active conflict. After 1780, when the fighting was over in the North, a baby boom began. If nothing else, the temporary slowdown in births slightly eased the pain of wartime shortages: there were thankfully fewer mouths to feed.[25]

The citizens of Concord did not quietly resign themselves to economic distress. Neither did people elsewhere. They looked for villains—for the speculators and price gougers they held responsible for inflation, for the engrossers and hoarders they blamed for shortages. In January 1777 the General Court passed "An Act to Prevent Monopoly and Oppression," fixing ceiling prices and wages on a wide range of goods and services and instructing town selectmen and committees of correspondence to enforce them. The Concord committee tried briefly to carry out the assignment. That spring the members heard at least five complaints against both merchants and farmers but found only one guilty of violating the law—a newcomer named Walker, who was ordered to repay what he had overcharged his customers. In other economic regulations, the committee moved to implement an embargo against exporting scarce goods from the state: in May, it stopped yeoman John Parlin from shipping five barrels of rum to a merchant in Cambridge and launched an investigation into the matter. The inquiry came to nought, as did the entire state anti-inflation program. Without strict, uniform enforcement of prices and wages throughout New England, it remained in the individual's self-interest always to make just one forbidden sale or to charge a little more than going rates as a hedge against future inflation. Country farmers and city merchants were soon bitterly blaming each other for the collapse of controls. In September 1777 the legislature repealed its nine-month-old anti-monopoly law. By then, the act was dead in Concord.[26]

That was not the end of the political struggle against inflation. In mid-1779, prices began one last upward spiral before Continentals lost all value and passed into oblivion. Alarmed by the rising cost of farm produce, Boston merchants launched a drive for voluntary price controls. Through their town meeting, they issued a call for a state convention to meet at Concord in July. Though they had not been consulted, Concordians quickly agreed to play host, pledging themselves to "Heartly Join in any Lawful measures" to stem that great "Evil," depreciation. The convention duly gathered with 171 delegates from all over the state. Concord was represented by its committee of correspondence. On a steamy summer's day the participants produced a detailed list of prices, promised to treat violators as "Enemies to this Country," and denounced the "Tories and Monopolizers" who were supposedly spreading those "Wicked and Malevolent Reports" of jealousy between country and city. Nevertheless, the delegates apparently doubted their handiwork would last. Before dissolving, the convention set the following October as the date for another conclave in Concord.[27]

After the mid-summer convention had ended, Concord set out in earnest to implement its resolves. In a unanimous vote the townsmen accepted a schedule of prices that were actually below those allowed by the convention. A special committee was named to "Inspect and keep a Watchfull eye over the People" and, if need be, to punish transgressors. But neither Concord nor any other town could hold back the inflationary tide. When the second price-control convention assembled on October 6, rural and urban delegates deliberated in an atmosphere of mutual distrust. Joseph Lee, now free to go where he pleased, observed their sessions. The delegates "Dispute, are Divided, Tangle & Labour," he wrote; they even met on the Lord's Day! After a week, a new agreement on prices came forth. ". . . If they have done good," Lee remarked, "it is well." But for all their labors, the convention's issue was stillborn. Although Concordians once again unanimously adopted the convention's resolves, three weeks later they had second thoughts. Merchants in Boston and elsewhere were already violating the official prices. There would be no move to form yet another agreement.[28]

Despite all these troubles, the people of Concord preferred paper money to no money at all, and when the state acted to take it out of circulation, they were quick to protest. Massachusetts kept her own financial house in fairly good order during the war, but through policies that frequently angered farming communities. As early as October 1777 the General Court called in the state's paper bills for redemption in bonds paying 6 per cent interest. Shortly thereafter, Concord was among a small minority of rural communities to petition against the move. It was far better, advised the town, to control inflation through regular taxes than to add the unnecessary burden of interest charges to the enormous cost of the war. The excesses of paper money could be cured. But the legislature eventually opted for radical surgery. In 1781, as the state was being buried under worthless Continentals, the General Court put Massachusetts on a hard-money basis and began imposing heavy taxes in gold and silver to pay off the state debt. These extreme deflationary policies were promoted by representatives of the richest, most commercialized communities of the commonwealth. As a center of trade and credit in central Middlesex, Concord placed solidly in this elite group of towns. But for the most part her delegation to the legislature rejected the alliance of privilege and sided with rural interests. Joseph Hosmer represented the town in the General Court for most of the war years, and he consistently voted for paper money and low taxes, as his constituents instructed. Captain David Brown spent a year in the House and did the same. Only James Barrett, Jr., who held his father's old seat in 1782, took a conservative, pro-creditor line.[29]

Cheap money, no matter how inflationary, answered a real economic need. Gold and silver coin had never been plentiful in the rural communities of Massachusetts, but after the legislature imposed its deflationary program, specie became a rare item in most homes. With so little money in circulation, farm prices plunged swiftly downward into a deep depression. Many yeomen were unable to pay their taxes and were in danger of losing their land. As money disappeared, Concord had trouble filling the post of constable. In 1780, even before paper was completely driven out of circulation, it became necessary to ask an unlikely pair of substantial citizens—Stephen Barrett and Jonas Lee, the doctor's son—to take the job after two small farmers flatly refused to make tax collector's rounds. Economic problems would only get worse in the next few years, and many were driven to the financial desperation that culminated in 1786 in Shays's Rebellion, an uprising by hard-pressed farmers to close the courts and prevent settlement of debts. Concord would ultimately be no supporter of the radicals' cause, but her spokesmen sympathized with popular discontent. At the war's end, Joseph Hosmer was back in the House, with his town solidly in the small farmers' camp.[30]

Amid the trials of inflation and deflation, good harvests and bad, military victories and defeats, war weariness gradually set in. For four years the calls for troops, for men to serve a few days, a few months, or even a few years, did not let up. 1775: 74 men; 1776: 212; 1777: 174; 1778: 139. Thereafter, the fighting was over for most

Concordians, but there were still soldiers to be raised and bounties to be paid at a time when costs were spiraling and willing bodies were getting scarce. In all, Concord was obliged to provide some 875 men for terms of two months or more—a figure more than two and a half times the eligible male population on the eve of the war. And that number does not cover the whole, does not include the men who fought on April 19 or answered later alarms, nor does it count the local citizens who enlisted on their own in units belonging to other towns. The demand for manpower was immense, but the town never failed to meet its quota, one way or another. In the process, though, the very character and social meaning of the war were transformed: from a voluntary struggle to a battle by conscripts and eventually from a community-wide effort to a poor man's fight.[31]

Throughout Massachusetts, voluntary enlistments were sufficient to fight the war until the summer of 1776. Then, with British troops attacking from Canada and Washington's forces beleaguered in New York, the General Court resorted to drafts and stuck to them over the next few years. Militiamen were conscripted for short terms of three or six months in theaters far from home—New York, New Jersey, the "Canady" country—as well as in nearby Rhode Island and in Massachusetts itself. There was often no time for ordinary recruitment campaigns, but even if there had been, men were no longer readily forthcoming in Concord or anywhere else. Enthusiasm could occasionally be whipped up in a sudden emergency. In September 1777, John Buttrick enlisted forty-six volunteers to stop Burgoyne only weeks after sixteen inhabitants had been drafted for the Saratoga campaign. But with few exceptions Concord did only what was required. Between July 1776 and April 1778 three quarters of the town's quotas were filled by pulling names from a hat.[32]

Not everybody who was drafted was expected to go. One could be excused by hiring a substitute or paying a substantial fine. Just to make sure no one forgot his obligation, the law occasionally threatened delinquents with a jail term. Although drafts favored the rich, who could buy their way out, they forced all social groups in Concord to contribute to waging the war. Indeed, conscription was carried out with ruthless efficiency. Half the men under fifty received a draft notice at least once; occasionally even the old, the crippled, and the women were not spared. To furnish men for the New Jersey front in November 1776 three aging deacons—Thomas Barrett, Ephraim Brown, and Simon Hunt—were called up along with sixty-nine-year-old widow Prescott. They presumably found substitutes.[33]

Conscription had long precedent in colonial Massachusetts, and it conformed to the same principles of participation that governed peacetime community life: citizens were expected to serve the public whenever they were asked and in ways appropriate to their social and economic rank. In fact, Concord developed its own supplement to the draft, applying tried and tested techniques of getting men to work. From 1777 to 1780 the selectmen, together with the militia officers, periodically estimated the town's war-related expenses and apportioned the sum to the taxpayers according to their wealth. Every individual was credited for the time he had spent at war or the money he had spent on substitutes or fines. He had to pay the difference; if the balance was in his favor, the surplus rested "in bank," to be deducted from the next year's tax. This was the same system Concord routinely used for building highways and bridges. In effect, the town recognized what many generations of soldiers have known: digging a ditch is still digging a ditch, whether at war or peace. Few men seek out the job.[34]

Through these devices, the military burden was widely shared in the years when demands for manpower were at their height. It was chiefly the old who escaped service and naturally the young who did the bulk of the fighting. Available records do not always distinguish between those who were drafted and those who actually turned out, making calculations uncertain, but in all likelihood most eligible men under forty put in their time. Stephen Barrett started as a Minuteman corporal in 1775 and ended in 1780 with a second lieutenant's commission in the militia. Along the way he helped guard the Massachusetts coast at Nantasket in 1776, where he joined in capturing three hundred Scottish Highlanders as they sailed into Boston, unaware of its evacuation by the forces of the king. The next year he was drafted to answer an alarm in Rhode Island. With a wife and three young children at home by 1780 and a farm to run, Barrett served some six to nine months in all, a little better than average.

Most of his contemporaries were credited with under half a year's time. They could count on the younger single men like Purchase Brown to take their places. Still landless and rootless, Brown spent a few weeks in camp at Charlestown in 1775–76, just missing the Battle of Bunker Hill, and made the Ticonderoga expedition later that summer. He had been home only half a year before being drafted with Stephen Barrett for the Rhode Island alarm. 1778 was one long furlough—unless records are missing—before doing guard duty in Boston for several months in 1779 and going off yet again to Rhode Island the next year. A few months here, a few months there, and never far from home for long: by 1780, Brown had accumulated a full year of service.[35]

Those who declined to serve had a variety of reasons. After his hard riding on April 19, Reuben Brown never entered the Army. He was drafted several times but always hired a substitute. Then in his late twenties, the saddler spent two years as a military supplier, employed in outfitting several companies. This could be profitable as well as patriotic work. Brown complained that he ended up losing $1,000 when a government contractor pocketed his pay. Perhaps. But Brown's wartime activities hardly slowed his rise in the world. In 1770 he had been warned out of Concord; by the 1780s he was the most active creditor in town.[36]

Other men were simply not cut out for war. John White, the pious storekeeper, nearly turned pacifist after experiencing combat. Born in Acton, he had moved to Concord about 1773. At age twenty-six he enlisted in the Minutemen to defend his country's cause and participated in the Concord Fight. He then tended his store for a while before marching with Buttrick's volunteers to Saratoga, where he "had the pleasure to see the whole of Burgoyne's [defeated] army parade their arms, and march out of their lines; a wonderful sight indeed; it was the Lord's doing, and it was marvellous in our eyes." That was the end of White's military career. He had found war, even with the Lord's backing, to be "a great calamity" and the life of a soldier uncongenial to his nature. In later years he often said that "though he discharged his musket many times . . . he hoped he had killed none of the enemy."[37]

There are no signs in Concord of opposition to the draft, nothing like the votes the town of Braintree took to indemnify its militia officers if they were fined for failing to carry out state levies. But after April 1778 the townspeople quietly ignored the General Court's orders to conscript and hired men to fill their quotas. This decision accentuated a change in the social character of recruits that had already begun the previous year. In January 1777, Concord was ordered to raise forty-four men for three-year tours in the Continental Army. These were the first long-term enlistments of the war. They had been persistently urged by General Washington as the only rational basis for running an army. Without them, the Continental forces had to be rebuilt every year almost from scratch, for by the time soldiers were well trained and battle tested, enlistments ran out and the Army melted away. Washington's proposal raised fundamental objections in New England. John Adams argued that respectable Yankee farmers and mechanics would not abandon their lands and shops for more than a year; the Army would be filled up with only "the meanest, idlest, most intemperate and worthless" sort. His moral judgments aside, Adams proved right. From 1777 on, the Continental ranks were manned largely by the lower social orders.[38]

Ezekiel Brown signed up right away. Upon his release from debtor's prison in March of 1776 he promptly turned his jailhouse medical studies to advantage and gained a commission as a surgeon's mate for six months in the regular Army. He returned to Concord by the following January, just in time for the birth of his third child. He was eking out a living as a schoolmaster when the call came for long-term Continental enlistments. With a growing family of five and only a few acres of land, no chance of resuming his store, and no visible prospects (except on the unprotected Maine frontier), Brown seized what opportunities there were in the Army. Despite his low circumstances, he was able to convert his medical training into a commission as a regimental surgeon—equivalent to a captain's rank—and enlisted not just for three years but "for the duration." By pledging to fight to the last, Brown qualified for a $20 bounty plus a promise of three hundred acres in the future. Over the next few years he participated in the brutal war on the western New York frontier, being stationed at Cherry Valley in November 1778 when

British-led Mohawks descended on the small settlement there and massacred more than fifty men, women, and children after resistance had stopped, and then going on Sullivan's retaliatory expedition to burn the Iroquois country to the ground. After four years Brown gained an early discharge and came home in January 1781, surely no better off than when he had left—his wages probably months in arrears and Congressional promises of land and seven years' half-pay still distant dreams for the future.[39]

Most of the ordinary Continental privates from Concord were, like Brown, men with little or nothing to lose by going off to war for three years or more. Surprisingly, after 1778, the soldiers hired by the town even for short terms in the militia were of the same sort. No longer did young men of substance volunteer for common duty in any sizable numbers. The war was now being fought principally by landless younger sons, by the permanent poor, and by blacks. In Massachusetts, as in every other state, necessity ultimately overcame prejudice. Concord, with a handful of slaves, hired blacks to fill up some 8 per cent of its Continental quotas. For slaves, army service was tantamount to a grant of freedom, although not always formally so. Squire Cuming's man Brister enlisted in 1779 as Brister Freeman, probably with Cuming's consent. Philip, James Barrett's slave, was still part of his master's estate when the colonel died in April 1779. Philip was then nineteen. By his master's will, he would have to labor for Peter Barrett, the colonel's youngest son, until he was thirty and then would obtain his freedom. But within a year Private Philip Barrett was stationed at West Point, obeying the orders of other superiors. At least one Concord slave definitely seized his freedom by enlisting. In January 1781 an eighteen-year-old black laborer named Richard Hobby was hired for a three-year term in the Continental Army while his owner, a newcomer to town, was out of state. On returning, Jonathan Hobby sued the Army for the release of his slave, on the grounds that his property had been taken without his consent. A military court of inquiry sympathized with this argument; belief in the sanctity of property was, after all, what had originally triggered the Americans' rebellion. But the Revolution against British-imposed "slavery" had dramatically undermined the notion that any man was, by right, a slave. Caught in the contradiction between property rights and natural rights, the judges temporized. They conceded master Hobby's claim, insisted on slave Hobby's military obligation, and passed the case up to higher authorities. The final disposition is unknown, but Richard Hobby, like many other blacks, probably gained his freedom by default.[40]

The longer the war went on, the poorer and more degraded in status were the recruits Concord supplied. The "three-year-men" who enlisted in the Continental forces in 1777 were generally poor, but at least they were Concord's poor. Three years later, only eight of the sixteen men who signed up for three-year terms had any known connection to the town. The poor who made up the peacetime army of transients were now welcome in Concord, as long as they stayed only long enough to have a drink, take their bounty, and go off to fight. For Concord, the Revolution was becoming a war by proxy. And it was not surprising that those who went, both the residents and the strangers, were often left by their countrymen to go barefoot, wrap themselves in thin blankets, and hunger in the cold. The soldiers represented the bottom of society, resembling in many ways the rank-and-file "lobsters" whom they fought. For both sides, life taught the same bitter lesson learned by Rudyard Kipling's trooper "Tommy" and others:

> O it's Tommy this, an' Tommy that, an' "Tommy go away";
> But it's "Thank you, Mister Atkins," when the band begins
> to play—
>
> . . .
>
> For it's Tommy this, an' Tommy that, an' "Chuck him out,
> the brute!"
> But it's "Saviour of 'is country" when the guns begin to
> shoot. . . .[41]

As the sounds of musket-fire grew distant and the character of the Army changed, many Concordians began resisting demands for more troops. At the outset the town had generously opened its treasury to pay for the war. But inflation and the sharp competition for volunteers had bid up enlistment bounties to dizzying heights. One could purchase a month and a half of a man's time with a single pound in 1775; by 1780 that sum commanded little more than a day.

Time after time the town instructed its officials to hire men at a given rate, only to have them return with the unhappy report that no one could be gotten for the price. Patience was fast running out. In 1780 the town met its quota "after many Debates." The next year, as they reeled under the impact of the sudden deflation, the citizens divided sharply over yet another requisition for three-year men. "After many Disputes," the measure finally carried by a narrow margin of nine.[42]

The war, combined with depression, left an exhausted people in its wake. Concord learned the news of the Treaty of Paris in a sour mood. Pausing only briefly to congratulate representative Hosmer on the restoration of peace "to this (of Late) Bleeding Land," the voters instructed him to investigate reports that Massachusetts had paid more than her fair share of the war. The conflict had begun in Concord with brave pledges to "go to the utmost with Lives and Fortunes" to defend the country's freedom. It was now ending in resentful muttering that the town had done too much.[43]

★ ★ ★

The strains of war and economic change inevitably took their toll of Concord's ideals. In 1774 the townspeople had set out only to protect their traditional community life against outside attack. But in the course of resistance to Britain their goal had become a revival of the community itself. Concordians sought not revolution but regeneration: an end to the bickering and fighting that had marked their prewar affairs and a rebirth of the virtue and public-mindedness that infused the ideal New England town. Elected magistrates would lead and people would follow; together they would preserve their rights, defend their interests, and secure the public good. Concord would be a community united in liberty's cause. But the price of liberty was too high to sustain this vision of a community transformed. The war imposed too many sacrifices, too unevenly spread. Once the immediate danger faded, old conflicts re-emerged, while the new issues of money and taxes produced divisions of their own. And as they struggled with the intractable problems of the war, the townspeople experienced their own mild "democratic" revolution.

They insisted, indeed required, that their leaders carry out the public will. At the end of the war a town majority had taken charge that was jealous of its powers, suspicious of outsiders, and intent on preserving its interests—even at the expense of conflict.

Concord embarked on revolution with a broad consensus of political ideals. During the decade of debate over British policies, the townspeople had steadily moved toward a republican philosophy, although without saying so explicitly and in language usually borrowed from others. Only a few months after the Declaration of Independence they spoke out boldly on their own and briefly became innovators and teachers of republican doctrine to the rest of the state. In the fall of 1776, Massachusetts was still operating under a makeshift government, the modified royal charter of 1691. But now that the province had rejected the sovereignty of the king, there was no longer any reason to retain the forms of his rule. It was time to break with the past. The General Court asked its constituent towns for permission to write a new constitution. Most of the ninety communities whose replies survive consented, but the voters of Concord said no, for reasons unique to themselves. They were the first anywhere in America to suggest that a constitutional convention was necessary to establish government of the people.[44]

When the legislature's request arrived in Concord, the townspeople were at first slow to react. The town meeting to consider the question had to be adjourned for a week because "the Inhabitants did not So Generaly attend as Could be wished." To drum up attendance, on the Sabbath beforehand everyone at church was reminded to come. The session drew a "very full" house. It should have; local officials had encouraged all adult males to turn out, whether or not they were qualified by property to vote. Town leaders thus signaled that they had something new in mind. When the meeting convened, it apparently followed a prearranged plan. The town voted unanimously that "the Present House of Representatives is not a proper Body to form a Constitution for this State," then appointed a committee to explain why. The members were those inevitable choices, Colonel Barrett and Ephraim Wood, plus James Barrett, Jr.—now Squire Barrett since his selection as a justice of the peace—Colonel John Buttrick, and Nathan Bond, son of the town treasurer and a recent Harvard graduate. For the sake of appearance, the committeemen probably withdrew briefly to look over once more the report they had already written and then returned to win a unanimous endorsement from the town. Concord easily reached the decision that was to be a landmark in American constitutional government.[45]

Far more than the battle of April 19 or even the Declaration of Independence, the formation of new governments, based upon the consent of the governed, ushered in the American Revolution. Americans everywhere recognized that they enjoyed an exhilarating opportunity given to few people before in history: the chance to wipe the slate clean, consult the most enlightened ideas of their age, and choose deliberately and rationally the forms of government under which they and their children would live. But how to translate the popular will into working practice? In 1776 the people in most states were content to let their existing legislatures prepare new constitutions. To the citizens of Concord this method nullified the whole point of establishing a written frame of government. A constitution, they said in much the same terms as they had used ever since the Stamp Act crisis, was "a System of Principals established to Secure the Subject in the Possession of, and Injoyment of their Rights and Privileges against any incroachment of the governing Part." If the legislature—"the governing Part"—had the power to write a constitution, then it had the power to alter it. But in that case, a constitution offered "no Security" at all.[46]

As an alternative to the legislature, Concord recommended the constitutional convention. The town proposed that delegates be chosen immediately from each town by a special electorate: all free male citizens, twenty-one years old and above. This suggestion represented a new departure in a society where only men of property had the right to vote. The inhabitants of Concord perceived that forming a constitution marked an extraordinary event in the life of a society; indeed, it could be said to create that society, since a constitution established the social compact by which men agreed to carry on their common life. All men were consequently entitled to share in making the fundamental law of their state—and also in ratifying it. Concord advised that the final product of the convention be published "for the Inspection and Remarks of the Inhabitants of this State." The town's proposal thus comprehended the major steps—from convening a constitutional convention to personal ratification by the citizens—that have come to constitute the American way of making and changing governments.[47]

Although Concord was soon joined by other towns in calling for a convention, the General Court ignored the advice and postponed any action until the following spring. Then it asked voters to authorize their ordinary House representatives to write a constitution. Concord duly named a committee to consider the request, perhaps with instructions to bury it; the committee was never heard from again. The legislature went ahead and wrote a constitution, which it presented to the towns for ratification in March of 1778. It was an ill-begotten document, too undemocratic for many western farmers, too weak for eastern moderates, racist in content—it limited the franchise to whites—and lacking a bill of rights. But to Concord the Constitution of 1778 was tainted forever by its illegitimate origins. The townsmen did not even bother to consider its provisions. After postponing action for several months, less than half of the eligible adult males turned out to reiterate—once again unanimously—their simple orthodoxy: no convention, no constitution. For this and many other reasons, the state's voters rejected the legislature's work. It was back to the beginning. The following February the House canvassed public opinion again: did the voters want a new constitution? And did they want it written by a special convention? A unanimous Concord seized the chance. "We . . . are now, and ever was of the mind to have a Constitution formed when the People at Large Shall have the Sole management of that affair and that as Soon as may be Consistant with peace and good order." This time the town's position prevailed. The constitutional convention opened in Boston on September 1, 1779, with delegates John Cuming and Ephraim Wood in attendance.[48]

For all its insistence that the people write the constitution, Concord remained ideologically a community of moderate Whigs. The constitution that was presented to the towns and ratified in 1780 established a far less democratic government than many rural reformers wished. It provided for a strong governor, equipped with a limited veto, to balance the power of the legislature. There was a Senate to represent the interests of property and to check the potential excesses of the people's House. And property qualifications restricted the right to vote and the right to hold elective state office. None of this upset more than a handful of voters in Concord. The town's ratification meeting again brought out about half of the eligible males, and they proceeded to accept the bulk of the constitution unanimously. They carefully scrutinized each section line by line. Three inhabitants dissented from the articles establishing the Senate and eight from the provision authorizing the Senate to try all impeachments brought by the House. The town did propose one minor check on the governor's power: his salary should be stated annually. But what concerned the voters at least as much as democracy was religion. The town wanted the governor to be not simply a Christian but a Protestant. Two "contrary-minded" citizens opposed the guarantee of freedom of worship in the Bill of Rights, while another eight, demanding greater separation between church and state, rejected the legislature's authority to require taxpayers to support a minister and attend on his words. The people of Concord thus did not carry their suspicion of "the governing Part" very far. Once a constitution was properly formed, they were ready, at least in political theory, to trust orthodox, elected magistrates to assure the common good.[49]

In the first years of the war, the townspeople continued to entrust their affairs to most of the same men of property and experience who had guided them before. The one major change was the retirement of sixty-five-year-old Colonel Barrett, who stepped down as General Court representative in 1776 and devoted the last years of his public career to recruiting men for the Continental Army. Lieutenant Joseph Hosmer, converting his Revolutionary popularity into solid political assets, took Barrett's place in the legislature and lodged himself almost as securely as his predecessor in the affections of his neighbors. In just about every other office, one saw the same faces in 1776 as before. Squire Cuming resumed his accustomed place as moderator of town meetings after his brief fall from public favor at the height of the Revolutionary crisis. Ephraim Wood remained the workhorse of the community—selectman and town clerk, member of the committee of correspondence, and now also justice of the peace. The selectmen hadn't changed; in fact, over the entire decade of the war, only five men would hold the office. And although some of the older men who were called to the committee of correspondence in the moment of crisis had dropped off, the body was more than ever a company of current and former magistrates. Of all the major figures who led the town through the explosive months of 1774–75 only Samuel Whitney disappeared, perhaps because of his panicky behavior in the wake of the Battle of Bunker Hill. Dr. Joseph Lee recorded in his diary for June 22 that "this day Mr. Saml Whitney a very zealous Whigg left ye Town in a fright with all his family." He soon returned to face political oblivion.[50]

War and revolution created potential opportunities for new leadership not only in politics but in the Army. In 1776 the legislature empowered the enlisted men in each company of militia to elect their field officers—the captains and subalterns—who would then be commissioned in due course by the Council. This new power was at first used quite conservatively in Concord. The militia officers chosen by the rank and file that year differed but little from the men who had previously been appointed by royal governors. All of the top militia posts went to the town's most distinguished military family, the Barretts, and to their relations. Thomas Barrett, the colonel's nephew; George Minot, his son-in-law; Thomas Hubbard, his brother-in-law, became captains of the three standing militia companies in town. Meanwhile, Nathan Barrett gained election to first major by all of the field officers of his regiment; soon he would succeed to his father's rank of colonel. To some extent Concord's enlisted men may have turned to middle-aged, middle- and upper-class officers because they had to. The Council actively intervened when the rank and file's choices went too far astray from its own notion of proper standards. Captain Thomas Barrett gained his commission only after the enlisted men's first choice, Silas Man, had been vetoed by the Council. The twenty-nine-year-old Man had been nearly propertyless only two years before the war, and there is no sign that he had gained an estate by the time of his selection. What the Council did not know, however, was that Man apparently had connections with the Barretts. In 1782 he would marry the colonel's niece and shortly be one of the wealthier gentlemen in town.[51]

The unquestioned dominance of town offices by a handful of wealthy, middle-aged gentlemen from a very few families was due in part to Concord's absorption with the exigencies of war. The luxury of the prewar squabbling, the questioning of the town's proven, established leaders could not be indulged in the emergency. The war, in any case, made normal town politics impossible. With so many men away in the Army, attendance at town meeting must have dropped off sharply; and once, when the militia was called out to Dorchester Heights, a session had to be canceled because of war. Old issues were temporarily set aside. The dissidents in the north part of town shelved their campaign for separation. Moreover, it was no longer possible to fight over the location of the grammar school: the town had given it up "on account of the Troblous Times." With Joseph Lee stigmatized as a Tory and William Emerson on leave as an army chaplain, religious conflict, too, had lost its spur.[52]

But Concord did not become a peaceable kingdom simply because the inhabitants were too busy to fight among themselves or even because they could now project their aggressions onto the "bloody-Handed" British foe. The war, as parson Emerson had hoped that March afternoon on the eve of the battle, had indeed stirred among his parishioners a spirit of self-sacrifice, of unity, of willingness to lead and to follow according to the traditional social code. The community's leaders rose honorably and effectively to the early challenges of war. Squire Cuming, it is true, put family above country in giving up the Ticonderoga command, but there were numerous examples of selflessness among the class of men who were expected to do the most—of William Emerson dying in the public service; of Colonel Barrett, in his sixties, riding from town to town to whip up army recruits; of Joseph Hosmer turning down a colonelcy because he thought "he could do the country more good by working at home for the army than by going to war." And work he did. Hosmer, who was elected captain of the town's volunteer Light Infantry Company and later commissioned as a brigade major, put his oratory to use as a muster-master, giving little speeches at country taverns to drum up enlistments, and he filled the post of collector of public stores without taking any pay, "simply, as he said, because it was somebody's duty to do so, and he might as well as another man."[53]

This deeply felt urge for the community to live and act as one reached its fruition just before William Emerson left for Ticonderoga. On July 11, 1776, a day of "Fasting, Humiliation, and Prayer," some sixty men, all full members of the church, representing all ranks of the community and including four of the eight aggrieved brethren still in town, renewed their covenant with one another. Besides avowing their shared belief in the Lord and in the orthodox Congregational way, besides promising to observe the Sabbath strictly and to "govern all in our Houses according to God's Word," they bore "solemn Testimony against ye Sins of ye present Day"—and of the recent past. They pledged themselves to avoid "All Fraud, Injustice and Deceit, especially in matters of an ecclesiastic Nature," to renounce "All Pride, Ostentation & Vanity in Apparel & Behavior," to watch more closely over the morals of their children and servants, and finally to abjure "All that unkind Neglect of friendly Rebuke and brotherly Admonition . . . And [all] that Want of Tenderness for ye good Name and Reputation of our fellow Creatures, especially fellow Xians, by indulging ourselves in slandering, backing and reproaching our Neighbour." An enduring peace appeared to have come to both town and church.[54]

Such harmony couldn't last. The first signs of conflict surfaced in the March 1777 election of the town committee of correspondence. The vote came at the end of the hard winter of 1776–77, a time of acute suffering throughout the country, when prices began to run away and nearly everyone felt the pinch. The Massachusetts Act against Monopoly and Oppression was but a month old, and the unwelcome task of enforcing it had fallen to the committee of correspondence, just as the members' one-year terms were expiring. On the outgoing committee were those magistrates to whom Concord assigned virtually all its important wartime business, men with the character and prestige to judge their neighbors' sins in the marketplace: Squire Barrett, Captain David Brown, Squire Cuming, Captain Jonas Heywood, Captain Joseph Hosmer, Captain George Minot, and, of course, Ephraim Wood. All were substantial farmers and tradesmen, better able to withstand the brunt of inflation than most of their constituents. Perhaps they were only beginning to impose the state's price controls, and perhaps they dragged their feet just a bit. Whatever the reason, enforcing prices was one job their townsmen did not trust them to do. Not one of the old committeemen was returned.

In their places the voters chose a mixed group of yeomen and artisans, none of whom had ever held a major town post before. New member John Buttrick was certainly as wealthy as his ousted neighbor David Brown, and three of his fellow incoming committeemen were also owners of sizable estates. But from the ranks of the "middling men"—the lesser yeomen and mechanics of the community—now came three members of the board: shoemaker Nathan Stow, housewright Josiah Meriam, and farmer Abishai Brown. Most of the newcomers, like the men they replaced, were middle-aged men. In what was apparently an effort to save the livings of their families, they were taking over the job of controlling prices from the squirearchs of the town.[55]

The challenge to Concord's establishment was short-lived. As we have seen, the new committee of correspondence tried bravely to hold back inflation but was overwhelmed; it soon gave up the exercise in futility. At the next year's election, the voters returned to their old ways, putting Barrett, Brown, Cuming, Heywood, and Wood back on the committee for good. Only Josiah Meriam, Colonel Barrett's son-in-law, and Colonel Buttrick, the town's military hero, who fought at the North Bridge, Bunker Hill, and Saratoga and was wounded on Sullivan's retreat in Rhode Island in 1778, retained their seats. Thereafter, the town's leadership was virtually frozen until the end of the war. The townspeople still turned naturally for leadership to their social elite and not to ordinary men. Yet, the voters had made their point. When the town undertook to enforce prices again in 1779, it assigned a number of small tradesmen to help the committee of correspondence do the job.[56]

Although men who wore silk and velvet and rode in chaises continued to dominate town government, their relationship with the lesser yeomen and mechanics who elected them changed dramatically over the course of the war. In the several decades before the Revolution, the townspeople had normally been content to defer to their magistrates' judgments on public affairs. They resorted to instructing their legislative representative only at moments of intense political agitation throughout the province, and even then it took a request from the Boston Committee of Correspondence or the General Court to prompt a binding statement of the town's position. During the final, fevered months of the Revolutionary movement, with mobs on the common and organized resistance to the courts, these traditional attitudes underwent considerable strain, and the voters began to reward and punish officeholders for their conformity to popular views. Once the crisis of the summer of 1774 broke and a united community went to war, the townspeople slid back toward their accustomed ways. But not completely: 1777 witnessed not only the brief rebellion against the town's governing class but also several attempts to revive the use of instructions.

That fall the General Court provided for redemption of the state's paper bills of credit in interest-paying treasury notes. As there was no roll call, representative Hosmer's vote is unknown. But in December, deacon Thomas Barrett and others asked the town to instruct Hosmer to work for repeal of the law. The proposal was turned down. Instead, Concord decided to petition the legislature for change. Between these two courses of action lay a major difference in attitudes toward representation: to petition was to supplicate, to ask a superior, equipped with the full authority of the people, to consider a policy in the name of the general good; to instruct meant to order one's agent to do the bidding of the local constituents who elected him. The voters reaffirmed their disposition to defer the following month when they declined to instruct Hosmer's vote on ratifying the Articles of Confederation and told him to "use his best Judgement." Still, attitudes were changing among some townspeople; now proposals for instructions were coming from within.[57]

By 1782 a revolution of opinion had taken place, as a result of the heavy taxes and hard money policies of the state. The townspeople did not simply oppose the legislature's deflationary program and then drop the subject when their position lost. Instead, out of the experience of political defeat and economic depression, many developed a deep distrust of all those magistrates who gathered in Boston far from their constituents' view and who, thus insulated from popular pressures, proceeded to spend the substance of the country, often to enrich themselves. The highest officials of the people appeared to be imitating the corrupt harpies and minions of the Crown! The voters' suspicions extended to even their own legislative representative. At the spring elections of 1782, the town handed its newly elected delegate, Squire Barrett, a set of rigid marching orders before sending him to court. It told him what bills to promote, what matters to investigate, what sort of men to appoint, all of which amounted to a single message: keep taxes and expenses down. The representative was less a magistrate than a bookkeeper charged with balancing public accounts and a secretary "to minute down the appropriations of Public monies . . . that you may be able to Exhibit an account thereof to your Constituents if Requested." He was allowed no discretion; if any matter arose that "should appear to your Mind Disputable," he was to come back to the town for directions. Squire Barrett could not even console himself with the pay: should the General Court set the representatives' salary at more than six shillings a day, he must return the "overplus" to the town. If he didn't like these conditions, Barrett was advised not to take the job. The town planned to watch him closely:

> We trust Sir you never will Swerve from our Reasonable Expectations from you, Either from Popelor applause or any other base motive whatever—as you will answer for such Conduct to us your Constituents.[58]

There was nothing personal in the town's attitude toward its representative. The voters showed no more respect for Joseph Hosmer's independent judgment the following year. Hosmer had served continuously in the House from 1776 to 1780, before moving up to a Middlesex County seat in the State Senate in 1781. Though Concord gave him its votes, Hosmer did not win re-election to the Senate; nor did he regain his seat in the House at the town election a month later. His omission from the House was probably an intentional rebuff, since the next year the town took pains to assure him that his election as representative was "a Proof of the confidence that we now have *(and ever had)* of your Integrity and abilities to Serve us in that Important trust." Perhaps Hosmer was flying too high. His instructions would certainly bring him down. The town told him, too, how to vote on each of the major issues ahead and pointedly reminded him that on his conduct hinged "the approbation and applause of us your constituants." Hosmer did not forget this message after he returned to the Senate from 1785 to 1793. Late one afternoon he rose to speak on a subject "which was obnoxious" to Governor John Hancock, then presiding over the Senate. "You are too late," ruled the governor. "The meeting will soon adjourn." Hosmer immediately asked for time in the morning. But before he could begin, Hancock abruptly cut him off: "Mr. Hosmer, I command you to sit down." "Did I stand here in my own behalf," he replied, "I could not too soon obey you but I was sent here to speak on a subject which lies near to the hearts of the people of Middlesex County and God willing I shall not set my face toward Concord until I have my say." Hosmer then proceeded to speak to a spellbound audience. When he had finished, he turned to the governor—"I wish your Honor a very good day"—put on his hat, and left the State House. As his footsteps rang out in the silence, one Boston gentleman observed to another spectator "that Mr. Hosmer of Concord fears not the face of mortal clay." Except, perhaps, that of his constituents.[59]

Suspicious of power in Boston, only eighteen miles away, the inhabitants of Concord were no less opposed to strengthening the distant Confederation government in Philadelphia. Back in 1774, as they embarked on the steps that would carry them to war, the townspeople gladly put their confidence in the emergency quasi-government of the colonies; they readily pledged to abandon the Solemn League and Covenant should the Continental Congress recommend other action. And four years later, as noted, they still felt enough attachment to the Continental cause to forgo their doubts about ratifying the Articles of Confederation and let Hosmer use his own best judgment. The new central government established under the Articles was, in fact, quite limited. It lacked the key power to tax and so had to depend upon grants from the states, foreign and domestic loans, and its own increasingly worthless currency to finance the Continental war effort. By the early 1780s these sources were plainly insufficient to meet the need. Congress asked the states for power to impose a 5 per cent duty on the value of nearly all imports. In Massachusetts, opinion was sharply divided on "the impost," as it was called, with the most commercialized communities first opposed and then in favor. But Concordians remained consistently unwilling to let the power over their purses slip into distant hands. In 1782 the voters instructed Squire Barrett to allow an impost for only a limited time; the next year they joined rural towns elsewhere in resisting outright any grant of a Congressional authority to tax. The townspeople were localists, intent on keeping the outside world at bay.[60]

For all their insistence on maintaining government close to home, Concordians were reluctant to extend their principles to a minority of their neighbors. As the immediate British threat receded, the inhabitants were once again confronted with sectional demands for separation, and they responded with no greater sympathy than before. The town did renew the northerners' exemption from the ministerial tax in 1778, provided that they hired their own preacher, but that concession was too little, too late. Those who lived farthest from Concord center were determined to have their own town, and with royal officials gone and the entire country engaged in a fight for self-determination, their prospects for victory in the state legislature looked better than ever. In September 1779, Captain John Green and a dozen of his neighbors joined with inhabitants from Acton, Billerica, and Chelmsford to ask the General Court for township status. The petitioners pled their distance from the meetinghouses of their respective towns and their long struggles to support their own preachers while paying for their communities' established ministers: ". . . Unless we have a mind to bring up our Children in a Heathenish Manner (which we dread) . . . we must be justified in our repeated Efforts to have the Gospel settled among us." The majority of Concord flatly opposed the request. Despite an appeal from the separatists to "put yourselves in [our] Place . . . and then say, Whether you wou'd not act as we have done, and ask for what we have ask'd for, and for all that we have asked for," the townspeople set out to defeat the bid. Concord, the mother country, refused to let her colony go.[61]

The townspeople pulled out all stops in their campaign to block the petition. A majority of residents within the bounds of the proposed town, including some former secessionists, were initially opposed to separation, and those who lived nearest to Concord were adamant. But the town was unwilling to rest its case on these facts. Opponents sought to discredit the secessionists as "a parcel of disaffected People to Ministers" and pointed as well to the eight or nine Baptist families who lived in the non-Concord portions of the proposed town. As if that were not enough, there were charges that the secessionists were too poor to support a church, despite the fact that Concord's separatists were richer, as a group, than their opponents. And in an effort to enhance the appearance of antisecessionist sentiment, Concord dispatched Squire Barrett, Jonas Heywood, and George Minot to appear before the legislature's investigating committee with a petition signed by North Quarter residents who would not be affected by separation. Or so John Green and his associates charged. None of these tactics worked. The legislative committee recommended in favor of the request. By March 1780 most of the opposition in the north had been won over: the original petitioners had promised not only to exempt them from the previous costs of building a meetinghouse but also to allow equal rights to its use. This compromise contrasted sharply with Concord's requirement, only nine months before, that the northerners pay their share of Ezra Ripley's settlement fee, even though they hired their own preacher.[62]

Faced with this political situation, the town majority tried subtler methods, agreeing to separation on conditions it expected the secessionists to reject. At the same time, six inhabitants demanded to be left out of the proposed town. Years before, in the 1750s, they had been included in the old district of Carlisle, an early effort by the northerners at separate existence. When that area ended its short, unhappy career and returned to Concord, the legislature promised not to set the residents off again without their consent. Now Samuel Kibby—the man with the fat daughters—and five other old-timers called in that pledge, but in terms appropriate to new times: "It is our oppinion a right every american ought to enjoy, and for which LIBERTY they have fought and Bled, and are still in Contest for, not to have their Rights taken from them without their Consent, or Receiving an Equavolent therefor."[63]

For a moment these tactics threatened to derail the independence movement. The original petitioners—John Green and company—went back to the legislature to protest all the conditions and requests. By then the General Court must have been weary of the interminable issue. On April 12, 1780, it granted some of Concord's demands, exempted the irreconcilables, and incorporated the district of Carlisle, with all the privileges of a town except the right to a legislative delegate of its own. The northerners would share representation with Acton. By this act Concord lost a tenth of its population and wealth.[64]

With the separation of Carlisle, all of the old issues were gone. Religious divisions did not revive after the death of William Emerson. The townspeople hired his successor, Ripley, by a vote of ninety-four to one, and that one, Ripley recalled fifty years later, had been motivated by the candidate's "Feeble appearance, and the expectation that I should live but a while." The new parson took over the parish, the widow Emerson, and the Old Manse, all with little controversy, and presided over a surprisingly peaceful flock. The few remaining Old Lights who had seceded during Daniel Bliss's ministry gradually trickled back into the church. The Revolution had finally extinguished the few flickering embers of the Great Awakening. Not until the 1820s would the Concord church again be split, and then the rift could not be healed. By that time nearly everyone had forgotten about the old fighting in the ministries of Emerson and Bliss. But not all: Ezra Ripley took over his predecessors' old grudges, too, and in later years, as he went riding through town with young Ralph Waldo Emerson, his step-grandson, he would tell anecdotes about the aggrieved brethren and show "how every one of . . . [them] had come to bad fortune or to a bad end."[65]

Even the wounds produced by Toryism slowly closed. In May 1778 the townspeople formally ended the social ostracism of those few residents who had refused to sign the Continental Association. It was now clear that whatever their doubts about the American rebellion, Joseph Lee and Duncan Ingraham—probable nonsigners—had cast their lot with their neighbors. Still, old resentments had not completely died. At that same meeting the voters could not restrain the urge to drop John Flint and Jonas Lee from the jury lists. The decision was reversed in 1782. With the British defeat at Yorktown, the townspeople could afford to be generous; Loyalism was a lost cause. Duncan Ingraham was already donning Patriot's clothes. In the spring of 1782, his clerk, Nathan Bond, observed that "even the Old Man talks of the Independence of *his* Country"; five months later he was eating "soup and garlic" with the French officers in Boston harbor. By 1788 in a conservative counter-reaction against Shays's Rebellion, the voters would send Ingraham to the General Court. Joseph Lee regained community acceptance, too. In April 1782 he actually got two votes for state senator. Four years later, at age sixty-nine, he finally achieved his long-standing ambition and, together with his devoted wife, Lucy, was admitted into the Concord church.[66]

There was no forgiving Daniel Bliss. He had deserted his fellow townsmen for the enemy. In his exile the land and houses he had left behind had been seized for the benefit of the country. For a while the town committee of correspondence had taken over management of the property and apparently had collected rents from Bliss's old tenants. But in November 1780, Bliss was tried *in absentia* and found guilty of "levying war and conspiring to levy war against the Government and People of this Province, Colony, and State." His real estate, which consisted of a few small but valuable parcels in the town center, was confiscated and sold at auction. Two artisans—a blacksmith and a carpenter—obtained it in what were their first purchases of land in Concord. The mechanic at whom Bliss once sneered, Joseph Hosmer, presided over the transactions as a member of the Middlesex County committee for selling confiscated estates. And two years later it was again Hosmer who voted, at the instructions of his constituents, to block the provision of the Treaty of Paris allowing the return of Tory refugees. That event, declared the townspeople, would be "one of the greatest evils that could fall upon us."[67]

If Bliss had come home, he would have found Concord not much different from the way he had left it. There was, on the surface, a new political world, but only on the surface. True, old issues were gone, and new state and national questions caught up the town—or at least its politically active part. The citizens were now proudly committed to the doctrines of republican government, to the people's right to rule, both in theory and, increasingly, in practice. Nonetheless, the underlying pattern of politics had barely changed. Although the militia leadership had opened a bit by the 1780s, responsibility for local government still belonged principally to the well born and the rich. Nor had the townspeople completely abandoned their old political conceptions. Even as they instructed their representatives, they remained tied to the rhetoric of the past, calling on them to "act with a single eye to the Glory of God, and the good of this People." The surge in popular power at the end of the war would soon recede. It was a fitful, defensive reaction against an unresponsive outside world and not a confident sign that the people's time had finally come. When the depression eased and state policies changed, town magistrates would govern with nearly as much discretion and independence as before.[68]

Socially and economically, too, Concord was worse off than before. At the war's end the town was sunk in economic depression. The land was still running out, and the prewar progress of agricultural improvement had actually been reversed. In the background the pressure of population on land remained a constant force. Many, perhaps most, of the young could find no opportunity at home; their teams and wagons continued to rattle their way down east and to the west. Concord was still more of a place to be from than go to. Indeed, in the constricted economic environment, the townspeople once again sent out the word that paupers were not welcome. In 1785, contrary to a new state law, they instructed the selectmen to resume warning transients out.[69]

Despite themselves, the townspeople could not close their borders to change. The war had exposed many individuals to new places, new values, new ideas. When the young Minuteman Ammi White was stationed in New York in 1776, he experienced greater religious diversity within a month than Concord had offered in his lifetime. He could attend Presbyterian services one week, a Low Dutch

Church the next, and a Baptist meeting soon after (where he heard "a very good Sermon"), and do so with a social freedom and tolerance that Concord never extended to its dissenters. Dr. Joseph Hunt could expand his horizons without having to leave home. In October 1782 he sat down to write a letter to his old friend and fellow townsman Tilly Merrick. The twenty-seven-year-old stepson of Duncan Ingraham was working in Amsterdam as an attaché in the American diplomatic service as well as carrying on his own international trade. For his contemporary Hunt, the very idea of writing to a place as distant as Amsterdam was a revelation:

> So small has been the Compass of my Travils and Acquaintance in the World that I have never had Occasion of conveying any Letter further than from the State of New York to that of Massachusetts and it seems new and strange to me to send this to Europe: but surely the Feelings of Humanity are not to be suppressed however distant the Objects which may excite them. . . .

Of course, having seen the attractions of a metropolis, a country youth might not want to come home. Merrick established himself as a merchant in Charleston, South Carolina, after the war. His friend Nathan Bond tired of Concord after working in Boston. "Of Concord," he wrote Merrick, "I can say nothing new. . . . But in Boston we have alwaise something new." [70]

Still, for all the young people it sent to the frontier or the city, Concord was more enmeshed in the wider world than before. Leaders like Squire Cuming had always been cosmopolitans. In the future, as they struggled with social and economic problems, many of his farmer constituents might be open to similar influences from the outside and more receptive to change.

★ 7 ★
A Bridge to the Future

FEWER than twenty years after the American Revolution, the people of Concord pulled down the venerable North Bridge. They were looking ahead to the future and not toward symbols of the past, and as a result of highway improvements, the old bridge was obsolete. Its planks were removed a few hundred yards down river to a new bridge near John Flint's farm. Only the stone abutments remained to remind passers-by of the stirring scenes that had happened there. Having served its historic purpose, "the rude bridge that arched the flood" was cast away, an early victim of progress.[1]

Concord took on a fresh look in the 1790s, the look of prosperity. As George Washington was assuming the presidency, trade was picking up, and by the time he left office, it was booming. Owing to the outbreak of war in Europe, neutral Americans became merchants to the world—the indispensable middlemen for everything from Jamaican sugar to Mocha coffee to Sumatran pepper—and as Boston and Salem got rich, so did their country cousins. The roads from Concord to the seaboard were filled with oxcarts, creaking under loads of barreled beef and pork, destined for West Indian plantations, and surpluses of wood, rye, and hay to build and feed the expanding port cities. Flourishing as never before, Concord farmers spent freely in the numerous stores and craft shops that dominated the village. Money passed over the counter so fast that deacon John White, a mediocre merchant, had only to buy his stock of goods "with ordinary care, mark them at the desired profits, and the sales would assuredly be made." The handsome profits of trade lured Boston merchant John Thoreau to open a store near White's on the common. A clock industry sprang up on the mill dam; it was brought to town by such newcomers as Asaph Whitcomb, who manufactured watches and also pulled teeth "bunglingly." On the Bay Road, Jonathan Fay, a Westborough native who had spent his senior year in Concord as part of the Harvard class of 1776, replaced Daniel Bliss as the town lawyer. Fay was conveniently located to argue cases in the elegant new county courthouse or to console losing clients in the new stone jail, the two buildings facing on opposite sides of the common.[2]

So active was business in the town center that a description of Concord in 1792 read much like a present-day Chamber of Commerce pamphlet. William Jones, the young Harvard-educated son of blacksmith Samuel Jones, boasted that "there are but few towns in the country where every mechanical branch of business is carried on with greater skill or industry. . . . The people are very industrious, enterprising, hospitable and patriotick." In all, a quarter of the townsmen earned an income from a trade or a profession. But no visitor to Concord could forget that the town's prosperity was based on agriculture. From eleven slaughterhouses and six tanneries came the periodic, heavy stench of offal and hides, which must have made many men eager to chop trees in the woods.[3]

With the coming of good times, the citizens began to create a new town for a new republic. New and straighter roads were but one sign of a growing spirit of improvement: the inhabitants faced up to obstacles they had previously gone out of their way to avoid. Men were beginning to sense that they could make their own world—that just as they had waged a revolution, broken with the past, and formed a new government, so they could start afresh in all their affairs. America would be a "New Order of the Ages." In Concord men set out to realize that dream by reversing the long decline of the town and directing the course of their social and economic evolution.[4]

At long last, farmers were taking up agricultural reforms. Wealthy gentlemen like Thomas Hubbard, Jr., kept in touch with the new Massachusetts Society for Promoting Agriculture and introduced the latest innovations. Frequently reminding his neighbors that "whatever is worth doing is worth doing well," Hubbard was patient whenever his farming experiments failed. "Well," he would say, "it is better to use money so, than to spend it for new rum." The example of Hubbard and other gentlemen-farmers apparently inspired their fellow townsmen. By 1801 most crop yields had risen above prewar levels. Yeomen were putting more labor into the land and rotating crops more carefully. More English clover was planted, which added nitrogen to the soil even as it produced better hay. And although its pastures still looked "indifferent" to one visitor in 1796, Concord was no longer fated to become a dilapidated home for undernourished cows. More than ever, farmers fattened their cattle on upcountry pastures, then drove them back to slaughter in town. Inevitably, more intensive farming brought an end to the easygoing habits of the past. Pigs lost the liberty to run at large, and each taxpayer was allowed to pasture only one cow along the public ways. A town pound stood on the common to pick up strays.[5]

A new social landscape took shape, too, as a result of the drive for improvements. Before the Revolution a man could go to church once a week, attend a few town meetings, and drill with the militia four times a year and he would have exhausted nearly all the organized social outlets in town. But now opportunities were expanding for a richer social life. The townspeople had discovered the secret of the voluntary association. "Two are better than one," announced the founders of the Charitable Library Society in 1795, "and a threefold cord is not easily broken." The Library Society was one application of this principle. To spread knowledge and virtue—without which, it was believed, the republic could not survive—the fifteen wealthy members made available to all of their neighbors, for a small fee, an impressive collection of books that included religious tracts, *Paradise Lost, Washington's Letters, The Wealth of Nations*, and a volume called the *Ladies' Library*. Even the inhabitants of the county jail could borrow books, although they were limited to heavily moralistic fare. Prisoners might also gain inspiration from the town's Corinthian Lodge of Masons, whose members strove to practice harmony, love, and order in all their affairs and thus to set an example for others. On a more mundane level, a Fire Society was organized to put out fires and a Harmonic Society to improve singing in church. These organizations were open to men in all parts of town, but it was principally residents of the village who joined. Outlying farmers could not or would not travel into the center simply to borrow a book or observe the fraternal rituals of Masonry.[6]

The founding of these societies owed much to another new association, the Social Circle. Established "to promote the social affections and disseminate useful communications among its members," the group was a gathering of the town political and social elite. David Brown belonged, as did Jonas Heywood, Joseph Hosmer, and Ephraim Wood. They were joined by such up-and-coming younger men as Reuben Brown, Jonathan Fay, John White, and Dr. Isaac Hurd, another graduate in the Harvard class of 1776. There was a total of twenty-five members, all residents of the town center and nearly all engaged in trade. Every Tuesday evening, from the first of October to the last of March, the men assembled in a member's parlor to enjoy each other's company. The group had originally grown out of the Committee of Safety, which was little more than a club by the end of the war, but it had broken up for a while, in part because of rivalry between merchants Elnathan Jones and Duncan Ingraham over who could throw more extravagant suppers for the members. Re-forming in 1794, the club settled for less lavish entertainment and perhaps more substantial conversation. The participants talked freely about the common subjects of the day—political news, religious ideas, farming reforms—and considered the needs of the town. In the process, the Circle effectively became a general improvement society. Most of the members sponsored the Charitable Library and helped found the Fire Society; Isaac Hurd joined every voluntary association in town. In the future the Social Circle would have a hand in all the important measures to come before the town.[7]

Even as it promoted the public welfare, the Social Circle weakened the old colonial community. Once, nearly everybody had a place in all the activities of the town—at least ideally. But now social leaders were distinguished from the common run of mankind not only by wealth or breeding but by membership in a formal organization. They were developing a distinctive identity as a group and potentially special interests of their own. Indeed, all of the voluntary associations served to set neighbors off from one another, to nurture attachments separate from the whole community. From one viewpoint, Concord had gained a livelier, more diverse social life. From another, the community had lost a certain moral unity.

Shops and stores, taverns, clubs, courts, the post office opened in 1795 at William Parkman's place, the new brick grammar school on the common—all imparted an urban flavor to life in the bustling town center. Indeed, Concord was linked more closely than ever to Boston and the cosmopolitan world it represented. A regular stage began running from Boston through Concord in 1791 along improved highways that shortened the journey. The routes carried not only men and goods but also ideas and institutions. High style came to town around 1790 in newcomer Jonathan Hildreth's sophisticated Federal-style house, with its brick ends, hipped roof, and four chimneys. The Social Circle was probably modeled upon the Boston Wednesday Club, a similar association. And when a town committee recommended rules for schoolmasters in 1799, it could think of "none more suitable than those expressed by the school committee of the town of Boston, in the year 1789." The suspicions that had flared between country and city during the postwar depression were gone. Boston influenced Concord's politics, its trade, and its culture—even its homes: young people now frequently took brides and grooms from the metropolis.[8]

But Concord was not content to be a satellite of the city. It aimed to be Boston's rival. During the postwar depression, Massachusetts farmers, angry at the unresponsive financial policies of the state, had demanded relocation of the capital in the countryside, and the townspeople of Concord had jumped on the bandwagon. What better capital could there be in a country of farmers than strategically located Concord, birthplace of the Revolution? In 1787 a legislative committee recommended Concord as a "suitable place" for the General Court to sit, but the full House turned down the suggestion. The issue did not die with the return of prosperity. In November 1792, as a gesture to the yeomanry, the legislature convened in Concord. It departed after two weeks, perhaps because smallpox had erupted in town. This was to be the last time the General Court sat in Concord, but Boston remained uneasy. Many years later a writer in the Concord *Yeomen's Gazette* recalled that Boston representatives had undercut a proposal in the 1790s to erect a monument to the

Revolution in Concord. "Everything . . . which had the smallest tendency to bring Concord into notice and consequence, was strenuously, not to say artfully opposed. . . ."[9]

If Concord could not be state capital, it bid fair to become the governmental center of Middlesex County. Since the Revolution, the county courts had met chiefly in Concord, and the Supreme Court came to town on circuit once a year. In the 1790s, with wide support in the countryside, the townspeople revived the colonial campaign to capture all the county institutions from Cambridge and Charlestown —with no greater success.[10]

The town's future seemed boundless. A writer in the *Massachusetts Magazine* in 1794 predicted that someday the name of Concord would bear the luster of "imperial Rome," and tourists were already coming to visit the first battle site of the Revolution. "From the plains of Concord," Yale College President Timothy Dwight mused in 1796, "will henceforth be dated a change in human affairs, an alteration in the balance of human power, and a new direction to the course of human improvement. Man, from the events which have occurred here, will in some respects assume a new character, and experience in some respects a new destiny." The people of Concord evidently agreed. They were beginning to translate these hopes into reality.[11]

★ ★ ★

BULKELEY, HUNT, WILLARD, HOSMER, MERIAM, FLINT,
Possessed the land which rendered to their toil
Hay, corn, roots, hemp, flax, apples, wool and wood.
Each of these landlords walked amidst his farm,
Saying, ' 'T is mine, my children's and my name's.'

. . .

Where are these men? Asleep beneath their grounds:
And strangers, fond as they, their furrows plough.
Earth laughs in flowers, to see her boastful boys
Earth-proud, proud of the earth which is not theirs;
Who steer the plough, but cannot steer their feet
Clear of the grave.

—Ralph Waldo Emerson, "Hamatreya"[12]

The changes that came to Concord after 1790 were largely the work of a new generation. Most of the old faces were gone. Colonel Barrett, Colonel Prescott, Squire Cuming, Honest John Beatton: all had passed away. Colonel John Buttrick died in 1791, memorialized as a Cincinnatus at the plow. Dr. Joseph Lee lived on till 1797; he actively managed his farm—still the largest in town—lent out money, and worried about the state of the world until his death at age eighty-one, too soon to see his son Jonas realize the father's political ambitions. Those Revolutionary leaders who remained stepped aside for younger men. Ephraim Wood left the selectmen in 1795 after a quarter century of service; he would spend the rest of his public career as a judge of the Court of Common Pleas, a justice of the peace, and an occasional moderator of town meetings. Joseph Hosmer retired from the State Senate to become high sheriff of Middlesex County. In all, only a third of the men who paid taxes just before the Revolution were still in town by 1795. They were overshadowed by their sons and by the many citizens—nearly a third of the town—who had moved in since the war.[13]

Even the Minutemen—the young men of the Revolution—had sought other fields far from home. By the mid-1790s more than half had departed the town they once fought to defend. Purchase Brown went back on the road to Ticonderoga, testing several places in Vermont before ending up in the town of Swanton on Lake Champlain, having endured the hardships of pioneering along the way. His first wife died in childbirth, he himself was "soarly visited with sickness," and once he nearly lost a leg when a ladle of "Scalding hot potash" fell on his foot. But it was worth the struggle. By 1800 he had acquired what he could not get in Concord: an "excellent" hundred acres of his own.[14]

Purchase Brown was not alone. Despite the commercial boom and the revival of agriculture, there was still not enough land in Concord for all the would-be farmers in town. As a result, families like the Browns continued to send their sons and daughters to the frontier. Purchase's brother Reuben joined him in Vermont, as did one sister for a while. Two sisters went with their husbands to Winchendon, Massachusetts; two brothers settled on their father's wild land in Barrettstown (now Baldwin), Maine, a community promoted by a successful Concord emigrant, the wealthy speculator Charles Barrett of New Ipswich, New Hampshire. The dispersal took its emotional cost. Though the family tried valiantly to keep in touch, visits inevitably became less frequent, and by 1798 sixty-five-year-old Captain David Brown simply hoped to see his sons in Maine "once more before I die." But for the Browns who moved it was a necessary change. They did fairly well—the sons in Barrettstown became selectmen, like their father—while the family's fortunes sank in Concord. Left on the homestead were two spinster daughters, a son who died young, a mentally deranged son, and Joseph, the youngest, who inherited the farm at his father's death in 1802. Joseph took over a good estate, but he fell on hard times and had to mortgage the property; after his death in 1821 the run-down farm was sold to pay his debts. The feeble-minded son, William, lasted in Concord the longest, the charge first of his family and then the town. When he died in 1849, Henry David Thoreau wrote to Ralph Waldo Emerson's daughter Ellen, "William Brown of the poor house is dead—the one who used to ask for a cent—'Give me a cent?' I wonder who will have his cents now!" [15]

Ezekiel Brown also moved to Maine, less in search of opportunity than because he had to. He was forced out by an unhappy repetition of the circumstances that had dragged him down just before the Revolution. On coming home from the war, Brown had energetically set about repairing his fallen estate. The army surgeon was ready to try anything, even a fisherman's life, but his offer to buy up the "shad fishery" for £540 ended in failure when he could not raise the funds. As a doctor, he did better, and he commanded wide respect for his military labors for the country, so much so that he was admitted to the Social Club—the predecessor of the Social Circle—in 1782. Then once again his world caved in. With the signing of the peace treaty, English creditors were legally entitled to recover prewar debts. Brown's old nemesis, Frederick William Geyer, who had taken refuge in London, went to work. He instructed his father-in-law, Duncan Ingraham, to reinstitute the old suit against Brown. The action succeeded; in April 1786 the plaintiffs won a judgment of more than £500. This decision came during the worst of the postwar depression, when hard money was scarce and paper money was nearly worthless. Brown's valuable village property was seized to satisfy the debt, but in the bad times it could not cover the whole. Brown offered to settle in the depreciated public securities he had received for army pay; Geyer insisted on his pound of flesh. The patriot surgeon was remanded to Concord jail at the instance of a Tory creditor who scorned the country's money. The move stirred much resentment in Concord, and the anger aroused by Duncan Ingraham's role in the suit helped to break up the early Social Circle. That was little solace for Brown. He broke out of jail but was quickly captured and later removed to Cambridge, where finally, in June 1789, after an imprisonment of two years and a month, Geyer released his grasp and set Brown free.[16]

There was no reason to return to Concord, where Brown had mainly been defeated and humiliated for all his pains. With his wife and eight children—the oldest son was fifteen—he headed for Clinton (now Benton), Maine, and at age forty-six he made a fresh start on the wild land he had obtained before the war. There, at long last, he thrived as a farmer, doctor, and tavern-keeper. He became a leader of his town, serving almost continuously as a selectman from 1797 to 1818 and also becoming a justice of the peace. By the time he received his bounty land in 1796 for army service, he no longer needed it, and he sold the property for cash.[17]

In his old age Brown's fortunes turned sour again. Around 1814, when he was seventy, he lost the use of his left arm and with it the ability to do any business at all. He turned to his government for help, applying for a military pension six years later. The law under which Brown applied imposed a strict and demeaning means test, but he could not afford pride. He was responsible for supporting his aged wife, Mary, two widowed daughters—one of whom was insane—and a fourteen-year-old grandson, all on an income of no more than $50 a year. He was once more deeply in debt, with his old house and one-hundred-acre farm held in mortgage. Brown got the pension. But in his declining years, he enjoyed little ease. His mind returned to the bitter scenes of the past. In 1822, two years before his death, the one-time member of the Social Circle wrote to Concord to ask if the society still existed and "if there be such a man living as Frederick Willam Geyer . . . son-in-law to Duncan Ingraham . . . who was the first founder of mischief in Concord." [18]

For the Minutemen and their leaders who remained in Concord, life generally went on in traditional ways. Joseph Hosmer attended meetings of the Social Circle and the Library Society dressed in a ruffled shirt and breeches and with his light hair, which never grayed, brushed back and curling on his neck. Hosmer and his contemporaries were poised between the old and the new. They were ready to improve their farming or to sponsor libraries, but in the interest of maintaining the world they had fought to preserve. Social values changed more slowly than the means to carry them out. Squire Barrett, Jonas Heywood, and Ephraim Wood were still seating the meetinghouse in 1792, assigning people to places according to their stations in life. The selectmen were still regulating individual morality, as the notorious tippler Oliver Wheeler discovered when tavern-keepers were barred from accepting his trade. And if the new school regulations emphasized reason over "threatenings and promises" in the education of children, they still taught the old virtues—belief in God and religious obligations, duty to parents and masters, "ye beauty and excellence of truth, justice, and mutual love," and "ye duty which they owe their country, and ye necessity of strict obedience to the laws." Ultimately, however, the application of reason could not be contained. Over the next generation, young people, born into a new republic and thinking for themselves, would cut their hair, adopt new fashions, and insist on carving out their own places in the world, free from the conventions of the past and the dictates of their parents. They would carry out a social revolution which the men of 1775 had not meant to inspire and which only a handful of Revolutionary veterans would live to see completed.[19]

The Barretts remained Concord's premier political family down to the Age of Jackson. They retained their influence, in large part, through well-calculated marriages; as much as ever, family ties furnished the bonds of political alliance and the means of access to office. Squire Barrett's daughter Patty married Joseph Hosmer's son Cyrus, and when Squire Barrett died in 1799, his widow wed Ephraim Wood. With his brother's death, it was Stephen Barrett's turn to carry the family's banner in town politics. Lieutenant Barrett, as he was known, entered the board of selectmen in 1802, serving for six straight terms before making way for his nephew, Major James Barrett, and going on to his father's and brother's seat in the General Court. By then he was a man of substance: a tanner and farmer, with eighty acres in Concord, another fifty nearby, and a half share in some four hundred acres in the town of Holden, in Worcester County, where he pastured large herds of cattle. He was indeed living much the same life his father had lived—just as he had always expected. And he, in turn, planned to pass on to his children the same advantages he had inherited. He raised his two eldest sons to be tanners like himself, married his three daughters off well—one to a son of Ephraim Wood—and settled all but one of his six children near him. On the surface, the passage from one generation to the next was unbroken.[20]

But Stephen Barrett could not repeat the past. He could not continue the family political dynasty in his own right nor assure his sons' fortunes in the world. And even the Barretts now had to cope with rebellious sons. Although economic opportunities were increasing, young people, especially farmboys, were still dependent on their fathers for their start in life. But the fathers, who as youths had been in a hurry to grow up, were in no hurry to make way for the next generation. Indeed, having won their birthright only after a struggle, the middle-aged men of the 1790s clung more tightly to their property than even their own fathers had. And as a result of the Revolution, with its stress on natural rights, eldest sons had lost their privileges and now gained no better treatment than their brothers.[21]

For Stephen Barrett, getting land proved easy, but it did not for his sons. Neither Stephen, Jr., nor Emerson, nor Cyrus Barrett ever received from their father a gift of land "in Consideration of Love and good will toward my sons." Lieutenant Barrett apparently intended to take his time before distributing his estate. But events intervened.

In the summer of 1799, Sally Barrett, the unmarried daughter of the lieutenant's first cousin Samuel, became pregnant, and the father turned out to be Stephen, Jr., age twenty-three. The news probably occasioned no great shock among the parents—premarital sex remained epidemic—but it hastened the young man's coming of age. Within less than a year after the marriage, Lieutenant Barrett provided his son with $1,400 to buy a farm and tannery in the western town of Shirley. The baby, born on April 19 at the opening of a new century, had secured its parents' independence.[22]

Gradually, over the first decades of the nineteenth century, the contest between the generations abated. Young men began to leave home sooner. They might spend winters clerking in a store, serving a short apprenticeship in a mill or shop, attending an academy, or lumbering in Maine before returning in the spring to work on the family farm. Although their fathers normally helped them out, the sons would take responsibility for their economic lives, choose their own occupations, and settle when and where they pleased. And if they ultimately established themselves on the paternal estate, they would pay their own way. This is what Emerson Barrett, the lieutenant's second son, eventually did. For years he worked as a tanner, probably in partnership with his father, saving his earnings and investing in land until he was ready to wed. Then in 1810, at age thirty-two, he married, moved into a house next door to his father, and five months later bought the house, fifteen acres, and the family tannery for $1,200 from the sixty-year-old lieutenant. The father had gained a retirement fund and the son his independence, free and clear. The tensions between the generations were resolved in a free and rational economic exchange.[23]

As it turned out, none of the lieutenant's sons did very well economically, however they came of age. Cyrus, the only child of Stephen Barrett's second marriage, died young and single before getting any land of his own. Stephen, Jr., abandoned economic striving altogether and joined a Shaker community. And for all his patient labors, Emerson could not hold onto what he had earned. Within two years of his father's death in 1824, his property was reduced to the house he and his family occupied. He never amassed much more. The standard of the Barretts passed to other branches of the family.[24]

Major Joseph Hosmer probably bridged the gap between the colonial world and the new republic as well as any of the Revolutionary leaders in town. He was, in many ways, a born activist, as the dramatic events of his career attest: he had quietly subverted Jonathan Barnes, had agitated against the Barretts, had challenged Daniel Bliss, fought the British, and defied the haughty Hancock. And in later years he was still occasionally refusing to resign himself to the word of authority. A friend once lay ill from typhoid fever, and the doctors had given him up for dead. Hosmer went to the sickbed, inserted a penknife between his friend's teeth, and poured in a few drops of brandy. Then he paused to consult his watch. Every few minutes he continued the remedy until the patient showed signs of improvement. The man got well and lived another twenty years. Hosmer was a natural candidate for the Library Society and the Social Circle: doing good, he had learned from boyhood, brought eternal rewards, no matter what parson Daniel Bliss might say.

Yet, life taught Hosmer a sense of limits—two of his children died in infancy, and he outlived a third—and a stronger respect for authority and hierarchy than many in the rising generation would show. In politics he became a "federalist of the old school" and a lifelong admirer of Alexander Hamilton—"the first man in America," he thought. In his role as high sheriff, Hosmer would improve where he could but accept what he must. Often, after his deputies had seized a man's goods for debt, he would ride after them the next day and give "a sorrowing and distressed" wife $5, $10, or $20—whatever he could spare. "It is a hard law," he would say, "but the laws must be obeyed. Here is a little for your present necessity." And once he was required to oversee the hanging of a poor wretch condemned to die, under an old English law, for stealing a watch. He spent the night before the execution consoling the widow-to-be and suffered intensely throughout the entire ordeal. When he returned home, his son recalled, "a deep gloom fell upon the household and for days after they hardly spoke above a whisper." Still, for all his pains, Hosmer never protested aloud; his good works were done in private. Another generation would campaign against the death penalty.

Within his own family, Hosmer could take pride in his four children. His two daughters married comfortably fixed farmers; his older son farmed successfully on the family domain; and the younger son, Rufus, attended Harvard, became a lawyer, and, settling in neighboring Stow, rose to prominence in the Middlesex bar and eventually won election to the Governor's Council. The major, once the leader of "all the young men in town," never lost touch with the next generation. He could often be seen, smoking his pipe, at the center of an admiring circle of young people, and on court days the young lawyers would gather about his chair to hear his predictions on the pending cases. "I never knew him make a wrong guess," recalled one. Hosmer also had a vast store of anecdotes about the Revolutionary war, which he constantly replenished. Whenever an old soldier wandered into town, the owner of the Middlesex Hotel would make him welcome at the bar and send for Hosmer to hear his stories—although sometimes the innkeeper's daughter protested, "Father, don't send for Major Hosmer; if you do, they will never go away." The major was the last of Concord's Revolutionary leaders to go, a vigorous and eloquent figure to his end at age eighty-five in 1821. "Patty," he told his daughter-in-law in what were supposedly his last words, "surely goodness and mercy have followed us all the days of our lives, and we will dwell in the house of our God forever." [25]

Lucy Hosmer had died three years before the major, but long before then she had apparently faded into the background of her husband's career. When Joseph received guests at the homestead in 1798, his favorite daughter-in-law, and not his wife, was on his arm: Patty Hosmer, the daughter of Squire Barrett, occupies the anecdotes in Hosmer's later life. Lucy is remembered only as an old woman grumbling about "those dark Concord woods" and reliving for her granddaughter her brief moment of rebellion—the one time she had dared to claim her freedom in a male-dominated society—before she took her subordinate place as the wife of the major and mother of his children.[26]

Like mother, like daughter. Lavinia—born "Lovina"—Hosmer was five months' pregnant on her wedding day in 1782, and her sister Lucinda may have continued the tradition in the next decade. Perhaps the young women were defying their father. Or better, perhaps the mother had prepared her daughters to assert their will in the one major life decision they could control—as a contemporary poem suggests:

Some maidens say, if through the nation,
Bundling should quite go out of fashion,
Courtship would lose its sweets; and they
Could have no fun till wedding day.

. . .

Some mothers too, will plead their cause,
And give their daughters great applause,
And tell them 'tis no sin nor shame,
For we, your mothers did the same.

In any case, after the marriages were made, the daughters, too, were caught up in bearing and rearing children—a dozen to Lavinia, eight to Lucinda. The Revolution initially made little difference in the lives and social position of New England women. Not until the early decades of the nineteenth century did courtship and marriage change, as young people came to exercise greater control over their own destiny. Women now chose their own mates, subject to their parents' veto, and not the other way around. They took their chances in the marriage market, where "fallen" women lost their value and where middle-class men, bent on establishing careers, were in no hurry to wed. Hence, chastity came back into fashion, and courtship lost its "sweets." Within marriage, too, prudence and reason held sway. Yankee couples no longer passively accepted the arbitrary decree that some families were fated to have a dozen children and others none at all. By 1820 they were consciously practicing birth control, limiting their families to a desired goal of four or five children. They thereby resolved the dilemma of too many children and not enough land for all. In the process—indeed, perhaps as a deliberate result—married women were liberated from wearying, foreshortened lives of one pregnancy after another. Self-repression became the means to the new freedom.[27]

For the blacks of Concord, the Revolution brought the most formal change but the least in substance. A series of court decisions, ruling that under the Massachusetts Constitution all men were "free and equal," gave the *coup de grace* to slavery. By 1790 there were no slaves in Concord or anywhere else in Massachusetts. That year the census taker did count twenty-nine blacks in town, almost double the number just before the war. Many were longtime residents or their wives and children; the black population was as strongly rooted in Concord as the white and perhaps even more so. Philip Barrett never came back from the war, but Brister Freeman and Caesar Minot did, and so, surprisingly, did Casey Whitney. Cato Ingraham and Cato Lee were still working for their former masters.[28]

Concord's freedmen now enjoyed the liberty to move about when and where they pleased, and a few even became accepted in white society. Thomas Dugan, a runaway slave from Virginia, came to Concord around 1791; after seven years of working as a farm laborer, he owned a house and two acres of land. Dugan, a mulatto, was an expert grafter of apple trees and supposedly harvested rye with the first cradle used in Massachusetts. His wife, Jenny, "a full-blooded Guinea Negro," made clothes. They were respectable folk, as was the family of Caesar Robbins, a former slave of Simon Hunt, on whom white ladies occasionally came calling for tea. But the success of these few only emphasizes the limits of possibility for most of Concord's blacks. A small plot of land, a good house, decent clothes, and a full stomach: this was the best blacks could do in the new republic, and it was not much better than John Jack had done in a land of slavery.[29]

Other blacks were worse off. They lived and worked at the edges of white society, on back lanes to the Great Meadows and Fields and in the vicinity of Walden Pond, an area reserved for town outcasts long before Henry David Thoreau took up residence in the woods. Of course, those freedmen who stayed with their former owners were well housed and well fed and were assured support for the rest of their lives. Dr. Joseph Lee directed his heirs to provide for "my faithful Servant" Cato, even after his laboring days were done—though on the condition that Cato remain "as diligent in business, and faithful to the family as he hath hitherto been." But when a black declared his independence, he lost his security in the white world. Cato gained Duncan Ingraham's permission to marry, only after agreeing to give up his claims on the former master. The wealthy Ingraham shortly thereafter moved to Medford, where his third wife lived. Cato continued in Concord and fell in need. Soon the former slave was paying a visit to Medford. When Ingraham reminded him of the agreement, Cato replied heatedly, "I don't want to hear any more about that; I tell you I am out of everything." The black was understandably desperate, for most likely Concord recognized no obligation for his support.[30]

Freedom could mean not only cold and hunger but also exposure to the malice of whites, with no hope of redress. Brister Freeman once passed by Peter Wheeler's village slaughterhouse minutes after a ferocious bull had been, with enormous effort, finally driven inside. As Wheeler and his men were wondering how they would ever kill the beast, they spied the hapless Freeman. Wheeler, "giving his men the wink," cheerfully asked after the Negro's health and told him "if he would go into the slaughter-house and get an axe, he should have a little job to do." The unsuspecting Brister opened the door and walked into a fight for his life. Meanwhile, Wheeler, son of the quick-thinking miller Timothy, and his laborers watched through the knotholes and cheered their victim on with roars of laughter. When the battle was over, a victorious Freeman emerged, his face "literally white with terror," and fled the scene without waiting for congratulations. As the frequent butt of such humor, it is no surprise that Freeman gained a reputation as "a very passionate man and often got into quarrels with the boys who loved to insult and plague him."[31]

The possibility of random abuse and violence must have hung over the lives of most blacks in Concord, keeping them always on their guard. But in their everyday comings and goings, they were more likely to encounter the sullen indifference of a world they inhabited only on sufferance. For years John Jack's tombstone, with Daniel Bliss's antislavery inscription, lay broken and overgrown with weeds next to the grave—a symbol of the town's unconcern for its blacks. It was not until the beginning of the abolitionist movement that a campaign was launched to procure a facsimile and restore the stone to its proper place. Ironically, the man who initiated that effort was Rufus Hosmer, the son of Bliss's old antagonist. The Tory lawyer's elegant lines were destined to become "the most famous epitaph in America," frequently copied by nineteenth-century visitors to town and printed in newspapers throughout the world. But that was small comfort for Concord's blacks. Though the white inhabitants were adopting all sorts of reforms and changing their most intimate habits within the family, they moved far more slowly to improve their treatment of their black townsmen. Racism remained the last stand of tradition and unreason.[32]

★ ★ ★

On September 2, 1824, the Marquis de Lafayette passed through Concord on his way from Boston to New York. The aging French warhorse of the American struggle for independence was just beginning a triumphal progress through the United States to receive the tributes of a grateful republic and to stand in, as it were, for his old friend George Washington at the fiftieth anniversary of the Revolution. Concord welcomed this opportunity to pay its respects to the past. A town committee arranged a reception in an open tent on the common, in front of the meetinghouse. But not everyone was invited within. Only town officials, the welcoming committee, a few old soldiers, and the women who served the cake and punch at the festivities were allowed into the presence of "the nation's guest." The rest of the townspeople had to catch a glimpse of the general from a distance, from outside the ropes that cordoned off the tent and were guarded by soldiers.

In their eagerness to get close, many inhabitants pressed against the barriers, the soldiers pushed them back, and as the crowd grew dense, tempers rose. Some people began to complain out loud that although "they were not as well dressed nor as educated in society . . . as those within . . . their fathers had served the country, some had fought with Lafayette at the battles of the Revolution, and they were as grateful for his services." Luckily, there was no riot. Lafayette departed within an hour or two. But the visit by the French aristocrat left bitterness toward Concord's own "aristocracy" in its wake.[33]

Lafayette had come to a very different community from the one the Redcoats entered on April 19, 1775. Then the townspeople accepted the existence of rank and privilege as part of the natural order of things. Now they no longer went quietly to their assigned places in life, whether at patriotic celebrations or on Sabbaths at the meetinghouse. Between the two attitudes lay a social and intellectual revolution that had transformed the town.

In 1775, Concord was a community in decline. The economy was stagnant, the land was worn out, the town was losing its young. Yet, men barely sought to reverse the course of decay. They were accustomed to resign themselves to circumstances. Their lives were determined by many forces—the weather, the changing seasons, the whims of death, the twists and turns of an international market—over which they had no influence and to which they adapted as best they could. In matters close to home, which they could control, they largely deferred to the wisdom of the past. The townsmen dressed old and thought old, choosing their magistrates from proven families and proven classes and turning naturally in a crisis to men of great years and experience. Even in their rebellions they looked backward. Young people were in a hurry to be like their mothers and fathers. Feuding leaders blamed each other for violating ancestral ideals. And the greatest rebellion of all was proudly undertaken in the name of tradition. They owed it to their forefathers, William Emerson had told them, to defy the assault on New England's sacred heritage.

Fifty years later the colonial world had nearly vanished, along with powdered wigs and silver-buckled shoes. Concord was swept up in the new—economically, socially, intellectually. The townspeople bent their energies to improving and mastering all their affairs, to subjecting life itself to rational control. The economy was growing, decade by decade, farming was improving, and opportunities in trade were wider than ever, although it was true that young people continued to go West and, increasingly, to the city and factory. Politically, the dominance of the old families and of the wealthy elite that sat inside the tent during Lafayette's visit would soon come under attack. Newspapers, Bible societies, temperance societies, lyceums, and libraries all promoted reform. Thanks to its location "almost in the suburbs of the city," as the town newspaper put it, Concord was exposed to the intellectual fads of the day—to exhibitions of ventriloquism and parades of lions and dromedaries and elephants. And if Americans still looked to England for ideas and models, within a decade the grandson of Concord's Revolutionary parson would sit in the Old Manse, look out over the battle site, and compose a declaration of intellectual independence. "Build therefore your own world," Ralph Waldo Emerson told his countrymen. "As fast as you conform your life to that pure idea in your own mind, that will unfold its great proportions. A correspondent revolution in things will attend the influx of the spirit."[34]

What explained the transformation? The men of 1775 had not gone to war to promote change but to stop it. Most would have preferred to ignore events in distant London—to pay loyalty to their king while going about their own squabbling business. But the outside world would not leave them alone. Boston kept sounding the tocsin, the British threat kept pressing closer and closer to home. Always in the background there was the town's downward slide, heightening the inhabitants' fears of the future and undermining their old, cherished ways—even a father's hold over his sons. Finally, they were forced to act if they wished to retain their traditional life. Indeed, they did. They rose in fury against the assault on their autonomy, and at the peak of the Revolutionary movement they were attached more strongly than ever to the ideals and values of the past. They would restore order to their lives by clinging to custom—and making revolution.

The strains of war deflated their hopes and made all their economic problems worse. At its end, the townspeople were once again on the defensive, struggling with financial depression and suspicious of the outside commercial interests they blamed for causing their plight. Yet, the war and revolution had opened the town to change. Army service exposed numerous individuals to new places and new ideas, while the flood of refugees from the metropolis brought Boston and Cambridge—the urban and intellectual capitals of the province—to Concord's doorstep, if only for a while. And as a result of the wartime mobilization, what the inhabitants did with their money and their lives was increasingly determined by decisions in Boston; they naturally responded by paying closer attention to state government than ever before. Most important of all, the people of Concord and the rest of Massachusetts had decisively and creatively broken with the past and established a new republican government, according to the most enlightened principles of the day.

Indeed, Concord contributed its own innovation to the novel work of making and changing governments—the idea of the constitutional convention. Popular government was a dynamic ideal. By the end of the war, the old deference to magistrates had weakened, and representatives were being treated not as "fathers" but as hired agents of the people. The citizens of Concord were taking control of their political lives.

The impact of that revolution in government was profound. It stood as an inspirational model of men's power to alter their own lives, to think new thoughts, to act on the best ideas of mankind, to liberate themselves from the dead weight of the past. When a new nation was securely established, when an unprecedented prosperity burst upon them, the people of Concord moved with remarkable energy to impress their will and their reason on all those forces that once held them in control. Thomas Jefferson declared that the earth belonged to the living, and after 1790 a new generation claimed possession.

The Revolution did not so much create the upsurge of confidence in human betterment as certify and encourage it and stimulate those dynamic, progressive forces that had been checked and submerged in colonial society.[35] In war, men grow up quickly, and perhaps the young soldiers who did the fighting—those same young men who had been pressing against paternal authority—felt they had earned their own as well as a nation's independence. No doubt the timing of the boom, at the outset of the new national government, did much, too, to heighten the desire for improvement.

But the good times came to an abrupt end in Concord with the events leading to the War of 1812, and by 1820 the clockmakers were long gone, the cabinetmakers had returned to farming, and the townsmen were just beginning to climb their way back to prosperity and uninterrupted economic growth. What remained were a readiness to innovate, to search out opportunity, and a rich network of self-help groups. The age of progress had begun. And it was fitting that the town of Concord, where the Revolution had its start, would eventually produce in Ralph Waldo Emerson nineteenth-century America's greatest philosopher of that progress and in Henry David Thoreau its greatest critic.

Notes

Abbreviations Used in Notes

CA	Concord Archives (nine boxes in Concord Free Public Library)
CAS Papers	Concord Antiquarian Society Papers (in Concord Free Public Library)
CFPL	Concord Free Public Library
CTR	Transcripts of the Ancient Records of Concord (seven volumes in Concord Free Public Library)
Emerson	Amelia Forbes Emerson, ed., *Diaries and Letters of William Emerson 1743–1776* (privately printed, Concord, 1972)
Lee	William Lee, comp., *John Leigh of Agawam . . . and His Descendants* (Albany, N.Y., 1888)
MSA	Massachusetts State Archives (in State House, Boston, Mass.)
Mid. Deeds	Middlesex County Registry of Deeds (in Middlesex County Courthouse, Cambridge, Mass.)
Mid. Prob.	Middlesex County Court of Probate (in Middlesex County Courthouse, Cambridge, Mass.)
NEHGS	New England Historic Genealogical Society (Boston, Mass.)
Old Conc. Docs.	Old documents relating to Concord, Mass. (in Lemuel Shattuck Collection, New England Historic Genealogical Society)

Shattuck	Lemuel Shattuck, *A History of the Town of Concord* . . . (Boston and Concord, 1835)
Shattuck's Hist. Notes	Manuscript Notes of Lemuel Shattuck for his *History of Concord* (in Lemuel Shattuck Collection, New England Historic Genealogical Society)
Social Circle	*The Centennial of the Social Circle in Concord, March 21, 1882* (Cambridge, Mass., 1882)

PROLOGUE

1. "Weather Observations, 1774–1780," anonymous manuscript, Safe File Dr. 1, CFPL; Arthur B. Tourtellot, *Lexington and Concord: The Beginning of the War of the American Revolution* (New York, 1963), p. 30; Shattuck, p. 100; Emerson, p. 59; Kenneth Lockridge, "The Population of Dedham, Massachusetts, 1636–1736," *Economic History Review*, 2nd series, XIX (August 1966): 339–41.

2. Evarts B. Greene and Virginia D. Harrington, *American Population before the Federal Census of 1790* (New York, 1932), pp. 21–25; Ezra Stiles, *Extracts from the Itineraries and Other Miscellanies of Ezra Stiles . . .*, ed. Franklin Bowditch Dexter (New Haven, 1916), pp. 345–46; Charles H. Walcott, *Concord in the Colonial Period . . . 1635–1689* (Boston, 1884), pp. 17–19; Ruth R. Wheeler, *Concord: Climate for Freedom* (Concord, 1967), pp. 34–36.

3. Allen French, *The Day of Concord and Lexington: The Nineteenth of April, 1775* (Boston, 1925), pp. 27–30; Bradford Torrey and Francis H. Allen, eds., *The Journal of Henry D. Thoreau*, 14 vols. bound as 2 (New York, 1962), VI: 79; CTR, 4: 213b–213c, 297b.

4. Ensign Henry De Berniere, "General Gage's Instructions . . . with a Curious Narrative of Occurrences," Massachusetts Historical Society *Collections*, 2nd series, IV (1846): 214–15; Tourtellot, *Lexington and Concord*, p. 92; French, *Day*, pp. 220–21.

5. French, *Day*, pp. 152–54; Wheeler, *Concord*, pp. 14, 88–90; *Boston Gazette, and Country Journal*, Dec. 18, 1775 (notice of court of probate); Elijah Wood, Jr., "Memoir of Ephraim Wood," Social Circle, p. 153. Daniel Taylor kept the tavern from 1765 to March 1775, then either hired or let it out to Amos Wright for several months. Wright was fated to play host to the British troops on April 19. Ever since, the building, still standing in the town center, has been known as the Wright Tavern. George Tolman, *Wright's Tavern* (Concord, 1902), pp. 15–17.

6. Wheeler, *Concord*, pp. 24–25; Tolman, *Wright's Tavern*, pp. 1–13; Ronald Boucher, "The Colonial Militia as a Social Institution: Salem, Massachusetts 1764–1776," *Military Affairs*, XXXVII (December 1973): 125; CTR, 4: 412a–412b.

7. For Concord's position in the provincial road network before the Revolution, see the Bickerstaff and the Ames almanacs for 1774 at the American Antiquarian Society, Worcester, Mass.; for the town's role as a trading center, see Chapter 4, n. 47; for military expeditions, Shattuck, pp. 66–73, and Alfred Sereno Hudson, notes and manuscript of vol. 2 of his

History of Concord, Box 2, File 18, CFPL; for the General Court in Concord, see *Journals of the House of Representatives of Massachusetts, 1715–1767*, 43 vols. (Boston, 1919–1974), 29: vii, 41: vii.

8. The residential distribution of the population was calculated from a list of persons assessed for the school rate in 1773; see 1773 Folder, Box 2, CA.

9. Evidence of a spring moving season appears in the lists of persons "warned out" of Concord. In these lists, which were presented to the county court every year, the Concord selectmen regularly noted the approximate time of a transient's arrival in town. The following table presents a percentage distribution of 243 persons warned out of Concord by season of the year. It covers the period 1725–69:

Jan–Mar.	*April–June*	*July–Sept.*	*Oct.–Dec.*
16	42	17	24

The data were collected from records of the Court of General Sessions of the Peace, Middlesex County, Office of Clerk of Courts, Superior Court, East Cambridge, Mass. On upcountry cattle drives, Wheeler, *Concord*, pp. 142–43.

10. James A. Henretta, *The Evolution of American Society, 1700–1815: An Interdisciplinary Analysis* (Lexington, Mass., 1973), pp. 31–33; Marc Harris, "A Demographic Study of Concord, Massachusetts, 1750–1850" (senior honors thesis, Brandeis University, 1973), pp. 108–9; Emerson, p. 81.

CHAPTER 1

1. 1764 Folder, Box 2, CA; Michael Zuckerman, *Peaceable Kingdoms: New England Towns in the Eighteenth Century* (New York, 1970), pp. 18–19, 32–45.

2. Susan Kurland, " 'A Political Progress': Processes of Democratization in Concord, Massachusetts, 1750–1850" (senior honors thesis, Brandeis University, 1973), p. 8; Robert E. Brown, *Middle-Class Democracy and the Revolution in Massachusetts, 1691–1780* (New York, 1955), pp. 80–93.

3. Richard D. Brown, *Revolutionary Politics in Massachusetts: The Boston Committee of Correspondence and the Towns, 1772–1774* (Cambridge, Mass., 1970), pp. 9–14; Richard L. Bushman, *From Puritan to Yankee: Character and the Social Order in Connecticut, 1690–1765* (Cambridge, Mass., 1967), pp. 9–13, 267–71.

4. Brown, *Revolutionary Politics*, p. 9; Bushman, *From Puritan to Yankee*, pp. 12–13. To study the relationship between office-holding and wealth, I ranked all resident male taxpayers on Concord's 1770 Province Valuation List from highest to lowest, according to the value of their assessed worth. The tax-paying population was then divided into five equal parts, or

quintiles. The quintile to which a taxpayer belonged served as a measure of his relative economic status. Thus, if there were 100 taxpayers, the twenty with the highest assessments would represent the top quintile (or Top 20%), the next twenty the upper-middle quintile (UM 20%), and so forth, down to the lowest quintile (Bottom 20%). By this measure, the thirteen selectmen in the period 1765–74 were drawn from the upper strata of the town:

	Top 20%	*UM 20%*	*Bottom 60%*
Percentage of selectmen	77	23	0

As a group, the selectmen of 1765–74 were somewhat less wealthy than the men chosen twenty years earlier. Using the Province Rate Lists of 1746, 1757, and 1770 as the source for the decades 1745–54, 1755–64, and 1765–74, respectively, one finds a trend toward somewhat less wealthy magistrates. The following table shows the percentage distribution of the selectmen in quintiles over time:

	Top 20%	*UM 20%*	*Mid 20%*	*Bottom 20%*	*N*
1745–54	81	12	6	0	16
175–64	71	18	12	0	17
1765–74	69	31	0	0	13

For the sources used in these calculations, see "A Copy of the Valuation and State Bill by which the Assessors of the Town of Concord Made the Rate for the Year 1770," MSA, 130: 466–91; 1770 Province Rate List, MSA, 132: 201–5; 1746 and 1757 Province Rate Lists, 1746 and 1757 Folders, Box 1, CA.

5. John Langdon Sibley and Clifford K. Shipton, *Sibley's Harvard Graduates*, 16 vols. (Boston, 1873–1972), XII: 117–19; Shattuck, pp. 388–89. In 1771, Cuming owned 130 acres of improved land in Concord. I have doubled this figure to estimate his total landed estate in town, since woodlands and unimproved lands probably represented 40–50 per cent of a farmer's acreage in the late colonial period. In 1784 woodlands and unimproved land made up 40 per cent of Concord's land area. For the 1771 Province Valuation, see MSA, 132: 199–210; for the 1784 Aggregate Valuation, MSA, 163: 51.

6. Lorenzo Eaton, "Memoir of Jonas Heywood," Social Circle, pp. 112–13.

7. Elijah Wood, Jr., "Memoir of Ephraim Wood," Social Circle, pp. 152–58; Shattuck, pp. 388–89.

8. The median age of selectmen on first election to office between 1745 and 1774 was forty-five.

9. Zuckerman, *Peaceable Kingdoms*, pp. 50, 65–72.

10. Zuckerman, *Peaceable Kingdoms*, p. 85.

11. Shattuck, p. 210; Evarts B. Greene and Virginia D. Harrington, *American Population before the Federal Census of 1790* (New York, 1932), pp. xxiii, 20. Following Greene and Harrington, I used a multiplier of four persons per poll to estimate total population size.

12. The term "outlivers" is taken from Bushman, *From Puritan to Yankee*, p. 54.

13. Bradford Torrey and Francis H. Allen, eds., *The Journal of Henry D. Thoreau*, 14 vols. bound as 2 (New York, 1962), III: 10; CTR, 4: 354a (March 2, 1772), 357a–357b (May 11, 1772); Edward Jarvis, "Traditions and Reminiscences of Concord, Massachusetts, or a Contribution to the Social and Domestic History of the Town, 1779 to 1878," CFPL, p. 130; Shattuck, p. 255.

14. Shattuck, pp. 73–74.

15. See votes on the grammar school issue at annual May meetings, CTR, vols. 4 and 5.

16. The under-representation of the North Quarter of town is evident from the following table, which compares the percentage of taxpayers in each section with the percentage of selectmen's terms held by their respective residents. The selectmen's terms cover the period 1765–74; residential location is identified from the 1770 Valuation List.

	East	*North*	*South*	*N*
1. Percentage taxpayers	28	40	33	281
2. Percentage terms	33	24	43	42

17. CTR, 4: 183a (May 19, 1760), 196c–197a (Nov. 2, 1761), 222b–222c (March 15, 1763).

18. Petition of Solomon Andrews and others, December 19, 1772, 1772 Folder, Box 2, CA.

19. Kenneth A. Lockridge, *A New England Town: The First Hundred Years* (New York, 1970), pp. 93–118.

20. Shattuck, p. 165; Sarah Blank, "Of Prayers and Negatives: Concord, Massachusetts, and the Great Awakening" (graduate seminar paper, Yale University, 1975), pp. 9–13.

21. Edwin Scott Gaustad, *The Great Awakening in New England* (New York, 1957); Sibley and Shipton, *Sibley's Harvard Graduates*, IX: 130; Daniel Bliss, diaries for 1740 and 1761 (entries for July 18, 1740, and July 29, 1761), Houghton Library, Harvard University; Daniel Bliss, *The Gospel Hidden to Them That Are Lost* (Concord, 1818), p. 17.

22. In 1739, thirty-one men and forty-five women belonged to the church, for a sex ratio of sixty-nine. This preponderance of women was not reflected in the entire adult population. In 1765, the date of the first available census, the adult sex ratio was eighty-eight, as a result of heavy male outmigration. Undoubtedly, twenty years earlier, the population was much more evenly

balanced. The average age of the male members was forty-five (n = thirty); 63 per cent were over forty, 30 per cent over fifty, and 17 per cent over sixty. By contrast, in 1746, 48 per cent of all male taxpayers were over forty, 14 per cent over fifty, and 12 per cent over sixty. Finally, the twenty-seven church members who appeared on the 1746 Province Rate List were overwhelmingly in the upper classes:

	Top 20%	*UM 20%*	*Mid 20%*	*Bottom 20%*
Percentage of members	50	36	11	4

See Concord First Church Record Book, 1739–1857, CFPL, pp. 1–3; J. H. Benton, Jr., *Early Census Making in Massachusetts 1643–1765, With a Reproduction of the Lost Census of 1765* (Boston, 1905); 1746 Province Rate List.

23. Shattuck, p. 168; Blank, "Of Prayers and Negatives," pp. 31–32; Sibley and Shipton, *Sibley's Harvard Graduates*, IX: 131–32.

24. Sibley and Shipton, *Sibley's Harvard Graduates*, IX: 132, 135; Shattuck, pp. 169–74.

25. Blank, "Of Prayers and Negatives," pp. 23–25; Shattuck, pp. 174–79; West Church Rate List, April 10, 1747, Old Conc. Docs. The sixty-eight West Church members who appeared on the 1746 Rate List formed nearly a cross-section of the total population of taxpayers:

	Top 20%	*UM 20%*	*Mid 20%*	*LM 20%*	*Bottom 20%*
Percentage of members	22	25	21	21	12

26. Lee, pp. 147–49.

27. Lee, pp. 149–50; CTR, 4: 255b–255c (March 11, 1765), 258a (Apr. 19, 1765), 261a–261b (Sept. 14, 1765); Petition of John Minot and others, August 19, 1765, 1765 Folder, Box 2, CA. Of the ten men who petitioned to "make void" the vote raising Emerson's salary to £100, eight were former members of the West Church and a ninth was the son of a former member. West Church members were identified from West Church Rate List, April 10, 1747, Old Conc. Docs. The turn-out rate for the 1765 meeting that chose Emerson as minister was 89 per cent. It was calculated as follows: there were 381 polls in Concord in 1765 (i.e., males sixteen years and over); this figure was reduced by 20 per cent to estimate the number of men twenty-one years and over, and reduced again by 30 per cent to estimate the total number eligible to vote. The resulting figure was 213; at the 1765 meeting, 190 people voted.

28. Franklin Bowditch Dexter, ed., *Extracts from the Itineraries and Other Miscellanies of Ezra Stiles . . . 1755–1764 with a Selection from His Correspondence* (New Haven, 1916), pp. 245–46; list of subscribers to singing school, November 11, 1773, Old Conc. Docs.; Emerson, pp. 14, 21–25; Sibley and Shipton, *Sibley's Harvard Graduates*, XV: 39.

29. For Lee's farming practices, see his interleaved almanacs: for 1758 and 1759, Concord Antiquarian Society, Concord; for 1769, 1775, 1778–80, 1782, and 1789, Massachusetts Historical Society. Lee purchased four hundred acres in Ashby in 1770 (Lee, p. 143). His money-lending activity is apparent from the debts due his estate in 1797 (Will No. 13934, Mid. Prob.). The average number of terms per selectmen in ten-year periods was: 3.3 in 1745–54; 2.7 in 1755–64; 3.2 in 1765–74. The median number of terms per selectmen for the same intervals was: 2.0, 2.0, and 4.0. In both series, the decade before the Revolution shows a noticeable increase in tenure of office-holders.

30. Zuckerman, *Peaceable Kingdoms*, pp. 60–61; Edward Jarvis, "Autobiography," (1873) Houghton Library, Harvard University, pp. 35–37.

31. Emerson, p. 20; Lee, p. 150; "Matters of Greveince" between Joseph Lee and the Concord church, Old Conc. Docs.

32. "Matters of Greveince," Old Conc. Docs.; complaint against Joseph Lee by deacons Ephraim Brown and Simon Hunt, March 7, 1769, Old Conc. Docs.

33. Complaint against Joseph Lee by deacons Brown and Hunt, Old Conc. Docs.; Shattuck's Hist. Notes.

34. "Remarks on Several Events in Concord since ye ordination of William Emerson," anonymous manuscript *circa* 1771, Old Conc. Docs.

35. Concord First Church Record Book, pp. 115–18 (Feb. 18, May 25, 1767; Aug. 21 and 31, Sept. 6 and 26, 1768).

36. Concord First Church Record Book, pp. 118–19 (Oct. 4, Dec. 6, 1768).

37. Concord First Church Record Book, pp. 120–27 (June 5, July 13, 1769; Jan. 3 and 23, Feb. 12, Apr. 9, Aug. 23, 1770), pp. 523–24 (result of council of April 1769).

38. Interview with Ezra Ripley, February 4, 1829, Shattuck's Hist. Notes.

39. Thaddeus Blood, statement on the Battle of April 19, *Boston Advertiser*, April 20, 1886; Concord First Church Record Book, pp. 315–23. The opponents of Lee were identified from a list of witnesses against him at the April 1769 council (Old Conc. Docs.).

40. Of the ten aggrieved brethren who appeared on the 1770 Valuation List, seven were in the top quintile of wealth-holders and three in the second highest quintile. For the names of the aggrieved, see First Church Record Book, p. 120.

41. Notes dated November 8, 1832, Shattuck's Hist. Notes; CTR, 4: 338b (May 13, 1771).

42. Ebenezer Hartshorn to Captain Stephen Hosmer, December 19, 1767, Old Letters of Concord, Mass., Lemuel Shattuck Collection, NEHGS.

43. "Remarks on Several Events," Old Conc. Docs.

44. *Boston Gazette*, August 17, 1772.

CHAPTER 2

1. Merrill Jensen, *The Founding of a Nation: A History of the American Revolution, 1763–1776* (New York, 1968), pp. 4–6, 42–43; Bernard Bailyn, *The Ideological Origins of the American Revolution* (Cambridge, Mass., 1967), pp. 160–229.

2. Bailyn, *Ideological Origins*, pp. 50–143; Pauline Maier, *From Resistance to Revolution: Colonial Radicals and the Development of American Opposition to Britain, 1765–1776* (New York, 1972), pp. 27–48.

3. Shattuck, p. 183.

4. Stephen E. Patterson, *Political Parties in Revolutionary Massachusetts* (Madison, Wis., 1973), pp. 34–41.

5. Jensen, *Founding of a Nation*, p. 134; CTR, 4: 263b–263c (Oct. 28, 1765); Ruth R. Wheeler, *Concord: Climate for Freedom* (Concord, 1967), p. 98; Shattuck, p. 76.

6. "Instructions of the Town of Braintree, Massachusetts on the Stamp Act," *Documents of American History*, ed. Henry Steele Commager, 2 vols. (New York, 1968), I: 56–57.

7. Bailyn, *Ideological Origins*, pp. 161–63.

8. Bailyn, *Ideological Origins*, pp. 164–69 (quote on p. 169), 175–97.

9. See Richard D. Brown, *Revolutionary Politics in Massachusetts: The Boston Committee of Correspondence and the Towns, 1772–1774* (Cambridge, Mass., 1970), pp. 174–77.

10. *Journals of the House of Representatives of Massachusetts, 1715–1767*, 43 vols. (Boston, 1919–74), 42 (1765–66): 215 (hereafter cited as *Mass. House Journal*); Patterson, *Political Parties*, pp. 258–59; William H. Whitmore, *The Massachusetts Civil List for the Colonial and Provincial Periods, 1630–1774 . . .* (Baltimore, 1969), p. 38; MSA, 99: 444; John Adams to Abigail Adams, June 30, 1774, *Adams Family Correspondence*, ed. Lyman H. Butterfield, 2 vols. (Cambridge, Mass., 1963), I: 116–17.

11. Jensen, *Founding of a Nation*, pp. 108, 134–35, 143–45; *Boston Evening Post*, April 28, 1766.

12. *Boston Evening Post*, April 28, 1766.

13. Robert J. Taylor, *Western Massachusetts in the Revolution* (Providence, R.I., 1954), pp. 54–57.

14. Arthur M. Schlesinger, *The Colonial Merchants and the American Revolution, 1763–1776* (1918; reprint, New York, 1957), pp. 106–10; CTR, 4: 291a–291b (Dec. 28, 1767), 298a (Mar. 7, 1768).

15. *Mass. House Journal*, 43, Pt. II (1767): 324; CTR, 4: 291a–291b (Dec. 28, 1767); petition of John Cuming, Joseph Lee, and Charles Prescott, for Concord, and of agents for Acton, Groton, Westford, Littleton, and Pepperell, Jan. 15, 1768, MSA, 44: 649–50; answer of Justices of the Court of General Sessions of the Peace, May 1768, MSA, 44: 660–63.

16. MSA, 44: 651–52; Robert E. Brown, *Middle-Class Democracy and the*

Revolution in Massachusetts, 1691–1780 (1955; paperback, New York, 1969), pp. 189–90. John M. Murrin observes that county institutions were a bastion of royal influence in Massachusetts. "Review Essay," *History and Theory*, XI (1972): 257–70.

17. Jensen, *Founding of a Nation*, pp. 249–50; Whitmore, *Massachusetts Civil List*, p. 89.

18. Unpublished Massachusetts House Journal, 1768 session, vote of June 30, 1768, on deposit at Massachusetts State Library, Boston; Maier, *From Resistance to Revolution*, p. 170; CTR, 4: 301a–301b (Sept. 22, 1768); Jensen, *Founding of a Nation*, pp. 294–96; William C. Swain, comp., *Swain and Allied Families* (Milwaukee, Wis., 1896), pp. 70–71.

19. Emerson, pp. 53–54.

20. Paul Brooks, *Trial By Fire: Lincoln, Massachusetts, and the War of Independence* (Lincoln, Mass., 1975), pp. 3–4.

CHAPTER 3

1. Richard D. Brown, *Revolutionary Politics in Massachusetts: The Boston Committee of Correspondence and the Towns, 1772–1774* (Cambridge, Mass., 1970), pp. 68–80.

2. Brown, *Revolutionary Politics*, p. 59.

3. Arthur B. Tourtellot, *Lexington and Concord: The Beginning of the War of the American Revolution* (New York, 1963), pp. 64–69; Brown, *Revolutionary Politics*, pp. 38–57.

4. CTR, 4: 362a–362b (Dec. 31, 1772); John Langdon Sibley and Clifford K. Shipton, *Sibley's Harvard Graduates*, 16 vols. (Boston, 1873–1972), XIV: 563–66; West Church Rate List, April 10, 1747, Old Conc. Docs.; 1771 Province Valuation, MSA, 132: 199–210.

5. CTR, 4: 362b–365b (Jan. 11, 1773).

6. Brown, *Revolutionary Politics*, pp. 100–15, 117–18.

7. Merrill Jensen, *The Founding of a Nation: A History of the American Revolution 1763–1776* (New York, 1968), pp. 434–37.

8. Brown, *Revolutionary Politics*, pp. 155–63.

9. Petition of Jonas Heywood and others, December 15, 1773, 1773 Folder, Box 2, CA.

10. CTR, 4: 386b–387a (Jan. 10, 1774), 388a–389a (Jan. 24, 1774).

11. Bernard Bailyn, *Ideological Origins of the American Revolution* (Cambridge, Mass., 1967), pp. 209–29.

12. "The Intolerable Acts," *Documents of American History*, ed. Henry Steele Commager, 2 vols. (New York, 1968), I: 71–76.

13. Brown, *Revolutionary Politics*, pp. 178–91.

14. Brown, *Revolutionary Politics*, p. 190.

15. Brown, *Revolutionary Politics*, pp. 199–209 (quote, p. 202).

16. Concord Solemn League and Covenant, June 27, 1774, Safe Floor, Item 5, CFPL; CTR, 4: 401a–403a (June 20 and 27, 1774).

17. John Richard Alden, *Geneal Gage in America* (1948; reprint ed., New York, 1965), p. 208; account of Ephraim Wood, Jr., 1776 Folder, Box 2, CA.

18. There was virtually no wealth bias in subscriptions to the covenant. The adult males on the 1770 Valuation List were traced to June 1774 on the basis of information from genealogies, the town records, and appearance on the 1773 School Money List. If an individual was absent from the 1773 list, I assumed—unless there was positive evidence to the contrary—that he had moved by 1774; if present in 1773 but absent from the list of subscribers, I assumed he was a nonsigner. The following table shows the percentage of individuals in each 1770 quintile who persisted till 1774 and signed the covenant:

	Top 20%	*UM 20%*	*Mid 20%*	*LM 20%*	*Bottom 20%*	*All*
1. Percentage of signers	82	89	86	80	78	84
2. Number of cases	55	53	52	51	32	243

The underrepresentation of signers in the bottom quintile is undoubtedly owing to my assumption that individuals on the 1773 School Money List were still in town the next year. For the poorest of Concordians—laborers and servants—this was often not the case. Men shifted about from year to year, looking for work. For School Money List, 1773 Folder, Box 2, CA.

19. Only one of nine known county appointees—Deputy Sheriff Joseph Butler—is known to have signed the Solemn League and Covenant. County officials were identified from the following sources: William H. Whitmore, *The Massachusetts Civil List for the Colonial and Provincial Periods, 1630–1774 . . .* (Baltimore, 1969), pp. 89, 138–39, 156; *The British and American Register, with an Almanack for the Year 1774* (Boston, 1774); Eben Putnam, comp., *The Holden Genealogy: Ancestry and Descendants of Richard and Justinian Holden and of Randall Holden*, 2 vols. (Boston, 1923–26), 1: 131. For the quote from John Adams, see *Adams Family Correspondence*, ed. Lyman Butterfield, 2 vols. (Cambridge, Mass., 1963), I: 116–17.

20. Seventy-six men persisted from 1749 to 1774. Of the fifty-one who had remained in the established church, 84 per cent signed the Solemn League and Covenant. In contrast, only six of the fifteen West Church persisters from 1749, or 40 per cent, subscribed. The figure is a bit higher for the West Church group when one traces the twenty members in 1747 who remained in town. In this case, eleven, or 55 per cent, took the pledge. Economic status was probably not the key to the differential responses of West Church persisters to the boycott of British goods, as the following comparison of the economic rankings of the men in 1770 shows:

	Top 20%	*Mid 40%*	*Bottom 40%*	*N*
Percentage of West nonsigners	37.5	25.0	37.5	8
Percentage of West signers	20.0	60.0	20.0	10

Calculated from: West Church Rate List, 1747; 1749 Provincial Valuation, 1749 Folder, Box 1, CA; 1770 Valuation List. On New Light-Old Light responses to revolution, see Alan Heimert, *Religion and the American Mind: From the Great Awakening to the Revolution* (Cambridge, Mass., 1966), pp. 239–92.

21. Jensen, *Founding of a Nation*, pp. 535–37, 550–62; Stephen E. Patterson, *Political Parties in Revolutionary Massachusetts* (Madison, Wis., 1973), pp. 95–105.

22. Proceedings of Middlesex County Convention, August 30 and 31, 1774, in *The Journals of Each Provincial Congress of Massachusetts In 1774 and 1775, and of the Committee of Safety* . . . (Boston, 1838), pp. 609–14.

23. *Boston Gazette*, September 19, 1774; Records of the Court of General Sessions of the Peace, September 1771 to September 1790, Office of the Clerk of Courts, Superior Court, East Cambridge, Mass., p. 134.

24. Brown, *Revolutionary Politics*, pp. 233–34; *Boston Gazette*, September 12, 1774; Shattuck, p. 89.

25. Shattuck, p. 89.

26. The following account of Lee's encounter with the mob is drawn from: Elijah Wood, Jr., "Memoir of Ephraim Wood," Social Circle, pp. 154–55; Jensen, *Founding of a Nation*, pp. 535–36; Shattuck, pp. 88–90.

27. Josiah Bartlett, "Memoir of Duncan Ingraham," Social Circle, p. 128; CTR, 4: 406a–407b (Sept. 26, 1774).

28. CTR, 4: 407b (Sept. 26, 1774). For the Real Whig concept of "well-ordered resistance" to tyranny, see Pauline Maier, *From Resistance to Revolution: Colonial Radicals and the Development of American Opposition to Britain, 1765–1776* (New York, 1972), pp. 27–48, 272–87.

29. Patterson, *Political Parties*, pp. 109–15; *Journals of Each Provincial Congress*, p. 16; Shattuck, p. 92; CTR, 4: 409a–409b (Nov. 21, 1774).

30. H. James Henderson, *Party Politics in the Continental Congress* (New York, 1974), pp. 32–45: " 'The Association,' Oct. 20, 1774," *Documents of American History*, ed. Commager, I: 84–87.

31. CTR, 4: 409a–409b (Nov. 21, 1774), 416a–417a (Feb. 6, 1775), 417a–417b (Feb. 20, 1775), 424b (Mar. 6, 1775); Shattuck, pp. 92–93.

32. William Brattle to Governor Thomas Gage, August 29, 1774, Massachusetts Historical Society.

33. CTR, 4: 406a–407b (Sept. 21 and 26, 1774); Proceedings of Worcester County Convention, September 21, 1774, in *Journals of Each Provincial Congress*, p. 643; Patterson, *Political Parties*, pp. 95–105.

34. CTR, 4: 406a–407b (Sept. 26, 1774), 408a–408b (Oct. 24, 1774),

412a–412b (Jan. 9, 1775), 414a–416a (Jan. 27, 1775), 416a–417a (Feb. 6, 1775); *Journals of Each Provincial Congress*, pp. 47–48; Emerson, p. 59; Lee, pp. 156–57.

35. Since most Minutemen were in their early twenties and had had little time to accumulate property, there was no point in studying their economic status *circa* 1775. Instead, I calculated a wealth distribution of the households from which the Minutemen came. All Minutemen who were unmarried and under 30 were assigned their fathers' economic ranks in 1770—even if the sons were themselves present on the 1770 Valuation List. On the other hand, young men who were present on the 1770 list and had no family in town were assumed to be laborers and were assigned to a quintile based on their own property assessments. This procedure is partly responsible for the underrepresentation of the lowest quintile in the Minutemen. The following table shows the economic status of Minutemen households:

	Top 20%	*UM 20%*	*Mid 20%*	*LM 20%*	*Bottom 20%*	*Missing*
Percentage	33	23	19	19	6	-
Number	21	15	12	12	4	40

For age distribution of Minutemen, see Chapter Four, n. 8. For the background of Brown, see sketch in Chapter Four. On Miles, MSA, 99: 444, and 1771 Province Valuation. For the town's loan of "fire armes" to the Minutemen, see CTR, 4: 414a–415a (Jan. 27, 1775).

36. Over half (54 per cent) the members of David Brown's company lived in the North Quarter; over half (52 per cent) of Miles's company lived in the South Quarter. As for underrepresentation of neighborhoods, the Bloods Farms school district included many of the northern secessionists. It included 11 per cent of all polls in 1773, but only 4 per cent of all Minutemen. For all the other school districts, there is no noteworthy pattern of under- or overrepresentation. Calculated from 1770 Valuation List and 1773 School Money List.

37. Concord First Church Record Book, 1739–1857, CFPL, pp. 141–43 (July 1, 1774); notes dated November 8, 1832, Shattuck's Hist. Notes; Lee, pp. 156–59. For the supposed Tory leanings of Lincoln pastor William Lawrence, see Shattuck's Hist. Notes.

38. The median age of the twenty-two Revolutionary committeemen in 1774–75 was 48.5, the average age 50.4; for the thirteen selectmen during 1765–74, these figures were 50.4 and 48. The real contrast is in the percentage of men over 60 in the two groups: 27 per cent of the committeemen, only 7 per cent of the selectmen. And in the twenty years between 1755 and 1774, only four out of 88 terms were filled by men over 60. As for wealth, the following table compares the economic status in 1770 of the committeemen and the 1765–74 selectmen:

	Top 20%	*UM 20%*	*Mid 20%*	*N*
Percentage of committeemen	71	19	10	21
Percentage of selectmen	77	23	0	13

39. Brown, *Revolutionary Politics*, p. 11; Shattuck, p. 110.

40. Frederick Clifton Pierce, comp., *Whitney: The Descendants of John Whitney, Who Came from London, England, to Watertown, Massachusetts, in 1635* (Chicago, 1895), pp. 91–92; Wheeler, *Concord*, p. 110.

41. Josephine Hosmer, "Memoir of Joseph Hosmer," Social Circle, pp. 116–17.

42. *Journals of Each Provincial Congress*, pp. 612–13; Brown, *Revolutionary Politics*, pp. 171–76; CTR, 4: 412a–412b (Jan. 9, 1775).

43. Shattuck, p. 81; CTR, 4: 362a–362b (Dec. 31, 1772), 378b (May 10, 1773), 399b–400a (May 16, 1774).

44. Concord First Church Record Book, pp. 144–45 (Jan. 26, 1775), 323–25 (Daniel Hosmer and wife; Joseph Hayward and wife).

CHAPTER 4

1. *The Journals of Each Provincial Congress of Massachusetts In 1774 and 1775 and of the Committee of Safety* . . . (Boston, 1838), pp. 33, 97, 505–13; Alfred Sereno Hudson, Notes and manuscript of vol. 2 of his history of Concord, Box 2, File 18, CFPL.

2. Allen French, *The Day of Concord and Lexington: The Nineteenth of April, 1775* (Boston, 1925), p. 26; Edward Jarvis, "Traditions and Reminiscences of Concord, Massachusetts, or a Contribution to the Social and Domestic History of the Town, 1779 to 1878," CFPL, pp. 12–13; Shattuck, pp. 97–98.

3. Shattuck, pp. 97–98. Cray was identified as Daniel Bliss's tenant from the records of the Committee of Safety, which took over management of Tory Bliss's land after war broke out. See Nathan Stow, Journal, 1776–1780, entry for March 24, 1777, Stow Family Papers, 1748–1777 Folder, CFPL.

The economic status in 1770 of the custodians of military stores was as follows:

	Top 20%	*UM 20%*	*Mid 20%*	*LM 20%*	*Bottom 20%*	*N*	*Missing*
Percentage of custodians	50.0	25.0	14.3	3.6	7.1	28	2

Economic rankings were determined from "A Copy of the Valuation and State Bill by which the Assessors of the Town of Concord Made the Rates for the year 1770," MSA, 130: 466–91. The preponderance of rich taxpayers among the custodians of stores is understandable, since men with substantial farms had the room to hide military provisions.

4. Shattuck, pp. 98–99; William C. Swain, comp., *Swain and Allied Families* (Milwaukee, Wis., 1896), pp. 70–71.

5. Shattuck, pp. 95, 99; CTR 4: 422a–424a (March 6, 1775); James Warren to Mercy Warren, April 6, 1775, in Worthington C. Ford, ed., *Warren-Adams Letters: Being Chiefly a Correspondence among John Adams, Samuel Adams, and James Warren*, 2 vols. (Boston, 1917–25), I: 45.

6. Emerson, p. 60; Shattuck, pp. 66–73, 94. I am indebted to Nancy Voye of Boston University for supplying me with the French and Indian War records of Concord Minutemen. For Buttrick, see MSA, 93: 187; for Hosmer, see Shattuck, p. 73.

7. Entry for March 13, 1775, "Weather Observations, 1774–1780," Safe, File Drawer 1, CFPL; Walter L. Dorn, *Competition for Empire 1740–1763* (New York, 1940), pp. 83–84; French, *Day*, pp. 17–19; Lorenzo Johnston Greene, *The Negro in Colonial New England 1620–1776* (New York, 1942), p. 127.

8. The age distribution of the Concord Minutemen was as follows:

	Under 21	*21–24*	*25–29*	*30 & over*	*N*	*Missing*
Percentage of Minutemen	29.7	27.5	14.3	28.6	91	13

9. The median age of the twenty-three Concord militia officers commissioned by the Crown during the period 1765–71 was forty-two, the average age 43.1. None were under thirty. As for their wealth, the officers' economic rankings on the 1770 province rate list were as follows:

	Top 20%	*Mid 40%*	*Bottom 40%*	*N*	*Missing*
Percentage of officers	52.6	26.3	21.0	19	4

The list of colonial officers is in MSA, 99: 75–76, 444–45; the province rate list is in MSA, 130: 466–91.

10. For the roster of the Concord Minutemen, see Ruth R. Wheeler, *Concord: Climate for Freedom* (Concord, 1967), pp. 227–28. For Cogswell, see Middlesex County, Records of the Court of General Sessions, 1761 to 1771, Office of the Clerk of Courts, Superior Court, East Cambridge, Mass., p. 54.

11. The sermon is printed in Emerson, pp. 61–70.

12. Stephen Foster, *Their Solitary Way: The Puritan Social Ethic in the First Century of Settlement in New England* (New Haven and London, 1971), pp. 11–40; on social stratification, see David Hackett Fischer, "America, A Social History. Volume I: The Main Lines of the Subject 1650–1975" (forthcoming), Chapter V.

13. James Russell Lowell, "Lines: Suggested by the Graves of Two

English Soldiers on Concord Battle-Ground," *The Complete Poetical Works of James Russell Lowell* (Boston, 1925), pp. 96–97.

14. Stephen Barrett, School Workbook, Safe, Shelf 14, Item 1, CFPL.

15. Barrett, Workbook, CFPL; 1771 Province Valuation, MSA, 132: 199–210. I have assumed that the title to Barrett's land was held by his father, since there is no record of Stephen's having purchased any property by 1771 in the Middlesex County Registry of Deeds. Although he operated his own farm, Stephen was probably still living in his father's household: in 1771 he owned no house of his own. The age composition of Concord schools was determined from a class roster in Nathan Stow's Journal, CFPL. In 1779, Stow kept a winter school in the East District. Of his twenty-one students, three were age five to nine; seven, age ten to fourteen; eight, age fifteen to nineteen; two were twenty or more. There were fourteen boys and seven girls.

16. On the importance of land in shaping relations between fathers and sons, see Philip J. Greven, Jr., *Four Generations: Population, Land, and Family in Colonial Andover, Massachusetts* (Ithaca and London, 1970), pp. 125–72, 222–38. That young men in Concord received their portions without too much delay is evident from an analysis of intragenerational economic mobility. As was done in the previous sections on wealth and political office-holding, the economic status of individuals was derived from their relative ranks on tax and assessment lists. Each male taxpayer was assigned to a quintile; movement from one quintile to another over time represented economic mobility. In this investigation, tax lists approximately twenty-five years apart were used so that the economic progress of individuals could be followed over the life cycle from young manhood to maturity to old age. Lest variations in form of wealth (e.g., realty as opposed to personalty) or in assessment procedures affect the final results, economic mobility was always measured on the same type of list. (For the colonial period, I used province rate lists to construct mobility matrices for 1733–57 and 1746–70; for comparisons between the prewar and postwar periods, I used town assessment lists for 1770 and 1795. The sources were: for 1733, 1746, and 1757, Box 1, CA; for both 1770 lists, MSA, 130: 466–91 and 132: 201–5; for 1795, Town Treasurer's Vault, Town Hall, Concord.) Finally, in the analysis reported here, I used "adjusted" quintiles as the measure of economic status; that is, the taxpayers who appeared on the early and later lists were ranked relative to each other and not to the total population. In this way, one eliminates the effects of migration, fertility, and mortality on the mobility rates. After all, an individual may rise in the world only because those with higher status have died; in such cases, economic mobility becomes more an accident of fate than a hard-won achievement (although the extent of that "achievement" may be doubted from the data presented below). For the methods used here, see Daniel Scott Smith, "Population, Family and Society in Hingham, Massachusetts 1635–1880" (Ph.D. dissertation, University of California at Berkeley, 1973), pp. 107–17.

At first glance, the mobility rates for colonial Concord revealed an extraordinarily volatile social structure. Most taxpayers changed their relative positions over the twenty-five-year periods. Between 1733 and 1757, about a quarter (23.5 per cent) of eighty-five persisters remained in the same quintile; 38.8 per cent moved up, 37.6 per cent moved down. There was even more movement between 1746 and 1770: a fifth (21.8 per cent) of 101 persisters were stable; 41.6 per cent moved up; 36.6 per cent moved down. But the appearance of instability was deceiving. Behind the high turnover in the economic ranks lay a remarkably predictable pattern: most of the younger men (age thirty or under) moved up a quintile or more; most of the older men (over thirty) moved down. This pattern is nicely summarized by the median age of taxpayers, classified according to their mobility experience:

Period	*Upwardly mobile*	*Stable*	*Downwardly mobile*	*N*	*Missing*
1733–57	27	29	41	81	0
1746–70	28	31	43	100	1

From this age pattern one can conclude that, as young men grew older, they succeeded to the property of their fathers and rose in the social structure until eventually they came full circle and, in turn, passed on estates to their sons. It is uncertain whether young men were obtaining their portions sooner than they had done in the first century of settlement. Greven's investigation of wills and deeds in colonial Andover would sustain this interpretation, as would Linda Auwers Bissell's study of economic mobility on tax lists in seventeenth-century Windsor, Connecticut. Bissell found that only 60 per cent of taxpayers changed their relative ranks between 1640 and 1676; in addition, twice as many taxpayers retained their ranks as would have been expected on the basis of chance. (Technically, the coefficient of association, C_d, was 2.0; the comparable measure for Concord was 1.18 for 1733–57 and 1.09 for 1746–70.) See "From One Generation to Another: Mobility in Seventeenth-Century Windsor, Connecticut," *William and Mary Quarterly*, 3d ser. XXXI (January 1974): 86 (n. 10), 99.

On the other hand, the intragenerational mobility rates for colonial Hingham, Massachusetts, suggest a very different trend: high mobility in the seventeenth century, followed by increasing stability over the eighteenth century. On tax lists approximately thirty years apart, 80 per cent of taxpayers changed their relative ranks in the seventeenth century; this figure fell to 60–65 per cent by the mid-eighteenth century. (C_d was 0.95 to 1.05 in the first century; by the period 1749–79, it was 1.98.) In other words, by the eve of the Revolution, mobility in Hingham had slowed to the earlier Windsor rate. See Smith, "Hingham," p. 118.

There is no ready explanation for the divergent findings for the seventeenth century (except perhaps that the number of cases in the seventeenth-century Hingham and Windsor studies is too small to yield statistically reliable results). I suspect that the mobility rates for eighteenth-century Concord reflect a real change from the previous century—that as a result of the land shortage in Concord, compared to the opportunities on the frontier, fathers were induced to pass on land faster than ever before if they wished at least some of their sons to remain in town.

17. A study of intergenerational mobility clearly demonstrates the failure of most fathers to pass on their economic status to their sons. In this analysis, the economic status of fathers on the 1746 province rate list was compared to the status of sons on the 1770 list. The quintiles were "unadjusted"; that is, the father's wealth relative to all men on the first list was compared to the son's wealth relative to all men on the second, since the issue at hand was how successfully sons inherited their fathers' places in the entire community. The answer can be summarized simply: not very well. Most sons were downwardly mobile. Only a quarter (25.2 per cent) remained in their fathers' quintile; 62 per cent occupied a lower rung, only 13 per cent a higher one. By this measure, intergenerational mobility in Concord was similar to the pattern in Windsor, where 60 per cent of sons were downwardly mobile over the period 1676–1702, and 30 per cent were stable. In both towns there was much greater movement than in Hingham (except for the 1647–80 matrix). This comparison was unchanged when adjusted quintiles were used to rank only the population of father-son pairs: again Windsor (1676–1702) and Concord proved more fluid than Hingham. (A coefficient called Yule's Q was computed to measure the improvement over chance in predicting the son's status on the second list, given knowledge of the father's status on the first. For Windsor, 1676–1702, the Q value was .554; for Concord, 1746–70, it was .566; for Hingham, after the 1647–80 matrix, it did not reach this low level until 1810–40.) See Bissell, "From One Generation to Another," p. 109; Smith, "Hingham," p. 113.

18. The annual linear rate of population growth (based on the number of polls) dramatically documents the early eighteenth-century boom and dates the beginning of the westward exodus in the 1720s:

	1708–19	*1719–25*	*1725–40*	*1740–53*	*1753–60*	*1760–70*
Percentage change	3.0	3.2	1.5	1.6	-0.8	1.0

The population density was 14.7 people per square mile in 1706; in 1754 it was 44.2, about average for Middlesex County. In estimating total population, I multiplied the number of polls by a factor of four, the figure suggested in Evarts B. Greene and Virginia D. Harrington, *American Population before the Federal Census of 1790* (New York, 1932), p. xxiii. I also adjusted the data to account for the setting off of new towns. For the population data, see Shattuck, pp. 212–13; A. P. Usher, "Colonial Business and Transportation," *Commonwealth History of Massachusetts: Colony, Province and State*, ed. Albert Bushnell Hart, 5 vols. (New York, 1927–30), II: 387–88; J. Potter, "The Growth of Population in America, 1700–1860," *Population in History: Essays in Historical Demography*, eds. D. V. Glass and D. E. C. Eversley (London, 1965), pp. 631–88.

19. My generalizations about Concord's demographic history are based on several sources: (1) a reconstitution of the families of all male taxpayers on the 1771 Province Valuation; (2) an analysis of age at marriage in all families started after 1740 and registered in the *Concord, Massachusetts Births, Marriages and Deaths 1635–1850* (Concord, n.d.); and (3) Marc Harris, "A Demographic Study of Concord, Massachusetts 1750–1850" (senior honors thesis, Brandeis University, 1973). For the importance of early age at first marriage on colonial population growth, see Daniel Scott Smith, "The Demographic History of Colonial New England," *Journal of Economic History*, XXXII (March 1972): 174–83.

20. Greven, *Four Generations*, pp. 25–29, 106–11, 185–96; Maris A. Vinovskis, "Mortality Rates and Trends in Massachusetts Before 1860," *Journal of Economic History*, XXXII (March 1972): 184–213.

21. The average landholding in 1663 was 259 acres (n = 60); by 1749, that figure had fallen to about 56 acres (n = 245). Shattuck, pp. 37–38; 1749 Province Valuation, 1749 Folder, Box 1, CA (the average holding of improved land, 27.8 acres, was doubled to include woodland and brush); Records of Proprietors of the Great and Common Fields, Subscription List dated March 1, 1690/1, Safe, Shelf 1, Item 7b, CFPL; Concord Village Proprietors' List, Allen French-Mrs. Caleb Wheeler Papers, CFPL; For similar trends in other parts of New England, see Kenneth A. Lockridge, "Land, Population and the Evolution of New England Society, 1630–1790, and an Afterthought," *Colonial America: Essays in Politics and Social Development*, ed. Stanley N. Katz (Boston, 1971), pp. 466–91.

22. The extent of paternal control over the marriage decisions of young men can be measured by two tests constructed by Daniel Scott Smith, "Parental Power and Marriage Patterns: An Analysis of Historical Trends in Hingham, Massachusetts," *Journal of Marriage and the Family*, XXXV (August 1973): 419–28: (1) If sons normally delayed marriage until they obtained farms or money from their fathers, Smith reasoned, then men whose fathers died young should have married earlier than men whose fathers survived to old age. The difference between the average age at first marriage of the sons in the two categories serves as a measure of parental power. Smith found for Hingham that parental power remained effective until the sons, born to marriages formed in 1741–60, came of age. The results for Concord were strikingly similar:

Period of fathers' marriage cohort	*Age at marriage of sons by age at death of fathers*		*Difference*	*Hingham Difference*
	Under 60	*60 or more*		
1701–20	25.0 (25)	26.4 (86)	+1.4	+1.6
1721–40	23.9 (25)	26.0 (94)	+2.1	+2.0
1741–60	28.3 (49)	27.5 (116)	−0.8	+0.4

(2) The second test is based on the expectation that fathers sought to influence the marriage decisions of their sons so as to preserve the social position of the family line. But most fathers lacked the economic resources to ensure good marriages for all their sons. In order to achieve their social goals, Smith maintains, fathers would have had to favor their eldest sons. Consequently, eldest sons should have been able, on the average, to marry daughters of wealthier men more often than were their younger brothers. This prediction was confirmed for colonial Hingham. Smith compared the wealth of fathers and fathers-in-law on tax lists approximately thirty years earlier than the lists on which the sons appeared. He found that eldest sons were about twice as likely as their brothers to marry upward on the social scale and only half as likely to marry downward. This pattern continued until the early nineteenth century. But in mid-eighteenth-century Concord, favoritism for eldest sons in marriage decisions had already weakened considerably: 35 per cent of eldest sons married into a higher quintile, compared to 32 per cent of younger sons, while 30 per cent of eldest sons married into a lower quintile, compared to 38 per cent of younger sons. (The sons appeared on the 1770 province rate list; the fathers and fathers-in-law on the 1746 list.) Thus, on these measures as well as in the analysis of economic mobility, Concord appears to have been a more fluid society in the eighteenth century than Hingham.

23. Shattuck, pp. 74–75; Roy Hidemichi Akagi, *The Town Proprietors of the New England Colonies* (1924; reprint, Gloucester, Mass., 1963) pp. 175–229.

24. Frederick Clifton Pierce, *History of Grafton, Worcester County, Massachusetts, From Its Early Settlement By The Indians In 1647 To The Present Time, 1879* (Worcester, Mass., 1879), pp. 37–38, 49–53; Charles Edward Potter, *A Genealogy of Some Old Families of Concord, Massachusetts* (Boston, 1887), p. 21; Albert Smith, *History of the Town of Peterborough . . . New Hampshire* (Boston, 1876), pp. 340–41. The Benjamin Barrett on the 1737 petition for the Peterborough grant was the brother of Colonel James and deacon Thomas Barrett. For a similar speculative venture by Concordians that did not involve the Barretts, see Benjamin Read, *The History of Swanzey, New Hampshire, From 1734 to 1890* (Salem, Mass., 1892), pp. 35–48.

25. Estate of Benjamin Barrett, Administration No. 1147, Mid. Prob.; Helen H. Foster, *Only One Cummington* (Cummington, Mass., 1974), pp. 199–201. James Barrett's gifts of farms to his sons can be traced in Mid.

Deeds, Bk. 58: 13; 63: 304; 65: 334, and also Estate of James Barrett, Will No. 1194, Mid. Prob. No grant of land from Colonel Barrett to his son Stephen has been found in the Registry of Deeds, nor did the father confirm any previous land transfers to Stephen in his will. However, on March 25, 1775, only three months before Stephen's wedding, the colonel bought a farm from Ebenezer Farrar in northwest Concord. Stephen Barrett's homestead was in this section of town. In all likelihood, Stephen received this land from his father after war had broken out, and he never bothered to register the transfer in Cambridge. Such omissions were common (and most annoying for later historians). See Mid. Deeds, Bk. 76: 515; Edward Jarvis, "Houses and People in Concord, 1810 to 1820," CFPL, p. 218.

26. 1771 Province Valuation; Mid. Deeds, Bk. 63:3. On the 1749 and 1770 Valuation Lists, about 10 per cent of all taxpayers were assessed for having money out at interest. I calculated the distribution of wealth from the 1746, 1757, and 1770 province rate lists in order to obtain a common basis for comparisons. Such tax lists do understate the true level of inequality, since even propertyless citizens were assigned some share of the total tax, if only a few pennies for a poll tax; in addition, a comparison between the 1770 rate list and the 1770 valuation revealed that the rich escaped paying their fair share of the total tax. However, what matters for the present analysis is not the absolute level of inequality but the trend over time. The following table, showing the proportionate shares of the total tax paid by the various parts of the tax-paying population, indicates a mild increase in inequality on the eve of the Revolution:

Percentage of Wealth Held in Each Category

Year	*Top 10%*	*Top 20%*	*Mid 40%*	*Bottom 40%*	*N*
1746	22.8	38.4	41.6	20.1	346
1757	23.2	38.8	40.9	20.2	289
1770	26.7	42.7	39.2	18.0	292

27. Mid. Deeds. Bk. 63: 304; 65: 334.

28. For a similar argument, see Greven, *Four Generations*, pp. 155–71, 241–58. Nearly every study of colonial New England demography to date has shown a declining age at first marriage for men over the first half of the eighteenth century. Since my data series at present begins after 1730, I have assumed that the same was true for Concord. See Douglas Lamar Jones, "Geographic Mobility and Society in Eighteenth-Century Essex County, Massachusetts" (Ph.D. dissertation, Brandeis University, 1975), Table 3-1, p. 73.

29. Potter, *Genealogies of Old Families of Concord*, pp. 105, 110. Between 1750 and 1780, eight Barretts and in-laws held 35 per cent of the available positions as selectmen and representatives. Susan Kurland, "'A Political Progress': Processes of Democratization in Concord, Massachusetts, 1750–1850" (senior honors thesis, Brandeis University, 1973), p. 96. In the period

1745–74, sons of town leaders (selectmen, representatives, moderators, and treasurers) first won election to the selectmen at a median age of forty-one; men without office-holding fathers had to wait until age forty-seven.

30. Ricardo Torres-Reyes, *Captain Brown's House: Historic Data* [research report for Minute Man National Historical Park, Concord, Massachusetts] (Washington, D.C., 1969), pp. 7–10.

31. George Tolman, comp., "Genealogy of the Brown Family of Concord, Massachusetts," NEHGS; Estates of Ephraim Brown, Administration No. 3003, and David Brown, Administration No. 2976, Mid. Prob., printed in Torres-Reyes, *Captain Brown's House*, pp. 18–32; John Demos, *A Little Commonwealth* (New York, 1970), pp. 46–51.

32. Ruth R. Wheeler, "North Bridge Neighbors: A History of Area B Minute Man National Historical Park," CFPL, pp. 88–93; John Shepard Keyes, "Memoir of David Brown," Social Circle, pp. 74–75; 1771 Province Valuation; Torres-Reyes, *Captain Brown's House*, p. 21.

33. Torres-Reyes, *Captain Brown's House*, p. 22. In 1771, 20 per cent of Concord's improved land lay in tillage, 40 per cent in meadowland, and 40 per cent in pasture. No figures are available on woodland and unimproved acreage until 1784, when such land accounted for 40 per cent of all acreage in town. Calculated from 1771 Province Valuation and 1784/6 Aggregate Valuation, 163: 51.

34. George Madison Bodge, *Soldiers in King Philip's War* . . . (Boston, 1906), p. 435; Torres-Reyes, *Captain Brown's House*, p. 21; Wheeler, "North Bridge Neighbors," p. 21; Emerson, p. 51; David Brown to Ephraim Brown, November 19, 1794, CAS Papers. Following methods developed by Daniel Scott Smith, I compared the economic mobility of eldest and younger sons over the period 1746–70. Eldest sons were only slightly more likely to be upwardly mobile than were their brothers, but were less than half as likely to be downwardly mobile. Over the same period, eldest sons were also more likely to inherit their fathers' tax ranking than were their brothers. See Smith, "Hingham," pp. 156–63, and Greven, *Four Generations*, pp. 227–28.

35. Percy Wells Bidwell and John I. Falconer, *History of Agriculture in the Northern United States 1620–1860* (1925; reprint, New York, 1941), pp. 89–98; Fischer, "America; A Social History," Chapter V, p. 22; Edward Jarvis, "Traditions and Reminiscences of Concord, Massachusetts, or a Contribution to the Social and Domestic History of the Town, 1779 to 1878," CFPL, pp. 43–58. My estimates of the land necessary to meet the consumption requirements of a family of six were derived in the following way. First, I relied on allotments for a widow's support, which colonial farmers frequently specified in their wills, to determine a middle-class standard of living. The provisions for widows were converted into total family requirements by assuming that women consumed about two thirds as much as their husbands and that children needed only half as much as adult men. Finally, I used farmers' estimates of the productive capacity of their

land to determine the necessary acreage in tillage, meadow, and pasture to meet the projected consumption needs. On this basis, two adults and four children required about eight to ten acres of tillage for their grain (rye and corn) and fourteen to sixteen acres of meadow and pasture to obtain their beef and dairy products. Add an additional acre of tillage to fatten hogs for pork and another acre for potatoes and vegetables. Thus, a minimum of twenty-four to twenty-eight acres was needed for a family of six. In 1765 the average household size in Concord was 5.9. To be sure, cattle often browsed along the public ways, so the pasturage requirements may be too high. On the other hand, no provision has been made for horses, sheep, and young cattle in this estimate. In addition, a farmer would also have needed woodland for his fuel. For methods and similar results, see James T. Lemon, *The Best Poor Man's Country: A Geographical Study of Early Southeastern Pennsylvania* (Baltimore, 1972), pp. 151–83; Charles S. Grant, "A History of Kent, 1738–1796: Democracy on Connecticut's Frontier" (Ph.D. dissertation, Columbia University, 1957), pp. 58–69 (note that Grant's estimates are too high because he has neglected the difference between live and dressed weights of livestock), and Robert E. Gallman, "The Statistical Approach: Fundamental Concepts as Applied to History," *Approaches to American Economic History*, eds. George Rogers Taylor and Lucius F. Ellsworth (Charlottesville, Va., 1971), pp. 71–74. For the calculation of the average household size, see Greene and Harrington, *American Population before 1790*, pp. 21–25.

36. In 1749, 37.6 per cent of all farmers kept no sheep, 56 per cent raised no flax, and 37 per cent owned no orchard. By 1771, nearly half (47.2 per cent) had no sheep. On the other hand, orchards were more widely distributed (only 23.6 per cent reported no cider production). No data on flax were collected in 1771.

37. These generalizations about Concord agriculture are derived from analysis of the 1749 and 1771 Provincial Valuations. Farmers were required to tell the assessors what their different types of land were expected to yield in a given year. I have used these reports to compute direct measures of productivity from the land (e.g., bushels of grain per acre of tillage) and have also carried out a statistical analysis of the effects of selected farm inputs (e.g., number of polls per acre of tillage) on land yields. My methods and results have been presented at length in two papers, "Minutemen in a New Nation: Concord, Massachusetts in the 1790's" (paper given at the Historic Deerfield Conference on New England Towns in the Early National Period, December 8, 1973) and "The Agricultural Crisis of Eighteenth-Century New England" (paper given at the annual meeting of the American Historical Association, December 29, 1975). For present purposes, I cite only the direct measures of productivity. In 1749 it took 1.4 acres of pasture to support a cow for a year; in 1771, 2.2 acres. Pasture accounted for 30 per cent of all improved land in 1749, 39 per cent in 1771.

38. In 1749 farmers obtained 13.2 bushels of grain per acre of tillage; in 1771, 12.2. Hay yields also fell: from .82 to .71 tons of hay per acre of meadowland. The average farm contained 27.8 acres of improved land (tillage, meadow, and pasture) in 1749, 34.1 acres in 1771. I have assumed that half of all Concord land was forest and brush in 1749 and have applied a reported Concord figure of 40 per cent unimproved in 1784 to the 1771 data. MSA, 163: 51. For a similar argument about the decline of fallows and diminishing returns in agriculture, see James A. Henretta, *The Evolution of American Society, 1700–1815: An Interdisciplinary Analysis* (Lexington, Mass., 1973), pp. 15–23.

39. In 1749 "English hay," as it was called, accounted for 15 per cent of the total hay crop; in 1771, 29 per cent. For contemporary agricultural reforms, see Jared Eliot, *Essays Upon Field Husbandry in New England and Other Papers, 1748–1762*, ed. Harry J. Carman (1934; reprint, New York, 1967), pp. 110–16. In 1749, 36 per cent of all farmers owned no oxen; in 1771, 32 per cent.

40. Jones, "Geographic Mobility and Society," *passim;* Douglas Lamar Jones, "The Strolling Poor: Transiency in Eighteenth-Century Massachusetts," *Journal of Social History*, 8 (Spring 1975): 32–39; Frederic Kidder and Augustus A. Gould, *The History of New Ipswich From Its First Grant in 1736 to the Present Time* (Boston, 1852), pp. 67–68; Louise Helen Coburn, *Skowhegan on the Kennebec*, 2 vols. (Skowhegan, Me., 1941), pp. 32–35, 129, 159–60, 648–49.

41. The following account of Brown's career is drawn largely from Grindall Reynolds, "Memoir of Ezekiel Brown," Social Circle, pp. 79–85.

42. Josiah Henry Benton, *Warning Out in New England* (Boston, 1911); Jones, "Strolling Poor," pp. 28–54.

43. Town of Woburn *vs.* Town of Lexington, petition regarding Mary Powers, March 15, 1768, File Papers for 1768, Records of the Middlesex Court of General Sessions. I am indebted to Dirk Hartog of Brandeis University for this reference.

44. Records of the Middlesex Court of General Sessions, 1761 to 1771.

45. Most newcomers were never warned out. Of thirty-three in-migrants who had moved to Concord after 1746 and appeared on the 1757 province rate list, only a quarter (24.2 per cent) were greeted by a constable; of thirty-eight in-migrants on the 1770 list who had arrived since 1757, nearly half (44.7 per cent) had been warned out. Concord's increasing wariness about newcomers—i.e., potential paupers—can be taken as a sign of worsening economic conditions. Most in-migrants who had been warned out came from within ten miles of Concord, but in the periods 1724–49 and 1750–75, 15–16 per cent arrived from Boston and Charlestown. Calculations are derived from the warnings out registered with the Middlesex Court of General Sessions.

46. Stuart Bruchey, *The Roots of American Economic Growth 1607–1861* (paperback ed.; New York, 1968), pp. 52–54.

47. In 1768, Concord had 0.13 businesses (warehouses, workhouses, and mills) per poll; the corresponding figure was 0.14 for the larger Essex County seaports and 0.12 for the smaller Essex ports. Jones, "Geographic Mobility and Society," p. 169; 1768 Aggregate Valuation List for Concord, MSA, 130: 128. In 1784, Concord ranked among the most commercial-cosmopolitan towns in Massachusetts, according to the index constructed by Van Beck Hall, *Politics Without Parties: Massachusetts, 1780–1791* (Pittsburgh, 1970), Appendix. For the Concord importer, see advertisement of Elnathan Jones, *Boston Gazette*, March 18, 1771; for innkeepers, Records of Court of General Sessions, 1761 to 1771, p. 518.

48. Marc Egnal, "The Economic Development of the Thirteen Continental Colonies, 1720 to 1775," *William and Mary Quarterly*, 3d Ser. XXXII (April 1975): 191–222. The decline in property values is evident from assessment figures that Lemuel Shattuck collected for his *History of Concord* from the Office of the Massachusetts Secretary of State. The original records have since been lost. I discovered a paper listing the property valuation of Concord at several points in the eighteenth century in Shattuck's Hist. Notes. Unfortunately, Shattuck did not indicate whether the valuations were in British or Massachusetts currency. I have assumed that they were expressed in Massachusetts "Lawful Money." For an indication of economic growth, I calculated the property valuation per poll and converted the results into constant money by applying the Philadelphia wholesale price index (*The Statistical History of the United States from Colonial Times to the Present* [Stamford, Conn., 1965], Series E68-82). The constant valuation per poll rose by 2.3 per cent between 1753 and 1760, then fell by 6 per cent between 1760 and 1771. Further evidence of hard times in the 1760s and early 1770s is found in the Middlesex County probate records. Of thirty Concord estates administered between 1760 and 1774, eleven were insolvent. By contrast, there had been only one insolvency among nineteen estates in the previous twenty years. For similar findings, see William Floyd Willingham, "Windham, Connecticut: Profile of a Revolutionary Community, 1755–1818" (Ph.D. dissertation, Northwestern University, 1972), pp. 74–84, 93–95.

49. Carleton Edward Fisher, *History of Clinton, Maine* (Augusta, Me., 1970), p. 280.

50. Robert A. Feer, "Imprisonment for Debt in Massachusetts Before 1800," *Mississippi Valley Historical Review*, XLVIII (Sept. 1961): 257–61; Nathan Bond to Tilly Merrick, December 9, 1788, Tilly Merrick Papers, CFPL.

51. For identifications of slaves and owners, see the following sources: Will of James Barrett, No. 1194, Mid. Prob.; Joan Trumbull, "Concord and the Negro," CFPL, p. 22 (Brister Cuming); Josiah Bartlett, "Memoir of Duncan Ingraham," Social Circle, pp. 129–30; Joseph Grafton Minot, comp., *A Genealogical Record of the Minot Family in America and England* (Boston, 1897), p. 20; Emerson, p. 73.

52. Lorenzo Johnston Greene, *The Negro in Colonial New England 1620–1776* (New York, 1942), pp. 15–49, 57–60; Bartlett, "Memoir of Duncan Ingraham," p. 128; Edgar T. McManus, *Black Bondage in the North* (Syracuse, N.Y., 1973), p. 41. In 1771 eleven taxpayers were assessed for ownership of a "servant for life," age fourteen to forty-five: nine were in the top 20 per cent of wealth-holders the previous year and two in the next highest quintile. They owned a total of thirteen slaves.

53. Emerson, pp. 103, 105, 119; McManus, *Black Bondage*, pp. 39–41, 61–83.

54. George Tolman, *John Jack, the Slave, and Daniel Bliss, the Tory* (Concord, Mass., 1902), pp. 16–18. Jack was assessed for £9.5 in personal estate and no real estate in the 1770 valuation.

55. McManus, *Black Bondage*, pp. 72–83; Greene, *Negro in Colonial New England*, p. 135; form for sale of slave by James Barrett, 1772, in Allen French-Mrs. Caleb Wheeler Papers, CFPL (this form closely resembles the sample wills and deeds in Stephen Barrett's school workbook); Bradford Torrey and Francis H. Allen, eds., *The Journal of Henry D. Thoreau*, 14 vols. bound as 2 (New York, 1962), X: 284–85.

56. Arthur Zilversmit, *The First Emancipation: The Abolition of Slavery in the North* (Chicago and London, 1967), pp. 55–108 (quote, p. 101); Tolman, *John Jack the Slave*, pp. 3–7, 19.

57. Benjamin Quarles, "The Colonial Militia and Negro Manpower," *Mississippi Valley Historical Review*, XLV (March 1959): 643–52.

58. The following account of the Hosmers is taken from Josephine Hosmer, "Memoir of Joseph Hosmer," Social Circle, pp. 114–19, and from a longer unpublished memoir by the same author in the CAS Papers.

59. Emerson, p. 30. From the 1740s on, prenuptial conceptions—births less than nine months after marriage—steadily increased in every decade: they accounted for 19 per cent of all first births in the 1740s; 26 per cent in the 1750s; 41 per cent in the period 1760–74. For a similar pattern in other communities and for the general argument, see Daniel Scott Smith, and Michael S. Hindus, "Premarital Pregnancy in America, 1640–1971: An Overview and Interpretation," *Journal of Interdisciplinary History*, V (Spring 1975): 537–70.

60. 1771 Province Valuation; Margaretta Markle Lowell, "Boston Blockfront Furniture," *Boston Furniture of the Eighteenth Century, Publications of the Colonial Society of Massachusetts*, 48 (Boston, 1974), 125.

61. Nancy Falik Cott, "In the Bonds of Womanhood: Perspectives on Female Experience and Consciousness in New England, 1780–1830" (Ph.D. dissertation, Brandeis University, 1974), pp. 40–41, 102, 220. In 1785, when he was a forty-nine-year-old father of four and a state senator, Hosmer finally purchased title to his farm from his own father for £300. Mid. Deeds, Bk. 89: 394.

62. Cott, "In the Bonds," pp. 31–33, 40–41.

63. In 1765, for every one hundred women over age sixteen in Concord there were only eighty-eight men. Given this low sex ratio, I have accepted as valid for Concord the evidence of increasing spinsterhood over the eighteenth century, which Daniel Scott Smith presents for Hingham. J. H. Benton, Jr., *Early Census Making in Massachusetts 1643–1765, With a Reproduction of the Lost Census of 1765* (Boston, 1905); Smith, "Hingham," pp. 279–81. On the limited economic opportunities for single women, Cott, "In the Bonds," pp. 11–20.

64. Alexander Keyssar, "Widowhood in Eighteenth-Century Massachusetts: A Problem in the History of the Family," *Perspectives in American History*, VIII (1974): 83–119; Jones, "Strolling Poor," p. 36; Smith, "Hingham," pp. 281–84.

65. The distribution of land shifted in favor of middling property owners between 1749 and 1771:

	Percentage of Land Held in Each Category			
	Top 20%	*Mid 40%*	*Bottom 40%*	*N*
1749	55	42	3	326
1771	48	48	4	285

As a result, I have underplayed the significance of the increasing inequality in the distribution of the province rate (see n. 26). It is true that the over-all measures of concentration rise noticeably between 1757 and 1770 (the Gini coefficient by 14 per cent, the Schutz coefficient by 16 per cent), but this result could have been produced by a shift in assessment practices: the tax system was regressive, and if the assessors had been assigning taxes more equitably in 1770 than in 1757, one would have found increasing inequality. Since the observed trend on the province rate lists runs counter to the trend in the distribution of land, and, in addition, since the distribution of assessed wealth on the 1770 valuation list was less top heavy than in some other towns of the same period, I have emphasized stability rather than change. On the other hand, if inequality actually was growing, this would strengthen the argument for a breakdown in the traditional social order. For the 1749 landholdings, see 1749 Province Valuation List, 1749 Folder, Box 1, CA.

66. For two treatments of these issues, see Jack P. Greene, "The American Revolution as a Social Movement: An Evaluation and Interpretation," *Political Science Quarterly*, LXXXVIII (March 1973): 1–22, and Kenneth A. Lockridge, "Social Change and the Meaning of the American Revolution," *Journal of Social History*, 6 (Summer 1973): 403–39.

67. The argument that changes within the colonial family were related to the American response to British policy is presented by Edwin G. Burrows and Michael Wallace, "The American Revolution: The Ideology and Psychology of National Liberation," *Perspectives in American History*, VI (1972): 167–306.

CHAPTER 5

1. John Richard Alden, *General Gage in America* (1948; reprint ed., New York, 1969), pp. 5–9, 11, 61, 202–4, 209.

2. Alden, *General Gage*, pp. 218–31.

3. Richard D. Brown, *Revolutionary Politics in Massachusetts: The Boston Committee of Correspondence and the Towns, 1772–1774* (Cambridge, Mass., 1970), pp. 224–35; Stephen E. Patterson, *Political Parties in Revolutionary Massachusetts* (Madison, Wis., 1973), pp. 109–15; Merrill Jensen, *The Founding of a Nation: A History of the American Revolution 1763–1776* (New York, 1968), pp. 554–67.

4. Jensen, *Founding of a Nation*, pp. 554–55, 584; Allen French, *The Day of Concord and Lexington: The Nineteenth of April, 1775* (Boston, 1925), pp. 12–14, 39–40.

5. French, *Day*, p. 44; Henry De Berniere, "Narrative of Occurrences, 1775," *Collections of the Massachusetts Historical Society*, 2nd series, IV (1816): 214–15; Ruth R. Wheeler, *Concord: Climate for Freedom* (Concord, 1967), p. 109.

6. John Howe, *A Journal kept by Mr. John Howe while he was employed as a British Spy during the Revolutionary War . . .* (Concord, N.H., 1827), reprinted in *The Magazine of History*, 33 (1927): 165–76.

7. Howe, *Magazine of History*, pp. 175–76; French, *Day*, pp. 12–14.

8. Allen French, *General Gage's Informers* (Ann Arbor, Mich., 1932), pp. 3–33.

9. Jensen, *Founding of a Nation*, p. 565; French, *Day*, pp. 41–42.

10. Emerson, p. 89; French, *General Gage's Informers*, pp. 20–24, 27–28.

11. Alden, *General Gage*, pp. 233–41; French, *Day*, p. 15.

12. Alden, *General Gage*, pp. 242–44; French, *Day*, 56–57.

13. French, *Day*, pp. 64–66, 68–69; *The British in Boston: The Diary of Lt. John Barker* (1924; reprint ed., New York, 1969), p. 29.

14. French, *Day*, pp. 70–78, 83–85, 100–2; Arthur B. Tourtellot, *Lexington and Concord: The Beginning of the War of the American Revolution* (New York, 1963), pp. 89–91; Shattuck, p. 104.

15. Frank Warren Coburn, *The Battle of April 19, 1775 . . .* (privately published, Lexington, Mass., 1912), pp. 32–34; French, *Day*, pp. 85–86, 88–90.

16. French, *Day*, pp. 91–92, 104; Wheeler, *Concord*, pp. 112–13.

17. Tourtellot, *Lexington and Concord*, pp. 22–23; Deposition of John Parker, *The Journals of Each Provincial Congress of Massachusetts In 1774 and 1775, and of the Committee of Safety . . .* (Boston, 1838), p. 665; French, *Day*, pp. 95–108.

18. French, *Day*, pp. 95–99; Tourtellot, *Lexington and Concord*, pp. 111, 129–30, 139.

19. Tourtellot, *Lexington and Concord*, pp. 114–16, 132; French, *Day*, pp. 103–5, 108.

20. Deposition of John Parker, *Journals of Each Provincial Congress*, p. 665; French, *Day*, pp. 120–21, 125–27.

21. *The British in Boston*, p. 32; Tourtellot, *Lexington and Concord*, pp. 134–35.

22. Emerson, p. 71; French, *Day*, pp. 148–52.

23. Wheeler, *Concord*, p. 115; Coburn, *Battle of April 19, 1775*, pp. 37–38; Josiah Adams, *An Address Delivered at Acton, July 21, 1835, Being the First Centennial Anniversary of That Town . . .* (Boston, 1835), p. 47.

24. Charles Henry Chandler, comp., *The History of New Ipswich, New Hampshire 1735–1914 . . .* (Fitchburg, Mass., 1914), pp. 75–76.

25. Shattuck, pp. 103–4.

26. Letter of Amos Barrett, *Journal and Letters of Rev. Henry True* (privately printed, Marion, Ohio, 1900), reprinted in Amos Barrett, *The Concord Fight* (privately printed, Boston, 1924), p. 12; Thaddeus Blood, "Statement on the Battle of April 19," CFPL, and published in *Boston Advertiser*, April 20, 1886.

27. Emerson, pp. 71–72; French, *Day*, pp. 160–64. An interview with Abel Conant, dated November 8, 1832, in Shattuck's Hist. Notes, was the source for Rev. Emerson's fiery statement quoted in Shattuck, pp. 105–6.

28. Shattuck, p. 106; French, *Day*, pp. 164–66.

29. Emerson, pp. 73–74, 92.

30. French, *Day*, pp. 162–66; French, *General Gage's Informers*, p. 33.

31. Shattuck, pp. 107–9.

32. Marquis De Chastellux, *Travels in North America in the Years 1780, 1781, and 1782*, trans. Howard C. Rice, Jr., 2 vols. (Chapel Hill, N.C., 1963), II: 481–82.

33. Coburn, *Battle of April 19, 1775*, p. 95; accounts of Reuben Brown, William Emerson and Abel Fisk, Dr. Timothy Minot, and Ezekiel Brown, 1775 Folder, Box 2, CA.

34. Shattuck, pp. 108–9.

35. Elijah Wood, Jr., "Memoir of Ephraim Wood," Social Circle, pp. 153, 155; Shattuck, p. 109; interview with Mrs. Peter Barrett, November 3, 1831, Shattuck's Hist. Notes.

36. Shattuck, p. 107; French, *Day*, pp. 172–73.

37. Josiah Adams, *Letter to Lemuel Shattuck, Esq., of Boston* (Boston, 1850), pp. 20–21; French, *Day*, pp. 184, 193–94.

38. Josephine Hosmer, "Memoir of Joseph Hosmer," CAS Papers; Shattuck, p. 111.

39. French, *Day*, p. 189; Ezra Ripley, *A History of the Fight at Concord, on the 19th of April, 1775* (Concord, 1832), p. 16; William Gilman, et al., eds., *The Journals and Miscellaneous Notebooks of Ralph Waldo Emerson*, 9 vols. (Cambridge, Mass., 1960–71), VI: 242; Bradford Torrey and Francis H.

Allen, eds., *The Journal of Henry D. Thoreau*, 14 vols. bound as 2 (New York, 1962), III: 412; Shattuck, p. 100.

40. Barrett, *The Concord Fight*, p. 13; statement of Thaddeus Blood, *Boston Advertiser*, April 20, 1886; French, *Day*, pp. 190–92; Shattuck, pp. 111–12.

41. French, *Day*, pp. 207–9; Barrett, *The Concord Fight*, p. 14; *The British in Boston*, p. 34.

42. French, *Day*, pp. 207–9; reminiscences of Nathan Barrett, Jr., Allen French-Mrs. Caleb Wheeler Papers, Safe, Shelf 13, Item 17, Folder 39, CFPL; Statement of Thaddeus Blood, *Boston Advertiser*, April 20, 1886.

43. French, *Day*, pp. 211–12; Jeremy Lister, *Concord Fight* (Cambridge, Mass., 1931), p. 27.

44. Peter Force, comp., *American Archives*, 4th Series, II (Washington, 1839): 630; Nathaniel Hawthorne, *Mosses from an Old Manse* (Boston and New York, 1882), pp. 18–19; interview with Mrs. Peter Barrett, November 3, 1831, Shattuck's Hist. Notes.

45. Henry Wadsworth Longfellow, *The Complete Poetical Works of Longfellow* (Boston, 1922), p. 209.

46. French, *Day*, pp. 215–18; Emerson, p. 72; Shattuck, pp. 113–14.

47. French, *Day*, pp. 218–19; Coburn, *Battle of April 19, 1775*, p. 97; Barrett, *The Concord Fight*, p. 14.

48. French, *Day*, p. 220; Tourtellot, *Lexington and Concord*, p. 178.

49. French, *Day*, pp. 220–24.

50. French, *Day*, pp. 226–35.

51. Coburn, *Battle of April 19, 1775*, pp. 123–28.

52. Coburn, *Battle of April 19, 1775*, pp. 142–44; Tourtellot, *Lexington and Concord*, pp. 197–98; deposition of Hannah Adams, *Journals of Each Provincial Congress*, p. 677.

53. Tourtellot, *Lexington and Concord*, pp. 202–3.

54. Henry Ames Blood, *The History of Temple, New Hampshire* (Boston, 1860), p. 328; Shattuck, *History of Concord*, pp. 114, 116; Wheeler, *Concord*, pp. 127–28. Ensign Brown's comment may have been a common quip. It was presumably passed on by his descendants to the author of the history of Temple, New Hampshire, where Brown moved after the Revolution. But Shattuck attributes the quote to Luther Blanchard, an injured Minuteman from Acton. Shattuck's information was probably derived from Nathan Barrett, Jr., whose mother dressed Blanchard's wound.

55. *Essex Gazette*, May 10, 1775, quoted in William Willes Hayward, *The History of Hancock, New Hampshire 1764–1889*, 2 vols. (Lowell, Mass., 1889), II: 641–42; Coburn, *Battle of April 19, 1775*, p. 107.

56. Shattuck, pp. 116–17; interview with Mrs. Peter Barrett, November 3, 1831, and note on Samuel Lee, Shattuck's Hist. Notes.

57. Lee, p. 160; interview with John Vose, November 8, 1832, Shattuck's Hist. Notes; Arlin Ira Ginsburg, "Ipswich, Massachusetts during the

American Revolution" (Ph.D. dissertation, University of California, Riverside, 1972), pp. 112–13.

58. Adams, *An Address*, p. 32; Lee, p. 160; Emerson, p. 75.

CHAPTER 6

1. John Shy, "The American Revolution: The Military Conflict Considered as a Revolutionary War," *Essays on the American Revolution*, ed. Stephen G. Kurtz and James H. Hutson (Chapel Hill, N.C., and New York, 1973), pp. 130–35; Don Higginbotham, *The War of American Independence: Military Attitudes, Policies, and Practices, 1763–1789* (New York, 1971), pp. 98–99.

2. Michael Zuckerman, *Peaceable Kingdoms: New England Towns in the Eighteenth Century* (New York, 1970), pp. 250–51; CTR, 5: 74b–75a (March 17, 1777), 86a (March 30, 1778), 71a–71b (June 2, 1777); *Essex Journal*, August 30, 1776 (committees of correspondence are ordered to keep prisoners of war within town limits); *Acts and Resolves, Public and Private, of the Province of the Massachusetts Bay (1692–1780)*, 21 vols. (Boston, 1869–1922), XIX: 259–60.

3. *The Journals of Each Provincial Congress of Massachusetts In 1774 and 1775, and of the Committee of Safety* . . . (Boston, 1838), pp. 175–77; "The Famileys and the Number in Each Family which came from Boston to the Town of Concord as Donation Poor from Boston," October, 1775, Miscellaneous Bound Volume, Massachusetts Historical Society; Shattuck, p. 120. As of January 1, 1777, Concord provided refuge for some seventy to eighty inhabitants of Boston and Charlestown (based on a reported eighteen polls, age sixteen or over), Shattuck's Hist. Notes.

4. Percy W. Brown, "The Sojourn of Harvard College in Concord," *The Harvard Graduates' Magazine* (June 1919), pp. 497–509; Samuel Eliot Morison, *Three Centuries of Harvard 1636–1936* (Cambridge, Mass., 1936), pp. 148–50.

5. Concord's population on the eve of the war was about 1,500. This figure was estimated as follows: in 1765 there were 381 polls (males over age sixteen) and a total white population of 1,537, for a ratio of 4.03 people per poll; in 1773 polls numbered 377. Multiplying by the 1765 ratio yields a population estimate of 1,519. I have assumed that this figure did not increase much by 1775. A year later, on March 20, 1776, Concord accommodated 1,927 people, of whom about 110 belonged to Harvard College and 80 were refugees from Boston and Charlestown. Evarts B. Greene and Virginia B. Harrington, *American Population before the Federal Census of 1790* (New York, 1932), pp. 31–33; Shattuck's Hist. Notes (for 1765 polls); 1773 School Money List, 1773 Folder, Box 2, CA; *Acts and Resolves*, V: 468–70 (census of 1776).

6. Emerson, pp. 81–83, 86. In December 1775 the House of Representa-

tives ordered Concord to supply five tons of hay for the Army at Cambridge. Farmers would be paid £5 per ton by the province. Partly because of the drought, it proved impossible to obtain the hay at that price. Concord had to offer an extra pound per ton to meet the quota. CTR, 4: 432a–432b (Dec. 29, 1775).

7. According to Shattuck, p. 124, fifty-six men signed up on April 20, 1775. This figure, which was derived from a document headed "Hartwell Brook the first Everidge," MSA, Revolutionary Rolls, vol. 55, File L, p. 23, is probably too low. Two companies, one under Captain Abishai Brown and another under Captain Joseph Butler, were raised from Concord and its environs for service in the Massachusetts Army in 1775. Brown's company had sixty-four men, of whom forty-four were from Concord. From the military service records compiled by the Massachusetts Secretary of State, I have determined that at least half of the 104 Concord Minutemen enlisted for the eight months' service. It seems likely that other young men who had not been Minutemen also enlisted, so that the true number of volunteers must be about sixty or seventy, and perhaps even as high as eighty, which would represent about a third of the eligible men, ages fifteen to forty. "Sergeant Nathan Stow's Orderly Book," *Putnam's Monthly Magazine*, I (1892–1893): 307–8; Office of the Secretary, Commonwealth of Massachusetts, *Massachusetts Soldiers and Sailors of the Revolutionary War*, 17 vols. (Boston, 1896).

8. Shattuck, pp. 124, 352.

9. Shattuck, p. 354; Emerson, p. 100.

10. Emerson, pp. 102, 108, 113, 115.

11. *Acts and Resolves*, XIX: 69, 102; Note on prisoners, Shattuck's Hist. Notes; *The New England Chronicle, or Essex Gazette*, December 14, 1775 (Barrett's gun shop); Shattuck, p. 352.

12. John Homer Bliss, comp., *Genealogy of the Bliss Family in America, from about the Year 1550 to 1880* (Boston, 1881), pp. 81–84.

13. Shattuck, p. 119, does not give the name of the former selectman. In May 1778, Flint was dropped from the jurors' rolls. He was the only former selectman known to suffer this treatment. CTR, 5: 91a, 91c (May 14, 1778).

14. Lee, pp. 160–63; Shattuck, pp. 119–20; Joseph Lee to Stephen Hosmer, May 2, 1776, Old Letters of Concord, Mass., Lemuel Shattuck Collection, NEHGS.

15. Stephen E. Patterson, *Political Parties in Revolutionary Massachusetts* (Madison, Wis., 1973), pp. 117–24; warrants for town meetings, May 22, 1775, February 27, 1776, March 4, 1776, 1775 and 1776 Folders, Box 2, CA; *Concord, Massachusetts Births, Marriages, and Deaths 1635–1850* (Concord, n.d.), p. 247; Rev. Caleb Gannett, Diary for 1776, Houghton Library, Harvard University; Emerson, pp. 94–95.

16. CTR, 4: 453a–458a; warrant for town meeting, September 18, 1776, 1776 Folder, Box 2, CA; *Acts and Resolves*, V: 484. Between May and

September, 1776, Concord effectively assumed its own sovereignty; warrants for town meetings were issued by the selectmen without reference to higher authority. See warrants for meetings of May 16 and July 26, 1776, in 1776 Folder, Box 2, CA.

17. Marshall Smelser, *The Winning of Independence* (Chicago, 1972), p. 150; Don Higginbotham, *War of Independence, passim.*

18. Smelser, *Winning of Independence*, pp. 101–4; Jackson Turner Main, *The Sovereign States, 1775–1783* (New York, 1973), pp. 222–68.

19. Main, *Sovereign States*, p. 245; CTR, 5: 94a–95b (June 1, 1778); report of committee to look into Ezra Ripley's salary, March 1, 1785, 1785 Folder, Box 3, CA; Ezra Ripley, *Half-Century Discourse Delivered November 16, 1828* (Concord, 1829), pp. 8–9.

20. William B. Weeden, *Economic and Social History of New England 1620–1789*, 2 vols. (Boston and New York, 1970), II: 789–92; Main, *Sovereign States*, pp. 230–31, 246. A fragmentary Valuation List for Concord in 1780 provides striking evidence for the increase in wool growing. Twenty farmers were assessed on both this list and the earlier 1771 valuation. They operated larger farms, on the average, than the typical yeoman in 1771, but for the present analysis, this wealth bias is an advantage: one would expect farmers with ample grazing lands to take the lead in sheep raising. Actually, in 1771, the twenty men were nearly representative of the farming population: 45 per cent kept no sheep, compared to 47 per cent of all farmers; their median holding was 5.0, compared to a mean of 6.1 for all sheep owners. By 1780, they had substantially expanded their flocks: only 30 per cent had no sheep, and the median holding had risen to seven. No doubt much of this increase was intended to meet the farmers' own household needs for cloth, now that British imports were no longer available. But there were clearly some wool growers in the group who were taking advantage of the new domestic market: while only one of them—Dr. Joseph Lee—raised over ten sheep in 1771, six did so in 1780. For the fragmentary valuation, see 1780 Folder, Box 2, CA.

21. Concord farmers only modestly increased their efforts at cattle raising. In 1771 there were 2.6 cows per poll; in 1780, 2.8. Colonel Barrett, one of the largest cattle farmers in town before the war, with seventeen oxen, eighteen cows, and twenty-five steers and heifers in 1771, apparently did not increase his herds to meet wartime demand. When he died in April 1779 he left twenty-five cattle to be fattened and slaughtered for sale that fall; in addition, another six cows and four oxen remained on the farm. (Administration No. 1194, Mid. Prob.) The limited returns from both sheep and cattle raising are evident from the fact that in both 1780 and 1784 pasturage was the lowest valued use of improved land; in 1780 it was assessed at even less per acre than woodland and unimproved. (1780 Province Valuation; 1784 Aggregate Valuation; Shattuck, pp. 212–13.)

22. Shattuck, p. 124.

23. The toll on Concord's stocks of draft animals is clear from the aggregate valuations: in 1771 there were 1.72 horses and oxen per poll; in 1781, 1.41; in 1784, 1.24. The evidence on declining land yields derives from the small sample of twenty farmers on the 1780 valuation. But the analysis is also supported from the aggregate data. The number of acres of tillage per ox can serve as an index of extensive cultivation, for in 1771 it was inversely correlated with grain yields per acre. This measure increased over the course of the war: in 1771, 3.5 acres tillage per ox; in 1781, 3.7; in 1784, 4.1. (Shattuck, pp. 212–13; 1784 Aggregate Valuation.) The declining capacity of pasture to support cattle was probably due largely to overgrazing by sheep; so long as sheep raising was profitable, the decline may not have posed a serious problem (although one cannot eat wool, and Americans generally shunned mutton). But by 1784, with the resumption of British imports, the wool boom collapsed, leaving exhausted grazing lands in its wake.

24. E. A. Benians, ed., *A Journal by Thomas Hughes . . . 1778–1789* (Cambridge, Eng., 1947), pp. 32–33; Shattuck, p. 126; Edward Jarvis, "Traditions and Reminiscences of Concord, Massachusetts, or a Contribution to the Social and Domestic History of the Town, 1779 to 1878," CFPL, p. 11. Using an estimate of four hundred pounds for the average dressed weight of fat cattle, I calculated the number of head necessary to fill the beef quota. The estimate was derived from various accounts in the town records, which indicate the weight of sides of beef, and from Richard Brigham Johnson, ed., "The Diary of Israel Litchfield," *The New England Historical and Genealogical Register*, CXXIX (April 1975): 152. As for the decline in livestock holdings, between 1771 and 1784 the number of oxen per poll fell by 32 per cent, of cows by 6 per cent, horses by 21 per cent, swine by 35 per cent, and sheep by 45 per cent. Shattuck, pp. 212–13.

25. The registered marriage rate was 6.5 per 1,000 for the period 1765–74, 5.8 for 1775–84, and 7.1 for 1785–94. The recorded birth rate was 24.5 per 1,000 for. 1769–73, 16.9 for 1775–79, and 24.5 for 1781–5.

26. Oscar and Mary Handlin, "Revolutionary Economic Policy in Massachusetts," *William and Mary Quarterly*, 3d ser., IV (January 1947): 7–25; *Acts and Resolves*, V: 583–89, 642–47; CTR, 4: 464a–466a; Nathan Stow, Journal, 1776–1780, Stow Family Papers, 1748–1777 Folder, CFPL.

27. *Acts and Resolves*, V: 1253–54; CTR, 5: 119b (June 16, 1779); *Proceedings of the Convention Begun and held at Concord . . . on the 14th Day of July, 1779 . . .* (Boston, 1779); Patterson, *Political Parties*, pp. 215–16.

28. CTR, 5: 120b–120c (July 30, 1779), 121a–121b (Aug. 9, 1779), 124b–124c (Nov. 1 and 22, 1779); List of Ceiling Prices in Concord, 1779, 1779 Folder, Box 2, CA; Handlin and Handlin, "Revolutionary Economic Policy," pp. 20–25; Joseph Lee, Diary for 1779, Massachusetts Historical Society.

29. Patterson, *Political Parties*, pp. 178–82; CTR 5: 75a–75b (Dec. 1, 1777); Van Beck Hall, *Politics Without Parties: Massachusetts, 1780–1791*

(Pittsburgh, 1972), pp. 94–130 and Appendix. I have traced the votes of the Concord representatives on the roll calls analyzed by Hall, pp. 102–3. Concord's wartime representatives were Joseph Hosmer (1780, 1783), David Brown (1781), and James Barrett (1782).

30. Main, *Sovereign States*, pp. 250–60, 360–61; Robert J. Taylor, *Western Massachusetts in the Revolution* (Providence, R.I., 1954), pp. 103–27; Shattuck, pp. 129–42; CTR 5: 138b (March 10, 1780). From 1760–79 only two men refused to serve as constables out of a total of sixty-three elected to the post. But in the next five years, 1780–84, nearly a third—seven out of twenty-two—declined to make the tax collector's rounds. In part, the recalcitrants were reluctant to dun their neighbors, but more important, under state law, if a constable failed to collect all of his assigned tax, he had to pay the difference out of his own pocket. Charles Francis Adams, *Three Episodes of Massachusetts History*, 2 vols. (Boston and New York, 1892), 2: 824.

31. Shattuck, pp. 123–26. For the various state levies on the towns, see James J. Tracy, "Revolutionary War Legislation of the Province and Commonwealth," *Soldiers and Sailors*, I: ix–xxxix, and Jonathan Smith, "How Massachusetts Raised Her Troops in the Revolution," *Proceedings of the Massachusetts Historical Society*, 55 (1921–22): 345–70.

32. Smith, "How Massachusetts Raised Her Troops," pp. 358–59; Tracy, "Revolutionary War Legislation," pp. xxii–xxiii; Higginbotham, *War for Independence*, pp. 392–93; Shattuck, pp. 124–25, 352–59. The shift from a voluntary to a conscript army can be traced in the table of military levies on Concord presented by Shattuck.

33. Tracy, "Revolutionary War Legislation," pp. xxii–xxiii, xxx–xxxi, "Hartwell Brook the first Everidge; Detachment with Col. Thatcher," MSA, Revolutionary Rolls, vol. 55, File L. My conclusions about the incidence of the draft and the distribution of military service were derived as follows. For all taxpayers on the 1771 Valuation who persisted in Concord till 1776, I compiled military service records from the information given in *Soldiers and Sailors*. The service records were then entered into my computer file for all 1771 taxpayers. I have analyzed the nature and depth of participation in the war over time, the relationship between military service and the variables of age, marital status, occupation, and wealth, and the varying opportunities for men of different social classes to attain officer status. To some extent, *Soldiers and Sailors* overstates actual participation in the war, since some records do not make clear whether an individual served himself, hired a substitute, or is credited for his sons' services. However, a comparison between the service records compiled from *Soldiers and Sailors* and the actual military services recounted by applicants for Revolutionary War pensions shows a close correspondence between the two sources.

34. CTR, 4: 462a–463a (March 3, 1777), 467a–467b (May 10, 1777); 5: 96b (June 15, 1778), 103b–103c (Dec. 9, 1778), 140a (April 4, 1780).

35. For Barrett, see *Soldiers and Sailors*, I: 684; for Brown, II: 676.

36. *Soldiers and Sailors*, II: 676; interview with Reuben Brown, Shattuck's Hist. Notes; William Whiting, "Memoir of Reuben Brown," Social Circle, p. 97; Brock Jobe, "Debt in Concord after the Revolution" (unpublished graduate seminar paper, Boston University, 1974), p. 20.

37. Daniel Shattuck, "Memoir of John White," Social Circle, pp. 143–44. White's record in *Soldiers and Sailors*, XVII: 92–97, indicates more service than his biographer mentions.

38. Adams, *Three Episodes of Massachusetts History*, II: 375; Shattuck, pp. 124, 355; CTR, 4: 462a–463a (March 3, 1777); Higginbotham, *War for Independence*, pp. 389–91.

39. *Soldiers and Sailors*, II: 621; 1777 Folder, Box 2, CA; W. T. R. Saffell, ed., *Records of the Revolutionary War* . . ., 3d ed. (Baltimore, 1894), pp. 403, 406, 413; Ezekiel Brown, Revolutionary War Pension File S2399, National Archives; Willard M. Wallace, *Appeal to Arms* (New York, 1951), pp. 199–200.

40. Benjamin Quarles, *The Negro in the American Revolution* (Chapel Hill, N.C., 1961), pp. 52–67; *Soldiers and Sailors*, I: 684; VI: 32; Estate of James Barrett, Administration No. 1194, Mid. Prob.; Transcript of "a Court of enquiry held in the 3^{d} Mass$^{us.}$ Brigade Feb$^{y.}$ 3^{d} 1783," copied from State Department records in the late nineteenth century at the behest of U.S. Senator George Frisbie Hoar, a Concord native, and now in CAS Papers.

41. See, generally, Charles K. Bolton, *The Private Soldier under Washington* (New York, 1902), and Edward C. Papenfuse and Gregory A. Stiverson, "General Smallwood's Recruits: The Peacetime Career of the Revolutionary War Private," *William and Mary Quarterly*, 3d ser. XXX (January 1973): 117–32; Rudyard Kipling, *Rudyard Kipling's Verse: Definitive Edition* (Garden City, N.Y., 1940), pp. 396–98.

42. CTR, 4: 431a–432a (Nov. 14, 1775), 472b (Dec. 29, 1775), 433b–434a (Jan. 1, 1776), 448a–449a (July 5 and 29, 1776); 5: 89b–89c (May 4 and 14, 1778), 99b (July 23, 1778), 119a–119b (June 16, 1779), 151a–151c (June 29, July 7, 1780), 162b–162c (Jan. 22, 1781).

43. CTR, 5: 230b–231a (May 26, 1783).

44. Robert J. Taylor, ed., *Massachusetts, Colony to Commonwealth: Documents on the Formation of Its Constitution, 1775–1780* (Chapel Hill, 1961), pp. 36–37, 45–46; Henry Steele Commager, ed., *Documents of American History*, 2 vols. (New York, 1968), I: 104–5.

45. CTR, 4: 451a–453a (Oct. 14 and 21, 1776).

46. Gordon S. Wood, *The Creation of the American Republic 1776–1787* (Chapel Hill, N.C., 1969), pp. 306–10; CTR, 4: 451a–453a (Oct. 14 and 21, 1776).

47. Wood, *Creation of American Republic*, pp. 288–90.

48. Patterson, *Political Parties in Revolutionary Massachusetts*, pp. 164–75, 182–96; CTR, 5: 86a (March 30, 1778), 90b (May 14, 1778), 95c (June 1,

1778), 96b (June 15, 1778), 117b–118a (May 17, 1779), 120b (July 30, 1779). In 1778, Concord contained 312 men, sixteen years old and above; of these, about 80 per cent, or 250, were over twenty-one. At the June 15, 1778, town meeting, 111 voters deliberated on the state constitution. Hence, the turn-out rate was 44 per cent. (Greene and Harrington, *American Population before 1790*, pp. 31–33.)

49. CTR, 5: 147b–148a (May 27, 1780); Oscar and Mary Handlin, eds., *The Popular Sources of Political Authority: Documents on the Massachusetts Constitution of 1780* (Cambridge, Mass., 1966), pp. 29–33; Patterson, *Political Parties*, pp. 218–46; Wood, *Creation of American Republic*, pp. 288–89. In 1781, Concord had 326 polls, but the population had been reduced by the separation of Carlisle the previous year. Adding 10 per cent to that figure—the approximate percentage of population that was lost to Carlisle—gives a population estimate of about 350, of whom 280 were over twenty-one. At the May 27, 1780, meeting, 147 voters attended, for a turn-out rate of 52 per cent. (Shattuck, p. 213.)

50. *New-England Historical and Genealogical Register*, L (January 1896): 15–19; Lee, p. 161. Forty-three men served on Revolutionary committees during 1775–83, charged with such tasks as recruiting soldiers, fixing prices, and drawing up resolutions on the state constitution. As a group they were much less wealthy than the committeemen of 1774–75 or the prewar selectmen, but this "democratization" of Concord's leadership class is misleading. A wealthy thirty-three-year-old committeeman in 1782 would have been only twenty-one years old and still dependent on his father in 1770, the year of the Valuation List used for this analysis. In addition, most committeemen served only once or twice, often in specialist roles (for example, militia officers were called on to recruit soldiers, and several artisans helped the town's magistrates set prices in their respective trades). If we look at the top ten leaders during the war, who held 63 per cent of all committee posts, we find a miniature of the town's prewar political elite:

	Top 20%	*Mid 40%*	*Bottom 40%*	*N*	*Missing*
Percentage of selectmen, 1765–74	77	23	0	13	0
Percentage of committeemen, 1774–5	71	29	0	21	0
Percentage of committeemen, 1776–83	48	43	9	33	10
Percentage of top ten committeemen, 1776–83	70	30	0	10	0

51. *Acts and Resolves*, V: 445–47; Shattuck, p. 353; report of officers commissioned for the Third Middlesex Regiment, March 25, 1776, Miscellaneous Bound Volume, 1776–77, Massachusetts Historical Society.

On reaching age twenty-one in December 1767, Silas Man paid a "full and compleat and Honourable Treat" to Hepzibah and Joseph Barrett and Persis Blood. Perhaps he was a ward or apprentice of the Barretts (Old Conc. Docs.).

52. CTR, 4: 428a–429a (May 22, 1775), 440a–440b (March 4, 1776).

53. Emerson, p. 92; Josephine Hosmer, "Memoir of Joseph Hosmer," Social Circle, pp. 117–18.

54. Concord First Church Record Book, CFPL, pp. 541–43.

55. Main, *Sovereign States*, pp. 232–33; *Acts and Resolves*, V: 583–89; CTR, 4: 462a (March 3, 1777).

56. CTR, 5: p. 83a (March 2, 1778), pp. 124b–124c (Nov. 1779); Shattuck, pp. 356–57.

57. CTR, 5: 75a–75b (Dec. 1, 1777), 79a–79c (Jan. 1 and 12, 1778); Wood, *Creation of American Republic*, pp. 188–96.

58. CTR, 5: 201a–204c (May 27, 1782).

59. CTR, 5: 230b–232a (May 26, 1783).

60. Jackson Turner Main, *The Anti-Federalists: Critics of the Constitution 1781–1788* (Chapel Hill, N.C., 1961), pp. 72–102, and Main, *Political Parties before the Constitution* (Chapel Hill, N.C., 1973), pp. 83–119; Hall, *Politics Without Parties*, pp. 147–57; CTR, 5: pp. 203c–204a (May 27, 1782), 231a–231c (May 26, 1783). Concord's representatives followed orders. See their votes on the roll calls analyzed by Hall, *Politics Without Parties*, pp. 148–49.

61. CTR, 5: 84b (March 2, 1778); MSA, 226: 157–60; petition of John Green and others, December 13, 1779, 1779 Folder, Box 2, CA.

62. MSA, 226: 157–92; *Acts and Resolves*, V: 1362–63, CTR, 5: 137a–138b (March 10, 1780).

63. CTR, 5: 137a–138b (March 10, 1780); *Acts and Resolves*, V: 1362.

64. *Acts and Resolves*, V: 1189–90, 1362–63.

65. Ripley, *Half-Century Discourse*, pp. 5–6, 30–31; Concord First Church Record Book, CFPL, pp. 159, 323, 325; Ralph Waldo Emerson, "Memoir of Ezra Ripley," Social Circle, p. 171.

66. CTR, 5: 91a, 91c (May 14, 1778), 95b (June 1, 1778), 96c (June 15, 1778), 145a (March 4, 1782), 96c (June 15, 1778); Josiah Bartlett, "Memoir of Duncan Ingraham," Social Circle, pp. 128–29; Concord First Church Record Book, CFPL, pp. 323–25.

67. Richard D. Brown, "The Confiscation and Disposition of Loyalists' Estates in Suffolk County, Massachusetts," *William and Mary Quarterly*, 3d ser., XXI (October 1964): 534–50; entries for March 24 and 31, April 22, 1777, Nathan Stow Journal, CFPL; Robert Treat Paine, Attorney-General, *vs.* Daniel Bliss, late of Concord, November 28, 1780, Inferior Court of Common Pleas Record Book, Office of Clerk of Courts, Middlesex County Court House, East Cambridge, pp. 1–4; Mid. Deeds, Bk. 82: 333–38, Bk. 83: 93, 437–38; CTR, 5: 230b–231a (May 26, 1783); unpublished Mass.

House Journal, 1783 session, votes of June 25, 1783, analyzed by Hall, *Politics Without Parties*, p. 139.

68. CTR, 5: pp. 204a–204c (May 27, 1782).

69. CTR, 5: 264a (March 7, 1785). The setback to agricultural improvement is indicated by the retrenchment of meadowland devoted to English hay. In 1771, 32 per cent of all meadowland was sown with timothy and clover, but ten years later, this proportion had fallen to 26.5 per cent; in 1784, it was 25 per cent. (1771 and 1784 valuations; Shattuck, p. 213.)

70. Ammi White, War Journal, Revolutionary War Pension File W18402, National Archives; Joseph Hunt to Tilly Merrick, October 26, 1782, Safe, Letter File 3, H-9, CFPL; George M. Brooks, "Memoir of Tilly Merrick," *Memoirs of Members of the Social Circle in Concord: Second Series, From 1795 to 1840* (Cambridge, Mass., 1888), pp. 58–62; Nathan Bond to Tilly Merrick, September 6, 1782, Tilly Merrick Papers, CFPL.

CHAPTER 7

1. CTR, 6: 26d (May 7, 1792), 45b (May 13, 1793); petition of Ezra Ripley and others, November 21, 1791, 1791 Folder, Box 3, CA; Henry David Thoreau, *A Week on the Concord and Merrimack Rivers* (New York, 1966), pp. 13–14; Plan of Concord, 1794, MSA, vol. 9, Map No. 1178.

2. Douglass C. North, *The Economic Growth of the United States 1790–1860* (Englewood Cliffs, N.J., 1961), pp. 24–58; David Hackett Fischer, "America, A Social History. Volume I: The Main Lines of the Subject, 1650–1975" (forthcoming), Ch. IV, pp. 10–15; William Jones, "A Topographical Description of the Town of Concord, Aug. 20th 1792," *Collections of the Massachusetts Historical Society*, I (1792): 237–39; Edward Jarvis, "Traditions and Reminiscences of Concord, Massachusetts, or a Contribution to the Social and Domestic History of the Town, 1779 to 1878," CFPL, pp. 12–13; Daniel Shattuck, "Memoir of John White," Social Circle, pp. 145–46; Walter Harding, *The Days of Henry Thoreau* (New York, 1965), pp. 4–5; Edward Jarvis, "Houses and People in Concord, 1810 to 1820," CFPL, pp. 139–40, 345–51; Jonathan F. Barrett, "Memoir of Jonathan Fay," Social Circle, pp. 108–9.

3. Jones, "Topographical Description," p. 239. The percentage of adult male taxpayers earning an income was calculated from the 1795 Town Assessment List, Town Treasurer's Vault, Concord Town Hall. There were only one slaughterhouse and five tanneries in 1792; by 1801 there were eleven and six, respectively. (Massachusetts General Court, Valuation Committee, 1801, Abstract of Valuation, 1792 and 1801, Middlesex County, Archives of the Massachusetts State Library, State House, Boston, p. 34.)

One striking sign of good times is the building boom of the 1790s. Although Concord's total population rose by 6 per cent over the 1790s and the number of polls by 15 per cent, the number of houses increased by 21 per cent and barns by 29 per cent. (The barns are also an indication of expanding agricultural production and growing livestock holdings: oxen increased by 30 per cent, cows by 20 per cent, horses by 25 per cent.) As for trade, the number of artisan shops doubled. For sources, see Shattuck, p. 213, and Valuation Committee, Abstract of Valuation, 1792 and 1801, p. 34.

The benefits of the new prosperity were spread widely throughout the population. The share of middling property-holders in the total assessed wealth of Concord gained at the expense of the very rich and the propertyless.

Percentage of Wealth

	1770	*1795*
Top 20%	56	54
Mid 40%	35	40
Bottom 40%	9	6
N	292	296

4. Shattuck, pp. 204–5; Richard D. Brown, *The Modernization of Preindustrial America, 1600–1865* (forthcoming, New York, 1976), Chapter 4, "The American Revolution and the Emergence of the Modern Personality," pp. 4–13.

5. Samuel Hoar, "Memoir of Thomas Hubbard," Social Circle, p. 121; Massachusetts Society for Promoting Agriculture, *Papers for 1807* (Boston, 1807); Timothy Dwight, *Travels in New England and New York*, ed. Barbara Miller Solomon, 4 vols. (Cambridge, Mass., 1969), I: 280; Jones, "Topographical Description," pp. 237–38; CTR, 6: 22c (March 5, 1792), 167a (March 3, 1800), 192b (March 2, 1801), 266b (April 1, 1805). Crop yields from plowland rose between 1771 and 1801: bushels of grain per acre tillage by 23 per cent from 12.2 to 15.0, tons of English hay per acre upland meadow by 36 per cent from .64 to .87. That such changes reflected more intensive cultivation is suggested by the fall in acres tillage per ox from 3.6 to 3.0. In addition, farmers renewed their shift from natural to cultivated grasses. Although English and upland meadows accounted for a smaller share of total meadowland in 1801 than in 1771 (27 per cent rather than 32 per cent), they produced an increasing proportion of the total hay crop—34 per cent in 1801, 29 per cent in 1771—thanks to improving productivity. As for pasture, its capacity to support cattle remained limited. In 1801 farmers reported that it took 3.7 acres to keep a cow for a year—a substantial increase over the extraordinary low of over five acres near the end of the war. But the share of pasturage in the total improved acreage was also falling: in 1784 it was 49 per cent and in 1791, 55 per cent; but in 1801, it represented only 48 per cent of improved land, which was 8 per cent more than in 1771. Sources: 1771 and 1784 valuations, already cited; Shattuck, p. 213; for 1801, MSA, 1: 34.

6. Shattuck, pp. 228–30; Richard D. Brown, "Voluntary Associations in Massachusetts," *Journal of Voluntary Action Research*, II (April 1973): 64–73; Jocelyn Schnier Goldberg, "The Library in America and the Reading American Public: An Evolution and a Case Study of Concord, Massachusetts" (senior thesis, Princeton University, 1974), pp. 51–56; Gordon S. Wood, ed., *The Rising Glory of America 1760–1820* (New York, 1971), p. 89. All of the ten original Masons, twenty-two of the twenty-five Charitable Library founders, and at least thirty-five of the original thirty-eight Fire Society members lived within a mile of the village. Residence was determined from the 1797 Highway Rate List, Town Treasurer's Vault, Concord Town Hall. Membership lists of the organizations are found in Louis A. Surette, *By-Laws of Corinthian Lodge of Ancient, Free and Accepted Masons, of Concord, Mass. . . .* (Concord, 1859); Concord Fire Society, Record Book, CFPL; Concord Charitable Library Society, Constitution and Records, 1775–1821, CFPL.

7. Social Circle, pp. 49–62. Based on the 1795 town assessment, 73 per cent of the 1794 Social Circle members ranked in the top quintile of wealth holders and 23 per cent in the second highest quintile. Two thirds of the Social Circle members joined the Fire Society and 62 per cent the Charitable Library. Only 14 per cent belonged to the Masons, most of whose members were new to Concord and engaged in trade.

8. Shattuck, pp. 204–5, 208; Susan Fondiler and Nina Meyer, "Vernacular Carpenters in Concord, Massachusetts 1790–1875" (seminar paper on New England architecture, Boston University, 1974), p. 37; Alexander W. Williams, *A Social History of the Greater Boston Clubs* (Barre, Mass., 1970), pp. 7–9; School Report, May 6, 1799, 1799 Folder, Box 3a, CA; Richard D. Brown, "The Emergence of Urban Society in Rural Massachusetts, 1760–1820," *Journal of American History*, LXI (June 1974): 29–51. From the 1750s through the 1780s, citizens of Boston and Charlestown never accounted for more than 2.5 per cent of all nonresident males marrying Concord women; in the 1770s and 1780s, no men from the metropolis took Concord brides. But in the 1790s, the percentage suddenly rose to 13 per cent (eight of sixty-one nonresident males). Since most weddings were held and registered in the bride's home town, there are few nonresident women listed in marriages to Concord men. Even so, the pattern is similar: no brides from Boston or Charlestown before 1785, then two out of twelve during 1785–94.

9. Van Beck Hall, *Politics Without Parties: Massachusetts, 1780–1791* (Pittsburgh, 1972), pp. 208–9, 218, 251; unpublished Mass. House Journal, Massachusetts State Library, 8 (May 1787 to March 1788): 110; 12 (May 1791 to March 1792): 307; Joseph Lee, Diary for 1792, entries for November, Massachusetts Historical Society; *Yeoman's Gazette*, March 11, 1826, p. 2.

10. Shattuck, pp. 145–47.

11. *Massachusetts Magazine*, VI (July 1794): 390; Dwight, *Travels*, I: 280–81.

12. Ralph Waldo Emerson, *Poems*, Volume IX of *Complete Works*, 12 vols. (Cambridge, Mass., 1883–93), p. 35.

13. Shattuck, p. 366; assessment of Lucy Lee, Joseph Lee's widow, on Massachusetts Direct Tax of 1798: Concord, NEHGS (microfilm at CFPL); Joseph Lee, Diary for 1794, Massachusetts Historical Society; John S. Keyes, "Memoir of Jonas Lee," Social Circle, pp. 135–37. A third (32.6 per cent) of the male taxpayers on the 1770 Valuation List were present on the 1795 list. The persisters represented about half (52.5 per cent) of all 1770 taxpayers who survived the twenty-five-year period. This "refined persistence rate," as it is known, was virtually the same as the corresponding rate for the period 1746–70 (53.1 per cent).

14. U.S. Bureau of the Census, *Heads of Families at the First Census of the United States Taken in the Year 1790: Vermont* (Washington, D.C., 1907), p. 37; David Brown to Ephraim Brown, November 19, 1794, and February 13, 1796, to David, Jr., and Ephraim Brown, February 15, 1800, CAS Papers; U.S. Bureau of the Census, *Heads of Families at the Second Census of the United States Taken in the Year 1800: Vermont* (Baltimore, 1972), p. 80. Of the 104 Minutemen, forty-one are known to have moved away, and another twenty-one either died without leaving a record in Concord (unlikely) or left town (more likely). At a maximum, then, nearly two thirds of the Minutemen emigrated from Concord.

15. David Brown to Ephraim Brown, November 19, 1794, and June 13, 1798, CAS Papers; W. W. Clayton, *History of Cumberland County, Maine* (Philadelphia, 1880), pp. 214–17; Ruth R. Wheeler, "North Bridge Neighbors: A History of Area B Minuteman National Historical Park," CFPL, pp. 91–108.

16. Grindall Reynolds, "Memoir of Ezekiel Brown," Social Circle, pp. 85–88; CTR, 5: pp. 167a (March 5, 1781), 193a (March 4, 1782); Mid. Deeds, Bk. 90: 297–99.

17. Carleton Edward Fisher, *History of Clinton, Maine* (Augusta, Me., 1970), pp. 28–29. I assume that Brown sold the bounty land, since his listing in National Genealogical Society, *Index of Revolutionary War Pension Applications* (Washington, D.C., 1966), states that his bounty land warrant was assigned to another person. No further record of this transaction is extant.

18. Ezekiel Brown, Revolutionary War Pension File S2399, National Archives; Social Circle, pp. 55–56. Brown originally qualified for the pension in April 1818 before a means test was imposed, but because of a flood of pension applications, Congress in 1820 required every veteran seeking or already receiving aid to submit a list of his property holdings in order to prove that he was "in need of assistance from his country for support." Brown promptly filed the required schedule of his real and

personal estate. W. T. R. Saffell, ed., *Records of the Revolutionary War . . .* , 3d. ed. (Baltimore, 1894), pp. 512–15.

19. Josephine Hosmer, "Memoir of Joseph Hosmer," CAS Papers; report of committee to seat the meetinghouse, January 1, 1792, and notice to innkeepers, August 1, 1792, 1792 Folder, Box 3, CA; school committee report, 1799 Folder, Box 3a, CA.

20. Susan Kurland, " 'A Political Progress': Processes of Democratization in Concord, Massachusetts, 1750–1850" (senior honors thesis, Brandeis University, 1973), pp. 90–94; Jarvis, "Houses and People," pp. 217–18; 1795 Town Assessment and 1798 Direct Tax; inventory of James Barrett, Administration No. 1194, Mid. Prob.; Mid. Deeds, Bk. 143: 66 and Bk. 198: 137.

21. The rate of intragenerational economic mobility slowed considerably after the Revolution. Whereas in the period 1746–70, 78 per cent of persisting taxpayers changed their relative economic ranks (based on adjusted quintiles), only 62 per cent of the men continuing from the 1770 valuation to the 1795 assessment list did so. (The coefficient of association, C_d, rose from 1.09 to 1.89.) This was slightly less movement than found for Hingham in 1772–1800, when 65 per cent of persisters changed ranks (C_d was 1.76). The reason for the slowdown is that older men were holding onto their property longer than before and thereby blocking upward movement by the younger generation. The following table compares the percentage of upwardly mobile, stable, and downwardly mobile men in each age group:

	% UM		*% Stable*		*% DM*	
Age group	*1746–70*	*1770–95*	*1746–70*	*1770–95*	*1746–70*	*1770–95*
30 & under	66	52	23	20	11	28
31–40	31	41	42	41	27	18
40 & over	13	0	3	52	83	48

The median age for upwardly mobile men during 1770–95 was twenty-eight, the same as in 1746–70, but the median age for stable taxpayers rose from thirty-one to forty-one and for downwardly mobile taxpayers from forty-three to 44.5.

The rate of intergenerational economic mobility slowed, too. Whereas 25 per cent of sons retained their fathers' economic ranks—based on unadjusted quintiles—in the 1746–70 matrix, 29 per cent did so in 1770–95. Downward mobility remained the norm for most sons, but the percentage who fell below their fathers was substantially lower after the Revolution than before (52 per cent, as opposed to 62 per cent). On the other hand, when adjusted quintiles are used for the rankings, there was somewhat greater intergenerational movement: in 1746–70, 30 per cent of sons retained their fathers' ranks; in 1770–95, 28 per cent. In this respect, Concord remained more fluid than Hingham (C_d was 1.45 for Concord in 1770–95, 1.72 for Hingham in 1772–1800).

Finally, the breakdown of favoritism for eldest sons is evident when the intergenerational mobility of eldest and younger sons is compared. Before the Revolution (1746–70), eldest sons were twice as likely to succeed to their fathers' positions as would be expected by chance (C_d was 2.24 for eldest sons and their father, 1.51 for the entire population of fathers and sons). After the Revolution (1770–95), the eldest were actually less successful than their brothers in inheriting their fathers' status (C_d for eldest sons was 1.27; for all sons, 1.45). Similar results obtain when the intragenerational mobility of eldest and youngest sons is compared. The eldest retained some advantage in 1770–95—they were 38 per cent more likely to move upward and 11 per cent less likely to move downward—but the advantage was less pronounced than in 1746–70 and was perhaps due as much to the simple fact of age than to the benefits of being born first. For methods and comparisons, see Chapter Four, n. 16.

22. In the period 1775–94, 39 per cent of all first births were conceived out of wedlock; this was slightly higher than the rate for 1755–74 (34 per cent) and equivalent to the level found for Hingham during 1781–1800 (39 per cent). Daniel Scott Smith and Michael S. Hindus, "Premarital Pregnancy in America 1640–1971: An Overview and Interpretation," *Journal of Interdisciplinary History*, V (Spring 1975): 560–65; Mid. Deeds, Bk. 143: 66; *Vital Records of Shirley, Massachusetts to the Year 1850* (Boston, 1918), p. 15.

23. Joseph F. Kett, "Growing Up in Rural New England, 1800–1840," *Anonymous Americans*, ed. Tamara K. Hareven (Englewood Cliffs, N.J., 1971), pp. 5–9; Smith and Hindus, "Premarital Pregnancy," pp. 552–59; Mid. Deeds, Bk. 177: 268–70; Bk. 198: 137.

24. Charles Edward Potter, *A Genealogy of Some Old Families of Concord, Massachusetts* (Boston, 1887), pp. 46–47; George Tolman, "Descendants of Humphrey Barrett and Mary Potter 1675–1884," NEHGS; 1826 and 1850 Town Assessment lists, Town Clerk's Vault, Town Hall, Concord, Mass.

25. This account is drawn from Josephine Hosmer's manuscript "Memoir of Joseph Hosmer," CAS Papers, and her published "Memoir of Joseph Hosmer," Social Circle, pp. 118–19, and also from Jarvis, "Houses and People," pp. 49–50.

26. Hosmer, "Memoir of Joseph Hosmer," CAS Papers.

27. Smith and Hindus, "Premarital Pregnancy," p. 548; Nancy Falik Cott, "In the Bonds of Womanhood: Perspectives on Female Experience and Consciousness in New England, 1780–1830" (Ph.D. dissertation, Brandeis University, 1974), pp. 1–41; Daniel Scott Smith, "Population, Family and Society in Hingham, Massachusetts 1635–1880" (Ph.D. dissertation, University of California at Berkeley, 1973), pp. 746–60; Marc Harris, "A Demographic Study of Concord, Massachusetts 1750–1850" (senior honors thesis, Brandeis University, 1973), pp. 58–73.

28. Arthur Zilversmit, *The First Emancipation: The Abolition of Slavery in*

the North (Chicago, 1967), pp. 112–16; U.S. Bureau of the Census, *Heads of Families at the First Census of the United States Taken in the Year 1790: Massachusetts* (Washington, 1907), pp. 139–40.

29. Joan Trumbull, "Concord and the Negro," CFPL, pp. 20–21; *Concord, Massachusetts, Births, Marriages, and Deaths 1635–1850* (Concord, n.d.), p. 345; *Concord Enterprise*, April 27, 1890; 1798 Direct Tax; Jarvis, "Houses and People," pp. 186–90.

30. Henry David Thoreau, *Walden*, ed. J. Lyndon Shanley (Princeton, N.J., 1971), pp. 256–62; estate of Joseph Lee, Will No. 13934, Mid. Prob.; Josiah Bartlett, "Memoir of Duncan Ingraham," Social Circle, pp. 129–30.

31. Cyrus Stow, "Memoir of Peter Wheeler," Social Circle, pp. 140–41; Jarvis, "Houses and People," pp. 97–99.

32. George Tolman, *John Jack, the Slave, and Daniel Bliss, the Tory* (Concord, Mass., 1902), pp. 3–7.

33. Edward Jarvis, Manuscript Notes to Shattuck's *History of Concord*, CFPL, pp. 392ff–392hh; *Concord Gazette, and Middlesex Yeoman*, September 4, 1824; *To The Inhabitants of Concord* (Concord, 1824), broadside in Letter File 4, L-2, CFPL.

34. *Concord Gazette, and Middlesex Yeoman*, May 14, 1825; Ralph L. Rusk, *The Life of Ralph Waldo Emerson* (New York and London, 1949), p. 209; Ralph Waldo Emerson, *Nature* (Boston, 1836), in Brooks Atkinson, ed., *The Selected Writings of Ralph Waldo Emerson* (New York, 1950), p. 42.

35. Brown, *Modernization of Preindustrial America*, chap. 4.

Index

The Minutemen and Their World brings to life the community of men who began the American Revolution on April 19, 1775, at the Old North Bridge in Concord, Massachusetts. Through intensive study of family genealogies, diaries, tax lists, and other public records, Robert A. Gross has re-created the daily pattern of pre-Revolutionary life: how individual farmers, artisans, and merchants earned a living, raised their families, and carried on their politics in a New England country town before the coming of war. Within this setting, Mr. Gross masterfully traces the growing intrusion of the Revolutionary crisis into the affairs of the town and shows how local conflicts shaped responses to British policy. His lively narrative carries through to the beginning of mobilization, and then follows individual Minutemen from the first battle through the succeeding war to their postwar careers.

The Minutemen and Their World is as entertaining as it is scholarly. Its fusion of solid research and vigorous writing, its blend of vivid detail and historical perspective, provide a new and exciting look at the human meaning of the American Revolution.